AF605968

ATUL BHALLA | YAMUNA WALK

MALIHA NOORANI

22KM: A JOURNEY INTO THE PRESENT

ATUL BHALLA | YAMUNA WALK

SEPIA EYE, NEW YORK
IN ASSOCIATION WITH
THE UNIVERSITY OF WASHINGTON PRESS,
SEATTLE AND LONDON

. . . THROUGH 22 KMS . . .

When did you last see the Yamuna?
When did you last touch the Yamuna?

I walk
I walk
The Yamuna
The city
The city
I walk
I walk . . . . . .

23 JANUARY 2007

11:30 AM

palla
northern border
delhi
delhi?
sand
and sand
space
mine
space
flow
flow
the river
dunes
fields
young wheat
flowers
marigolds
mustard
saplings

fishermen
small boat
little catch
large hearts
and broad
smiles
great hope
reflections
clear
air
water
clear
mining
sand
machines
across
the border,
U.P.
sky
rested
the earth
the river

me?
walk,
evening
spread,
creeping
water,
level
abandoned
fields
hope
shallow
crossings
deeper
I walk
the Sun
against
sucking
eucalyptus
evening
jagatpur

5:30 PM

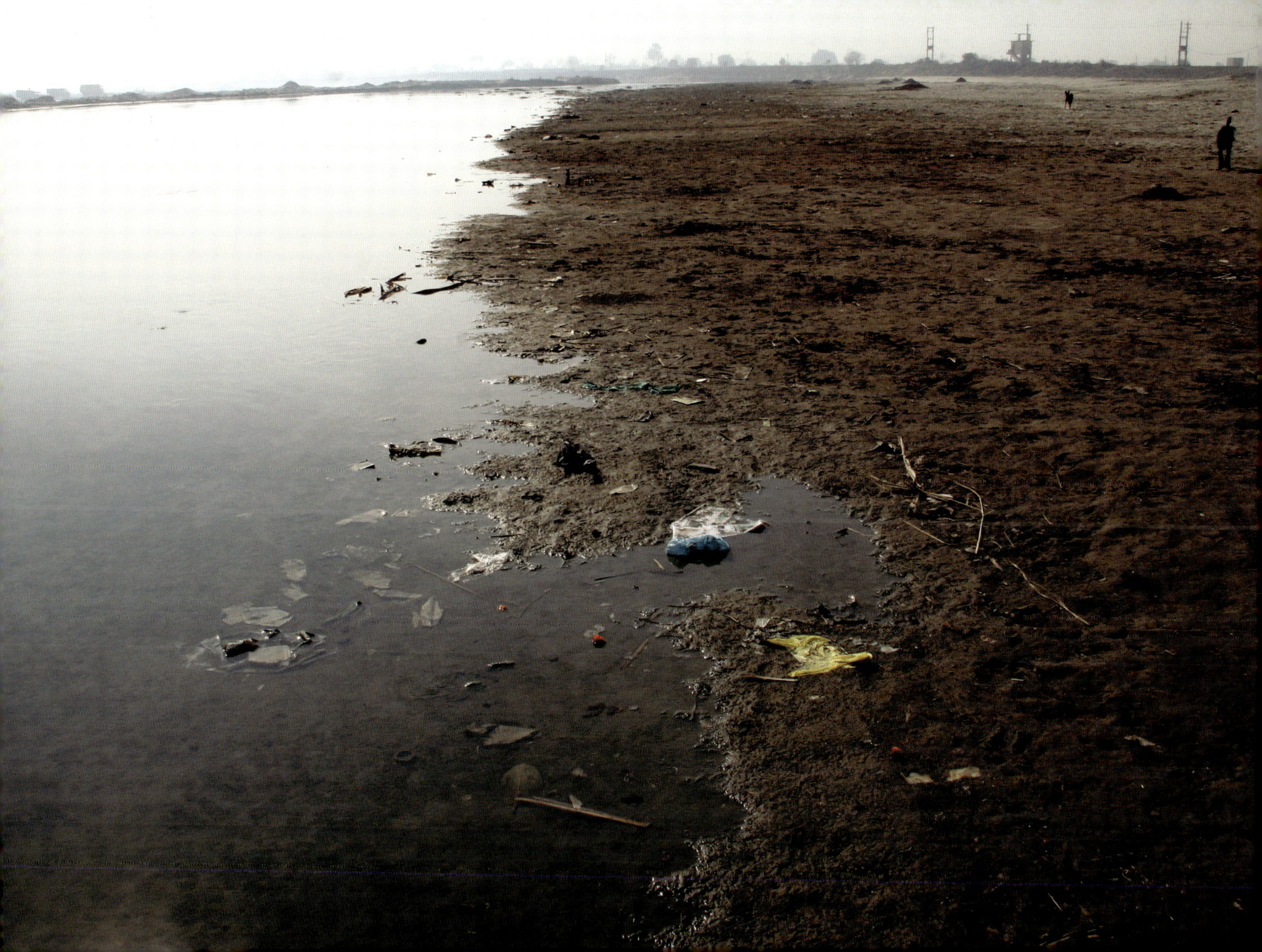

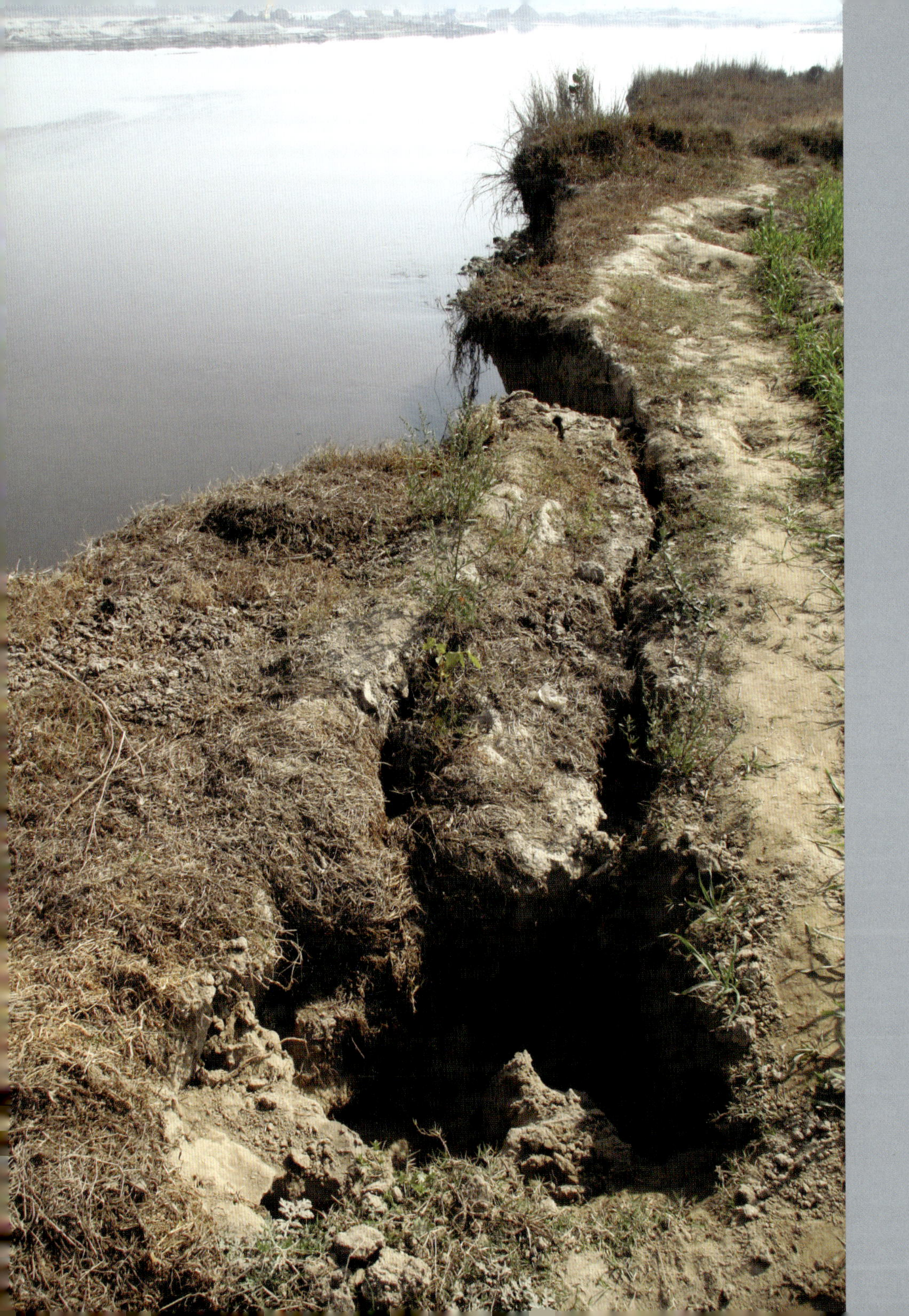

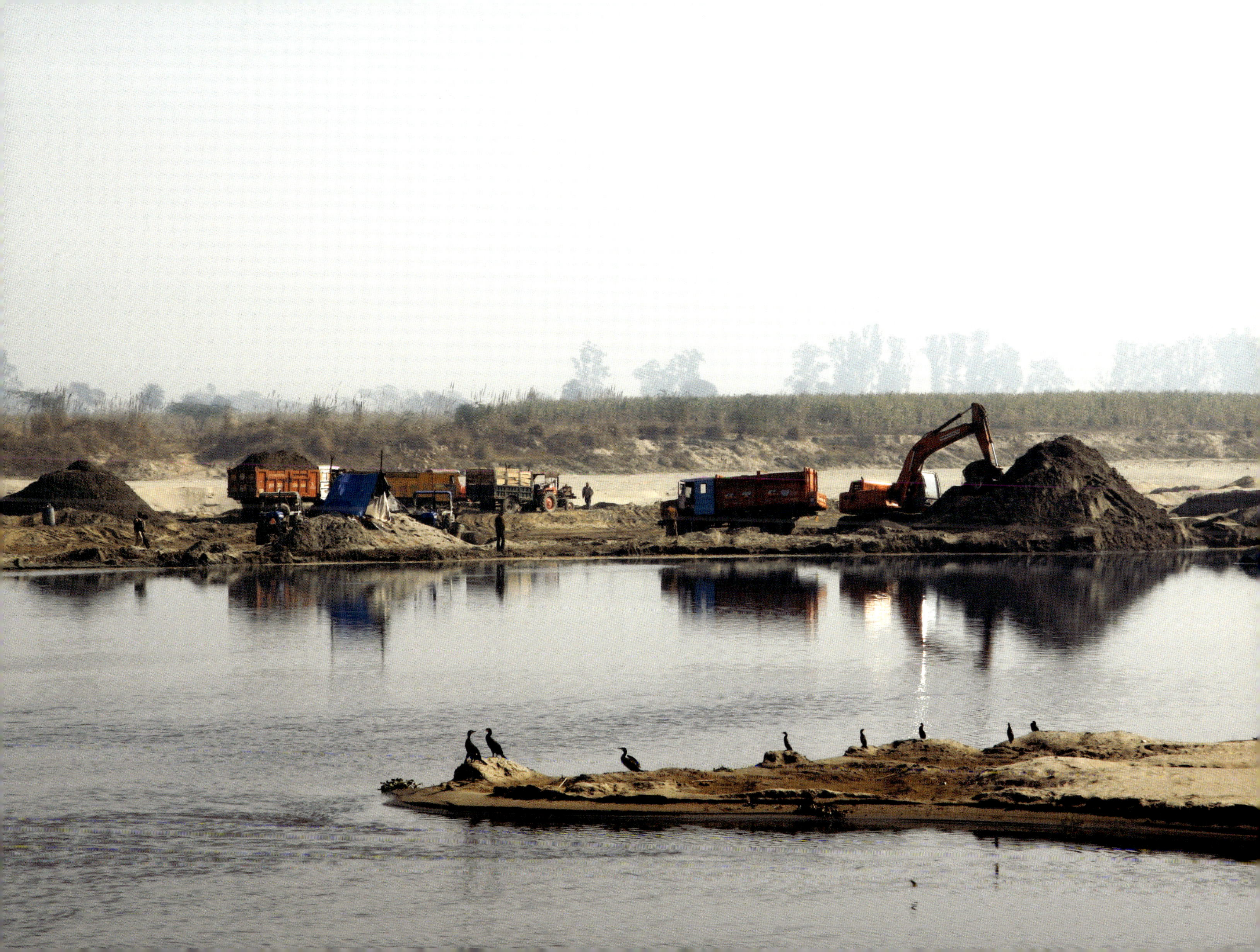

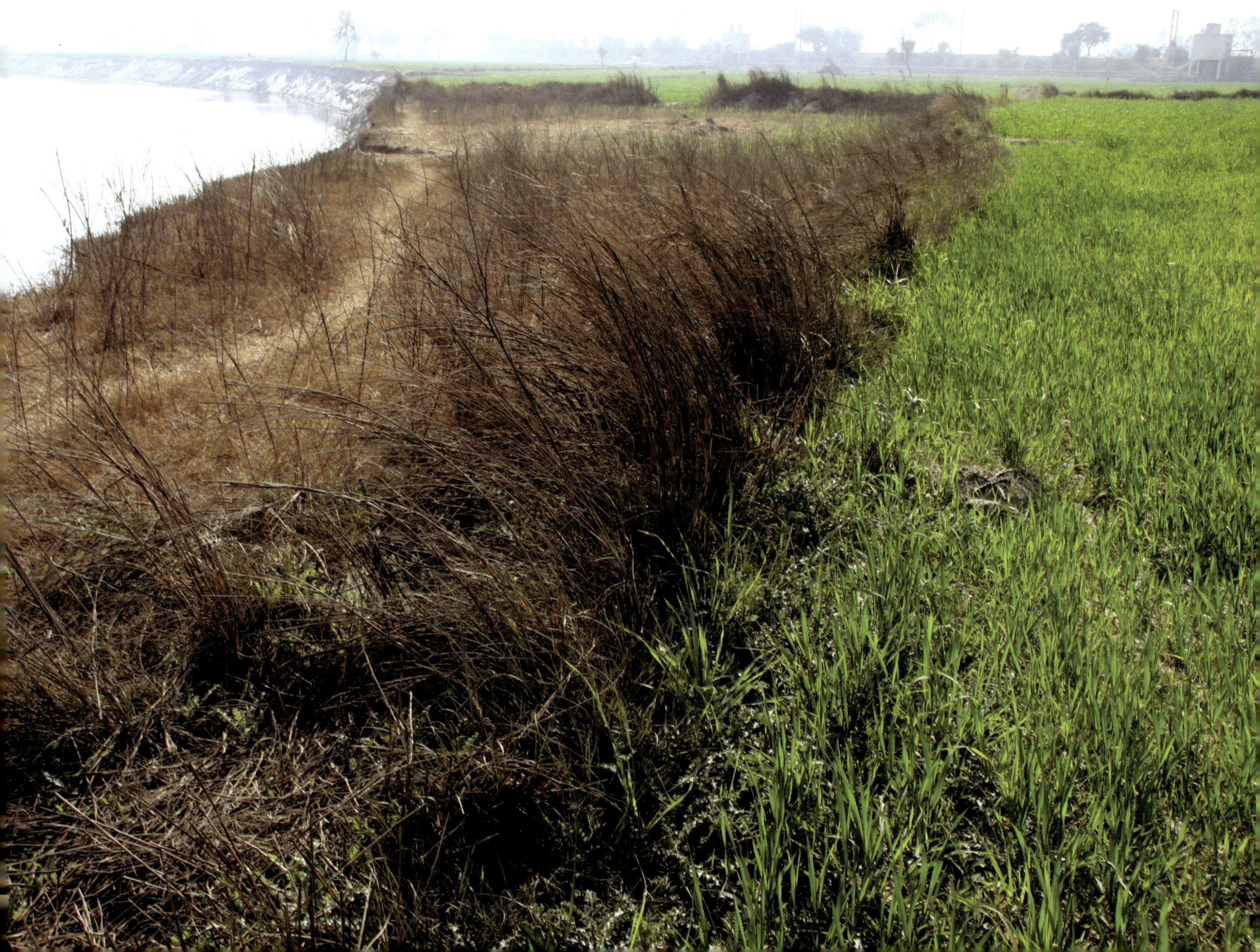

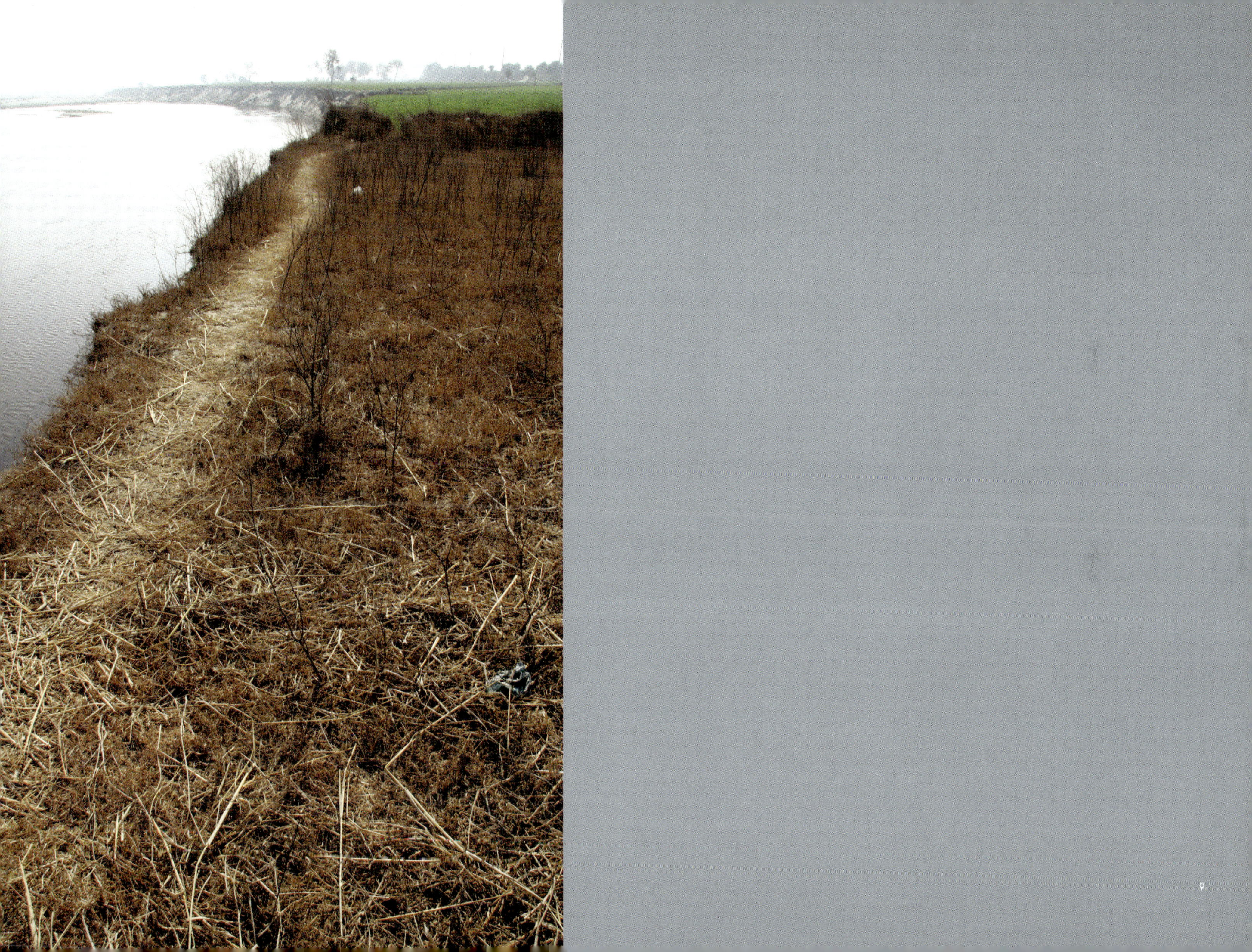

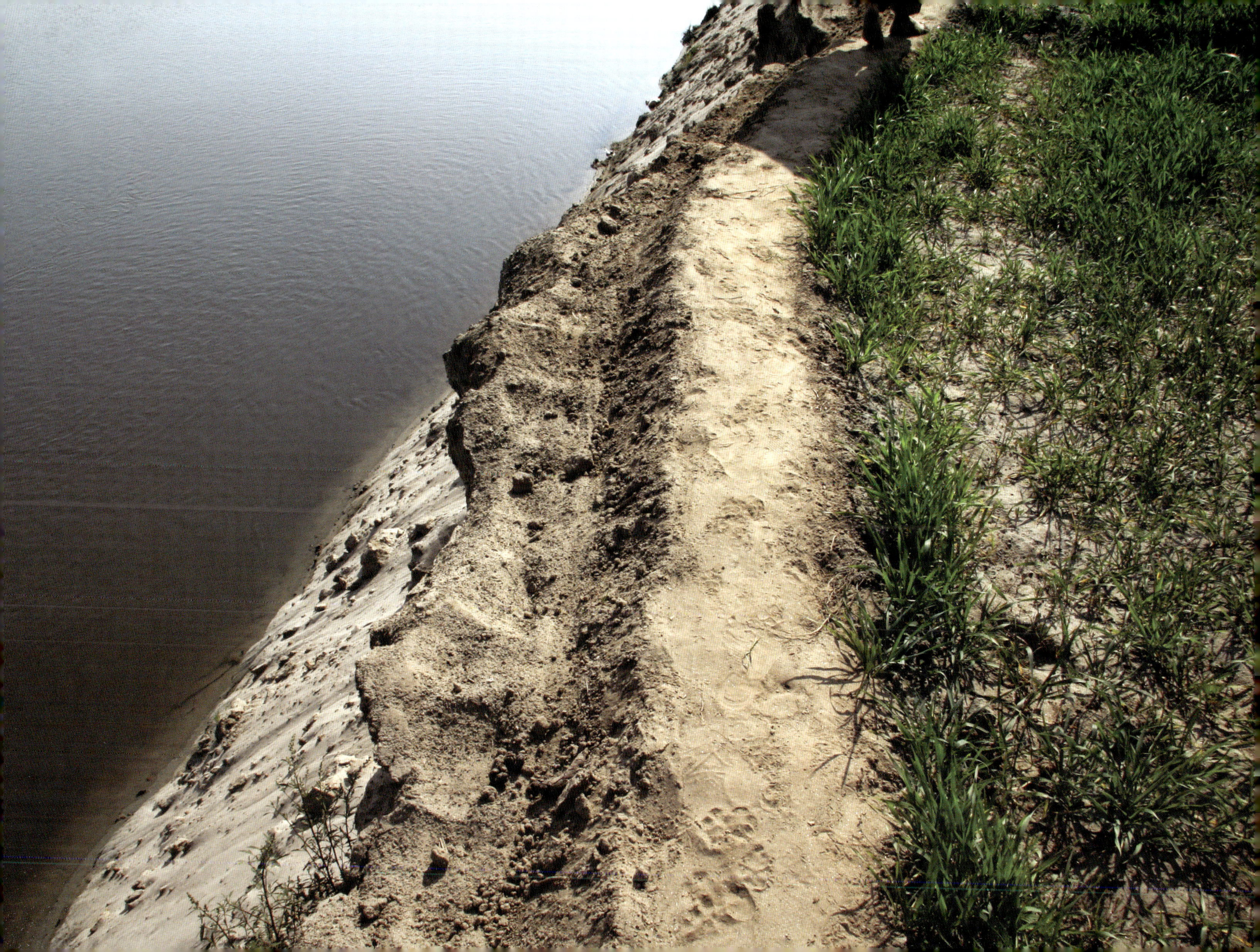

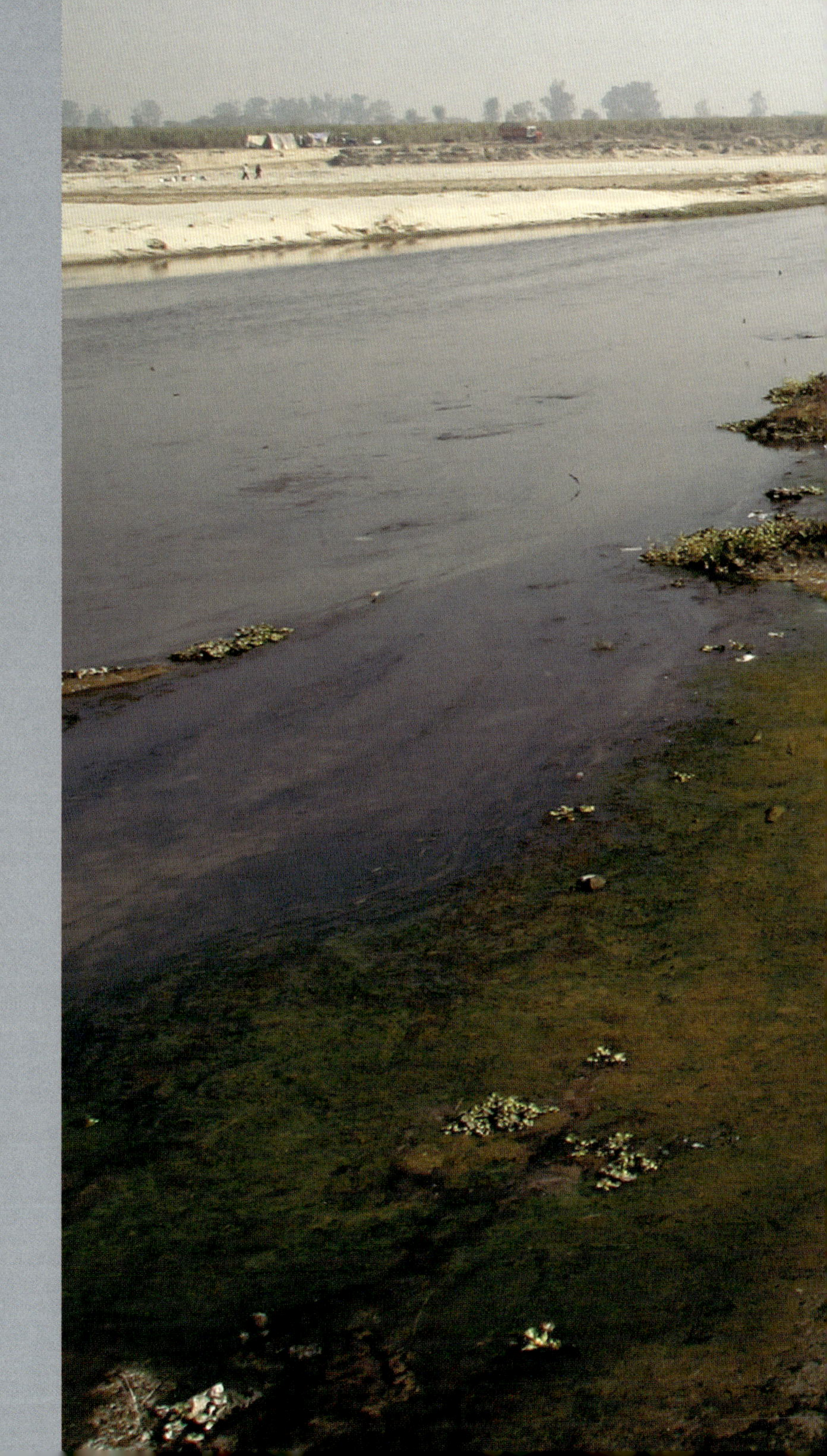

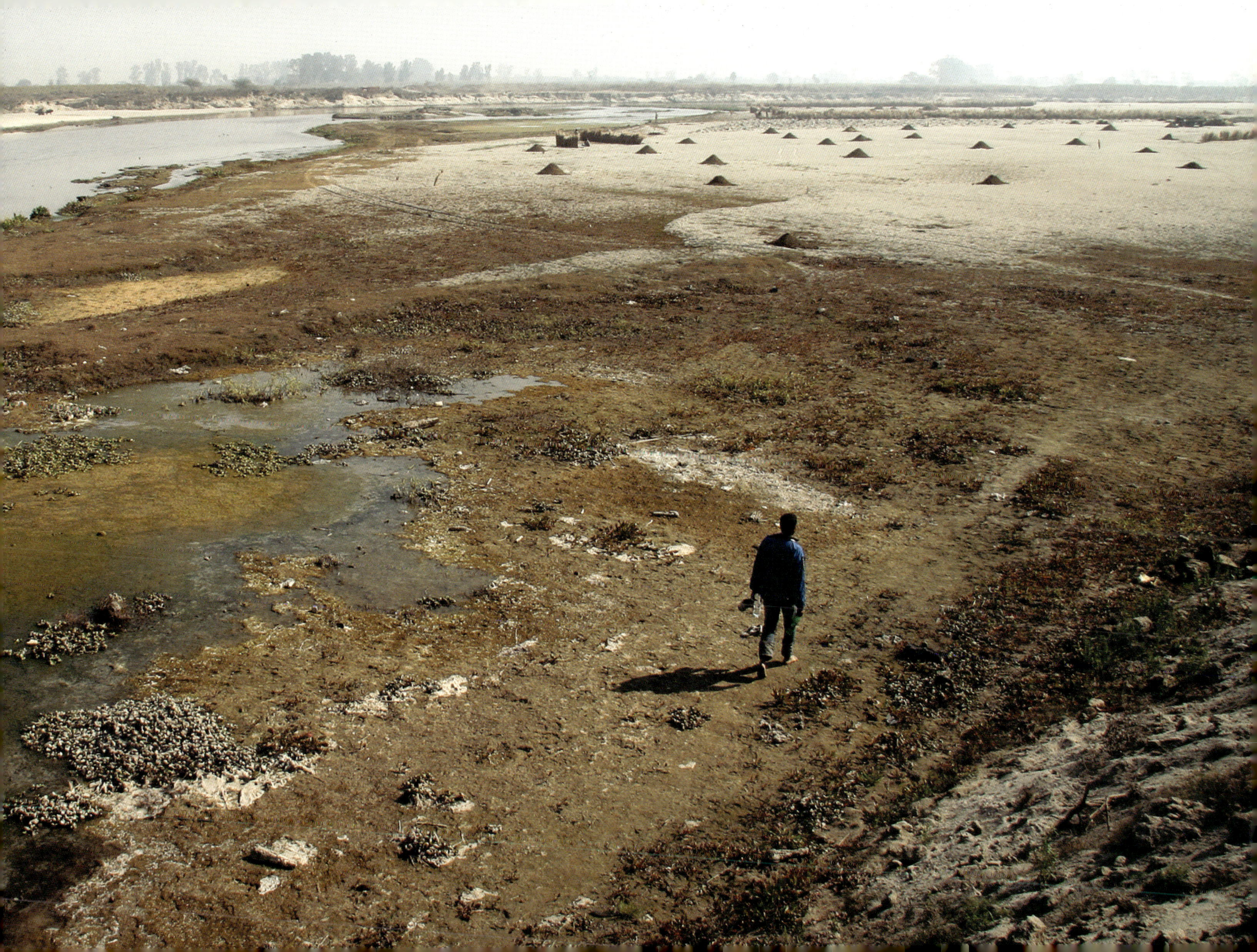

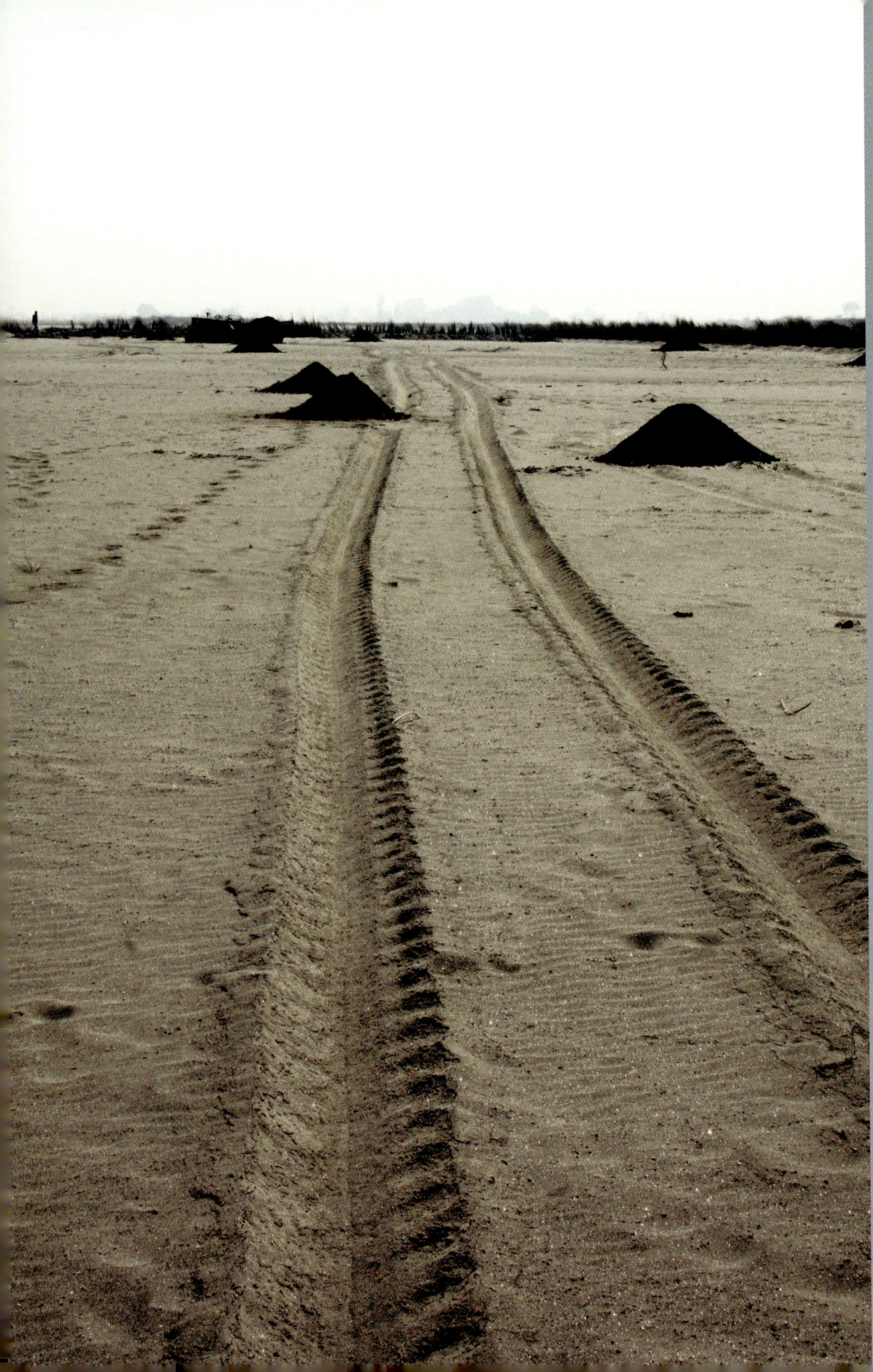

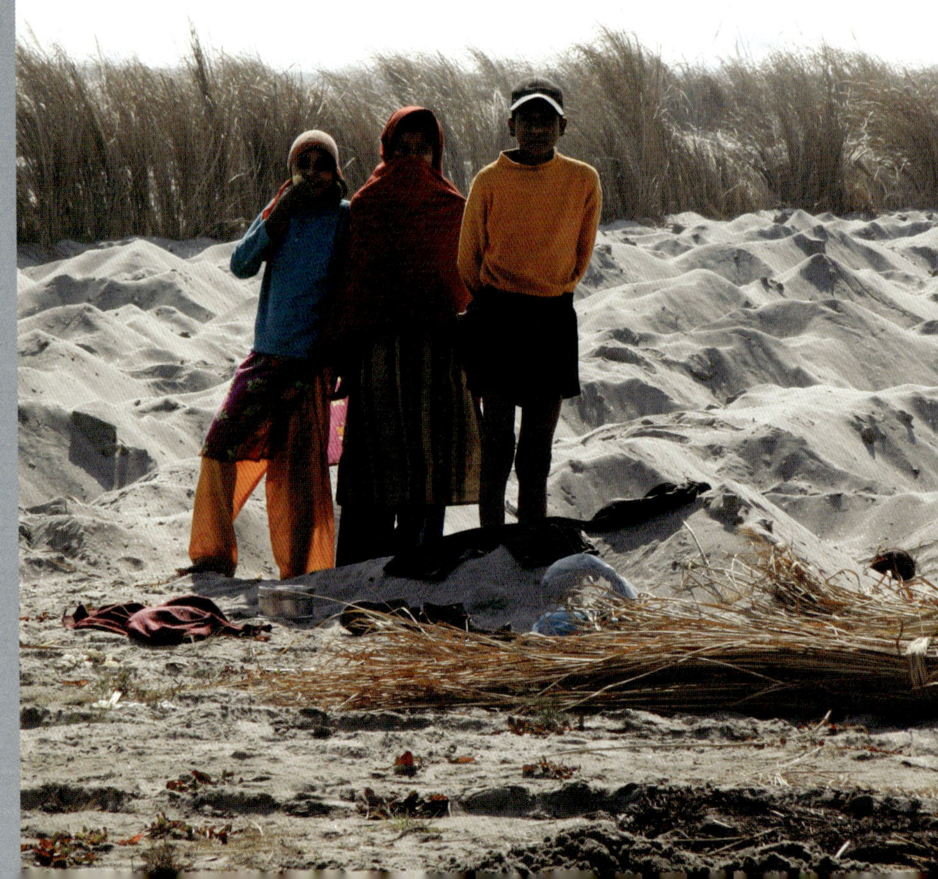

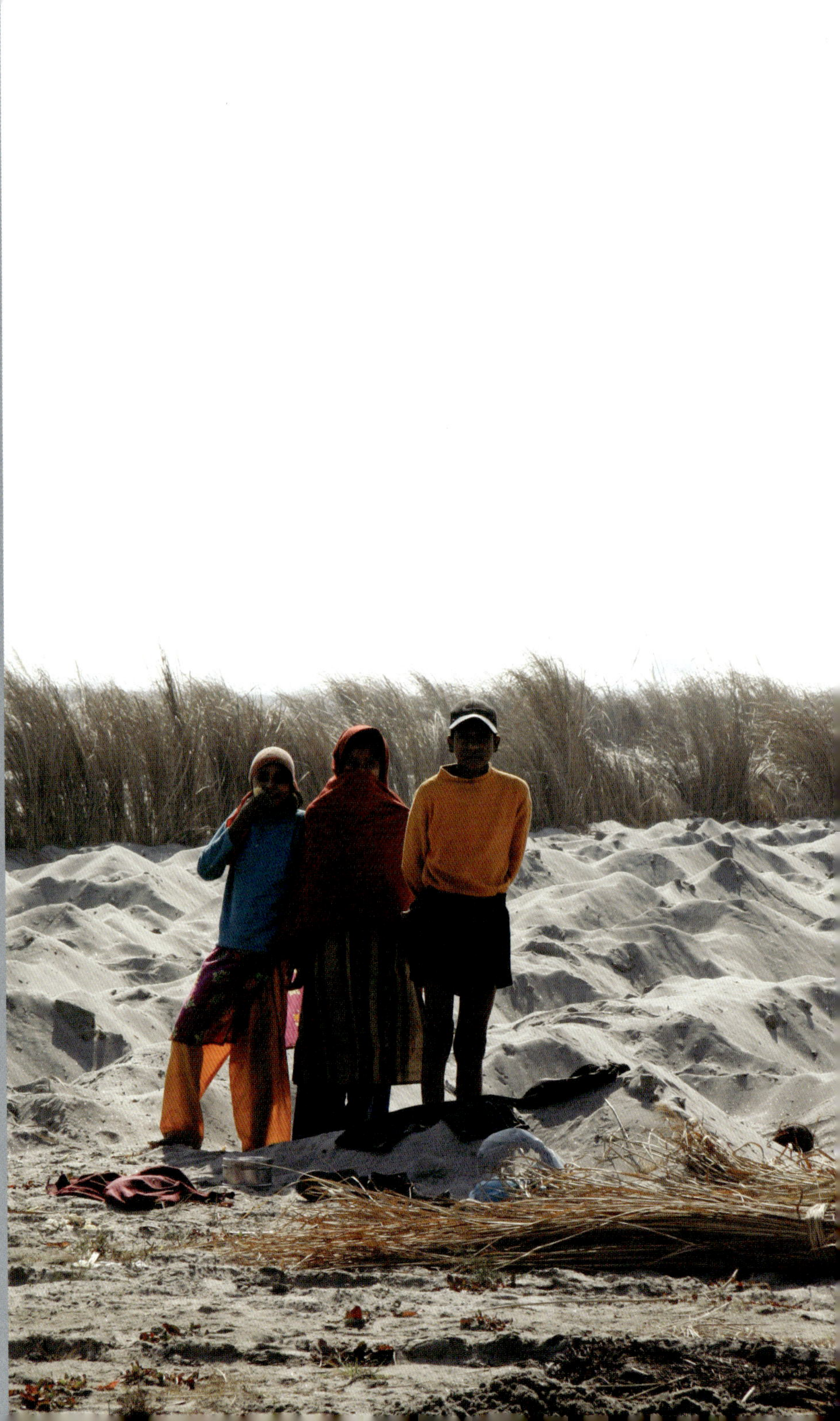

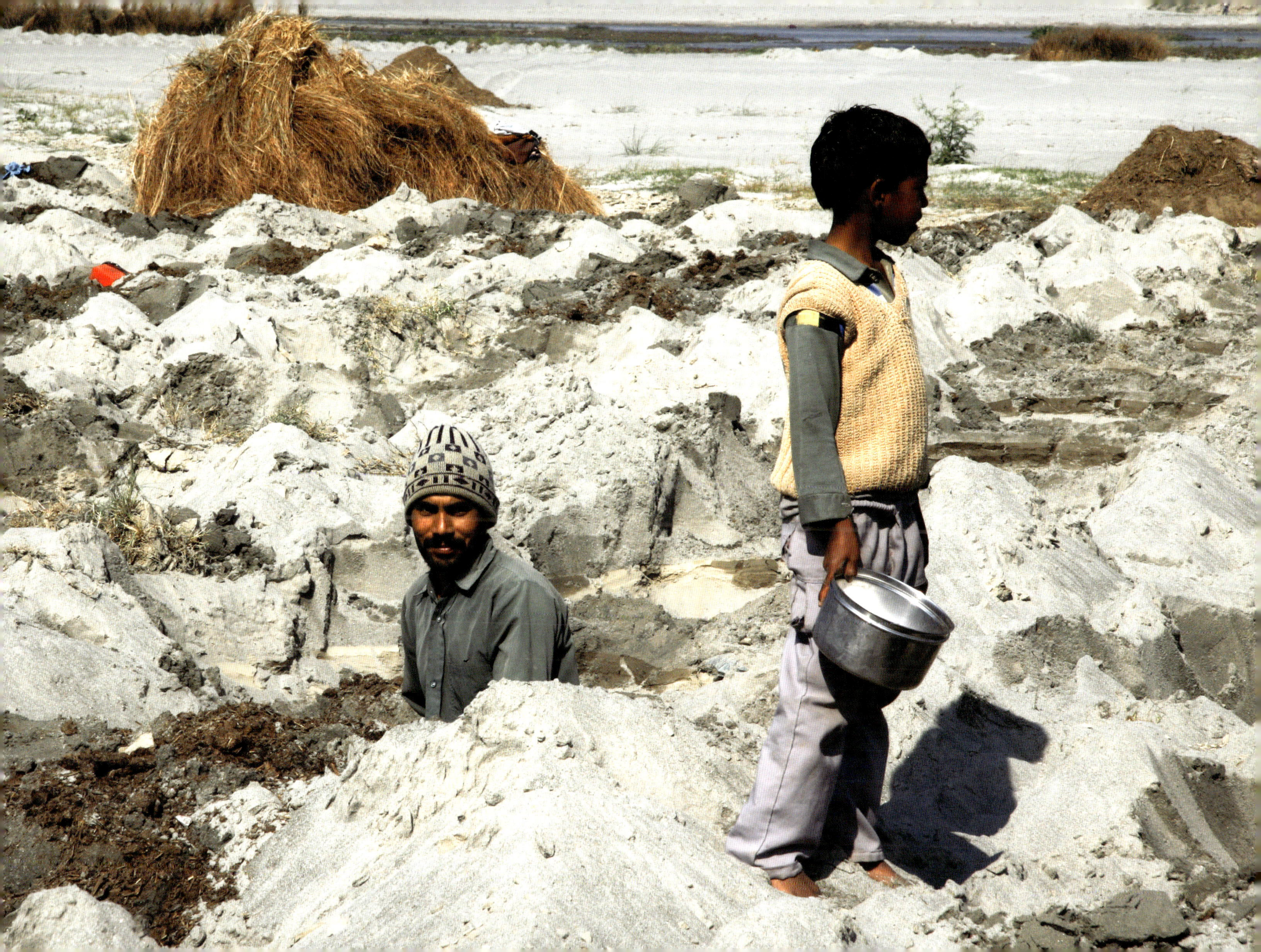

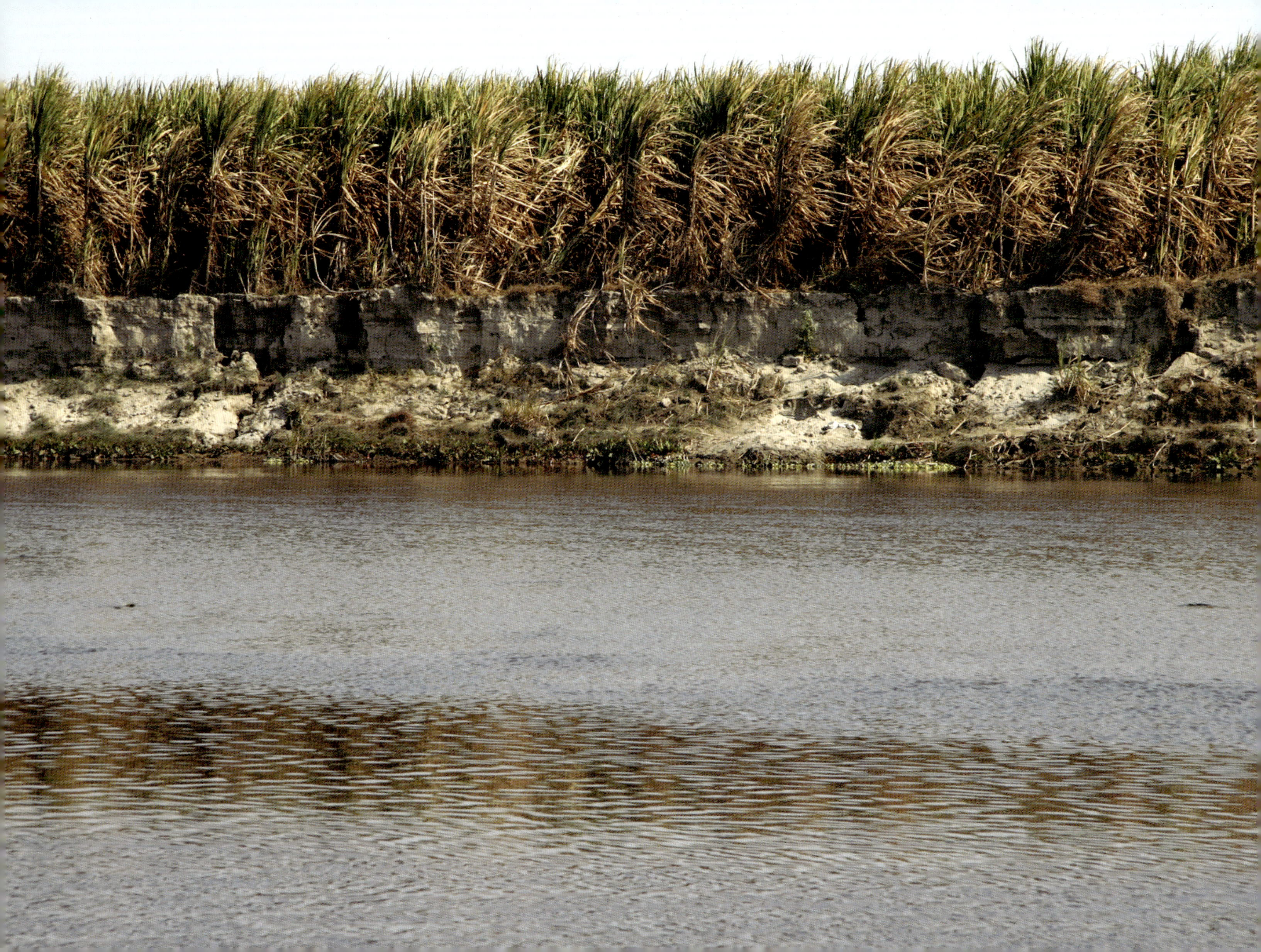

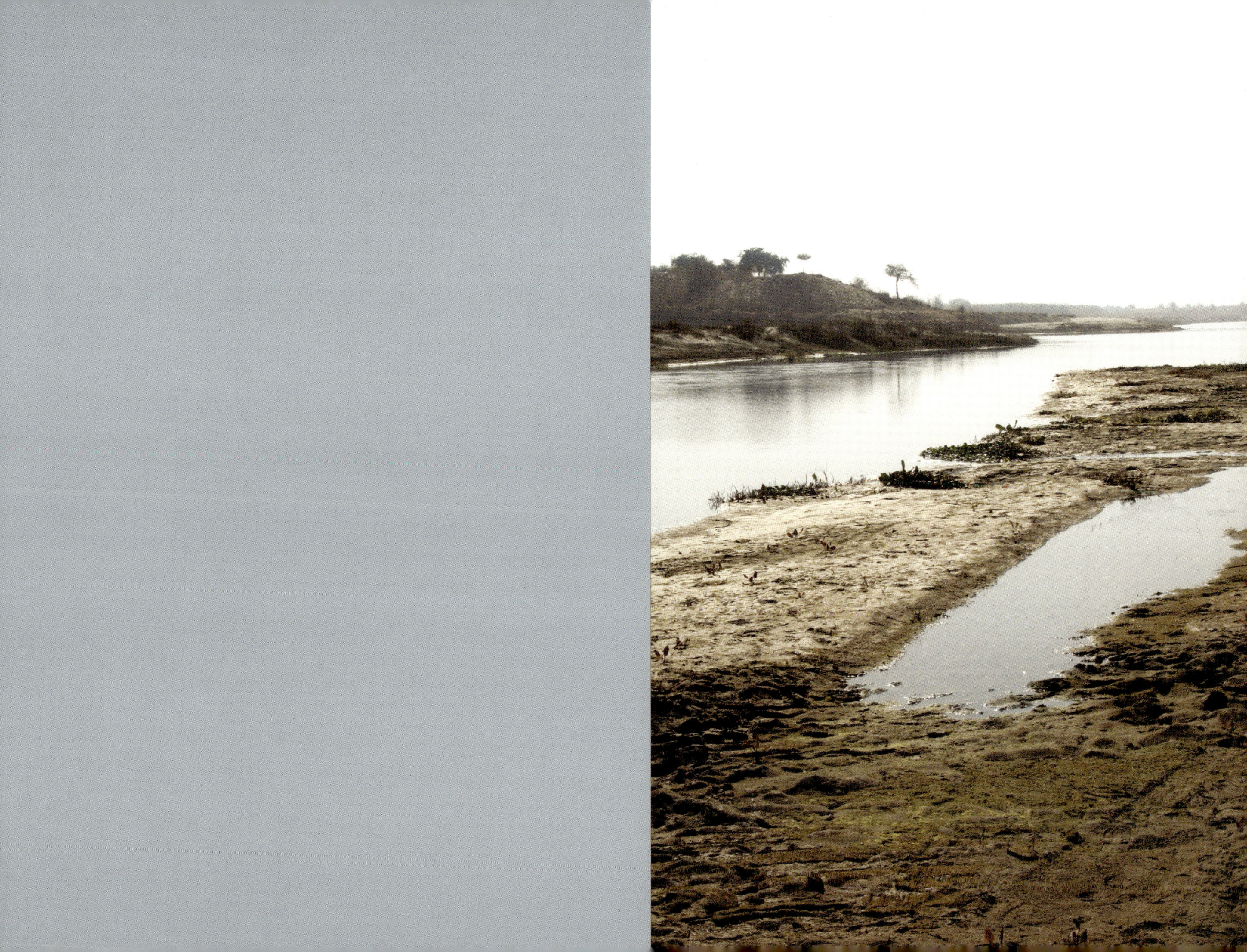

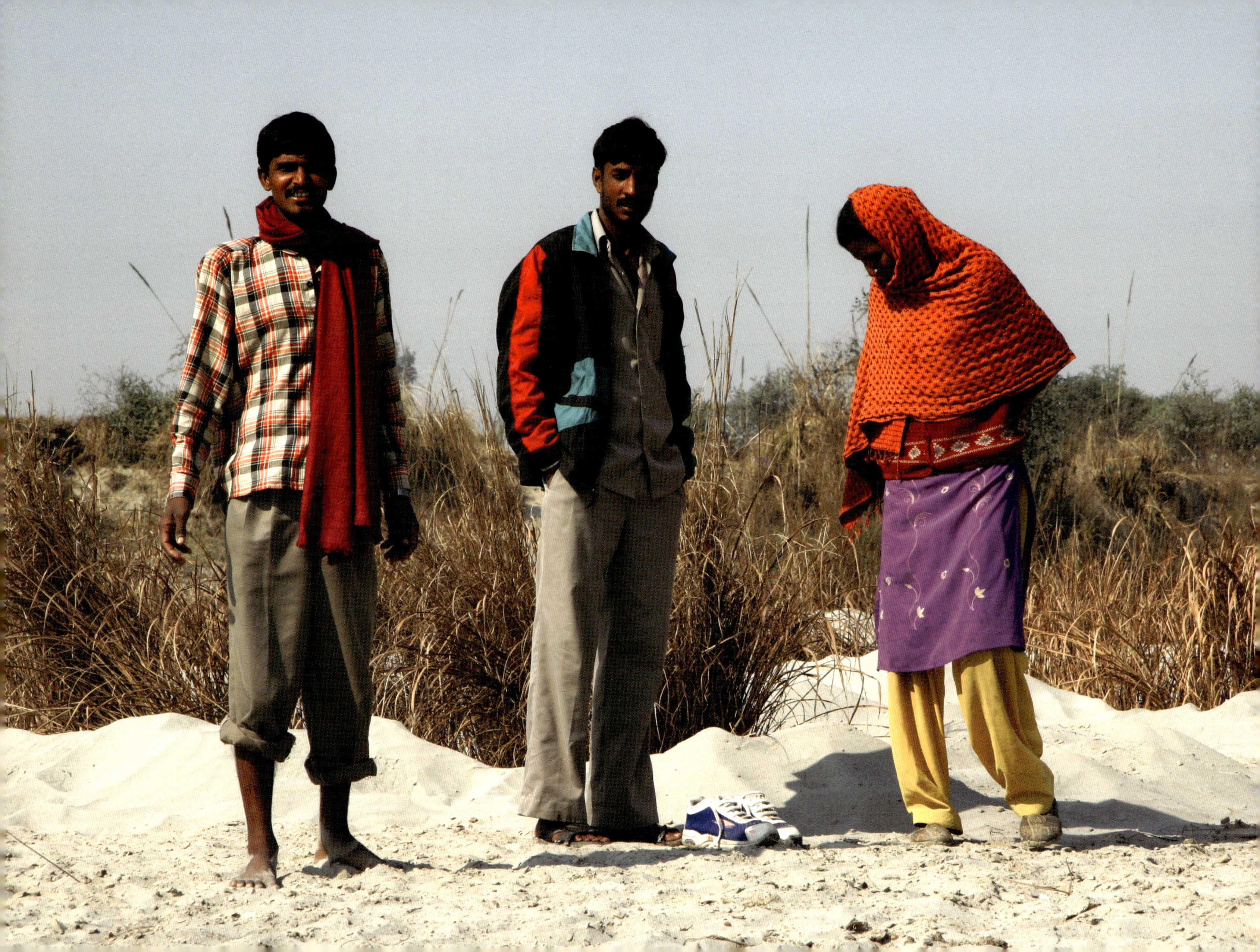

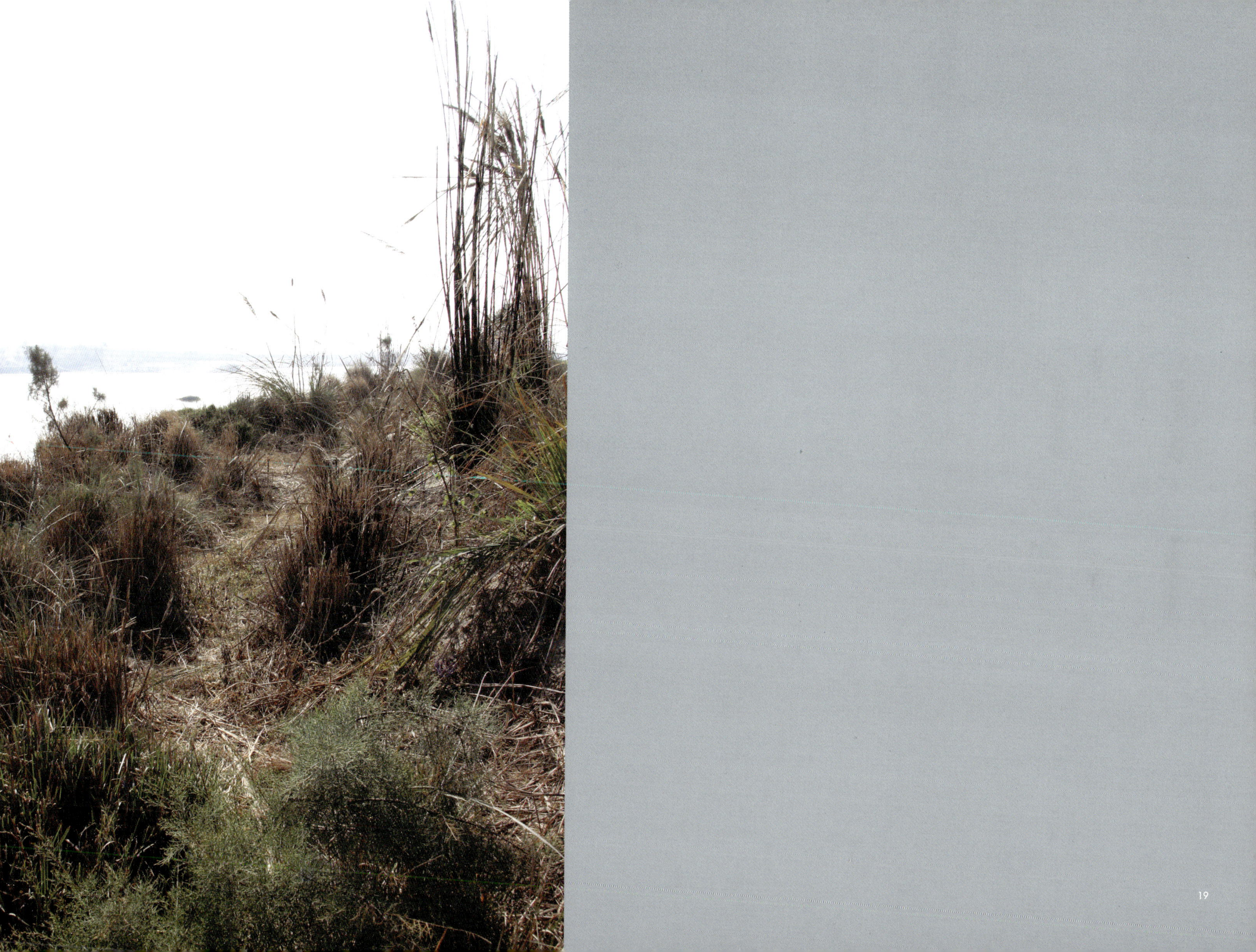

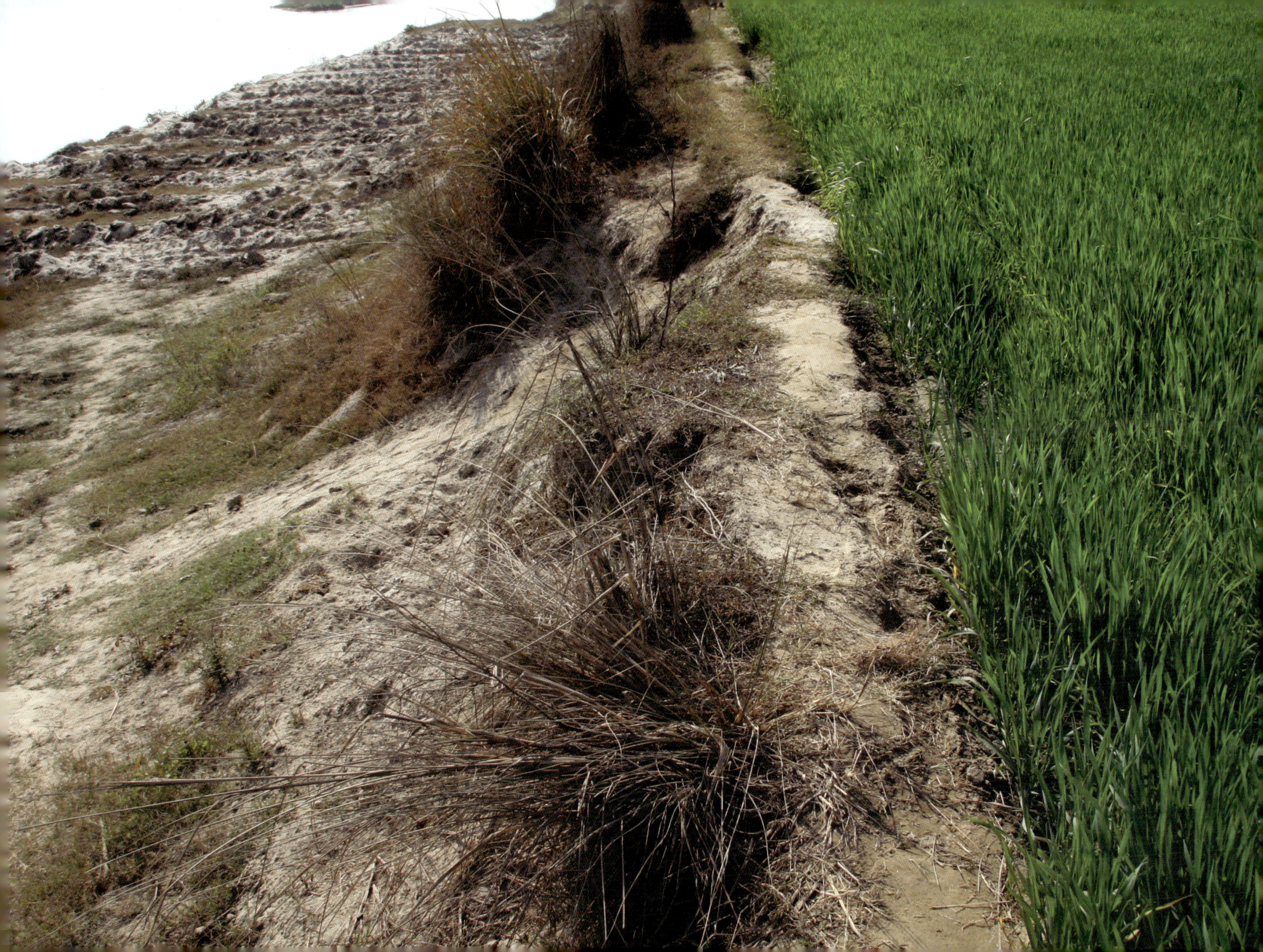

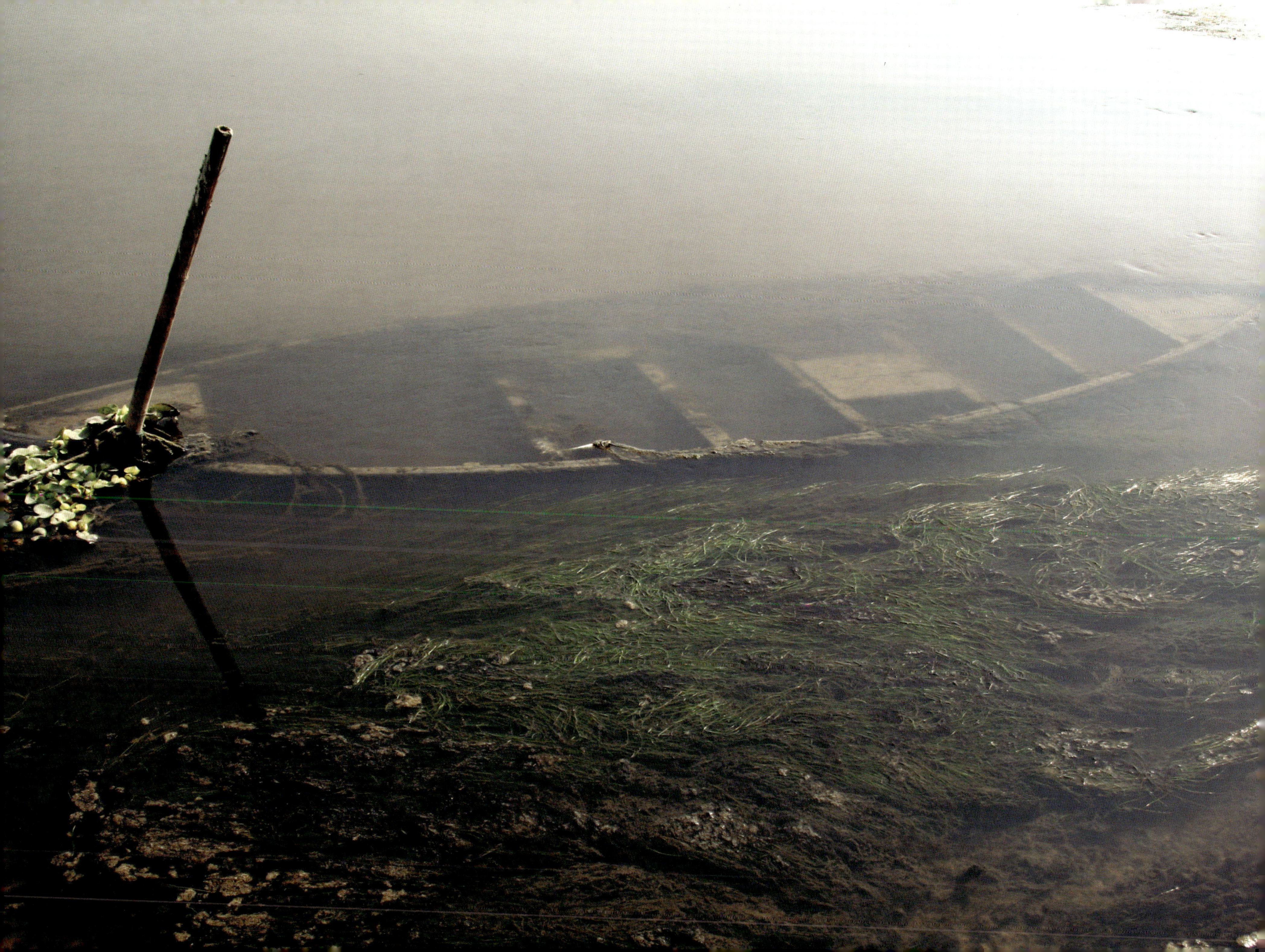

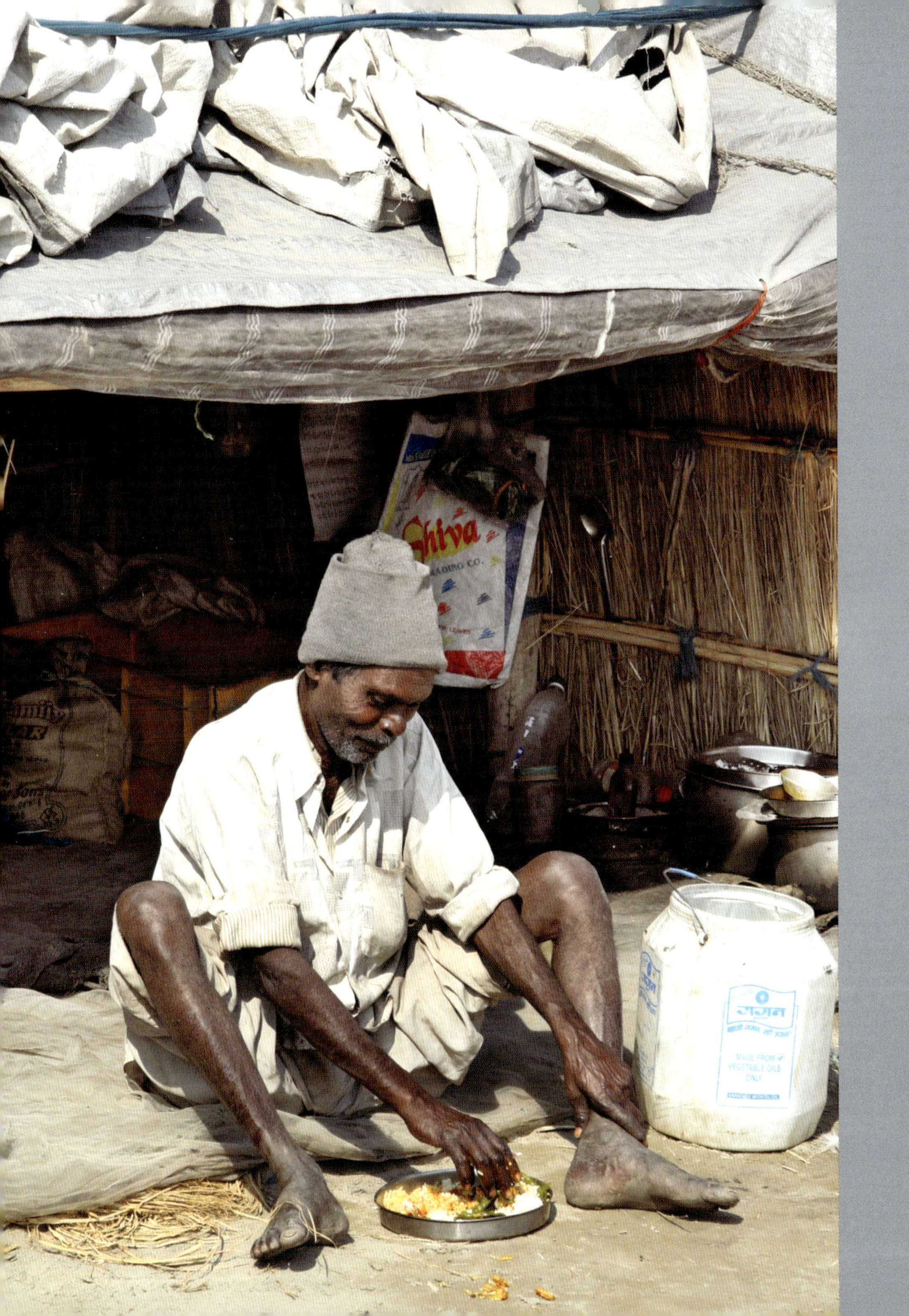
Shiva

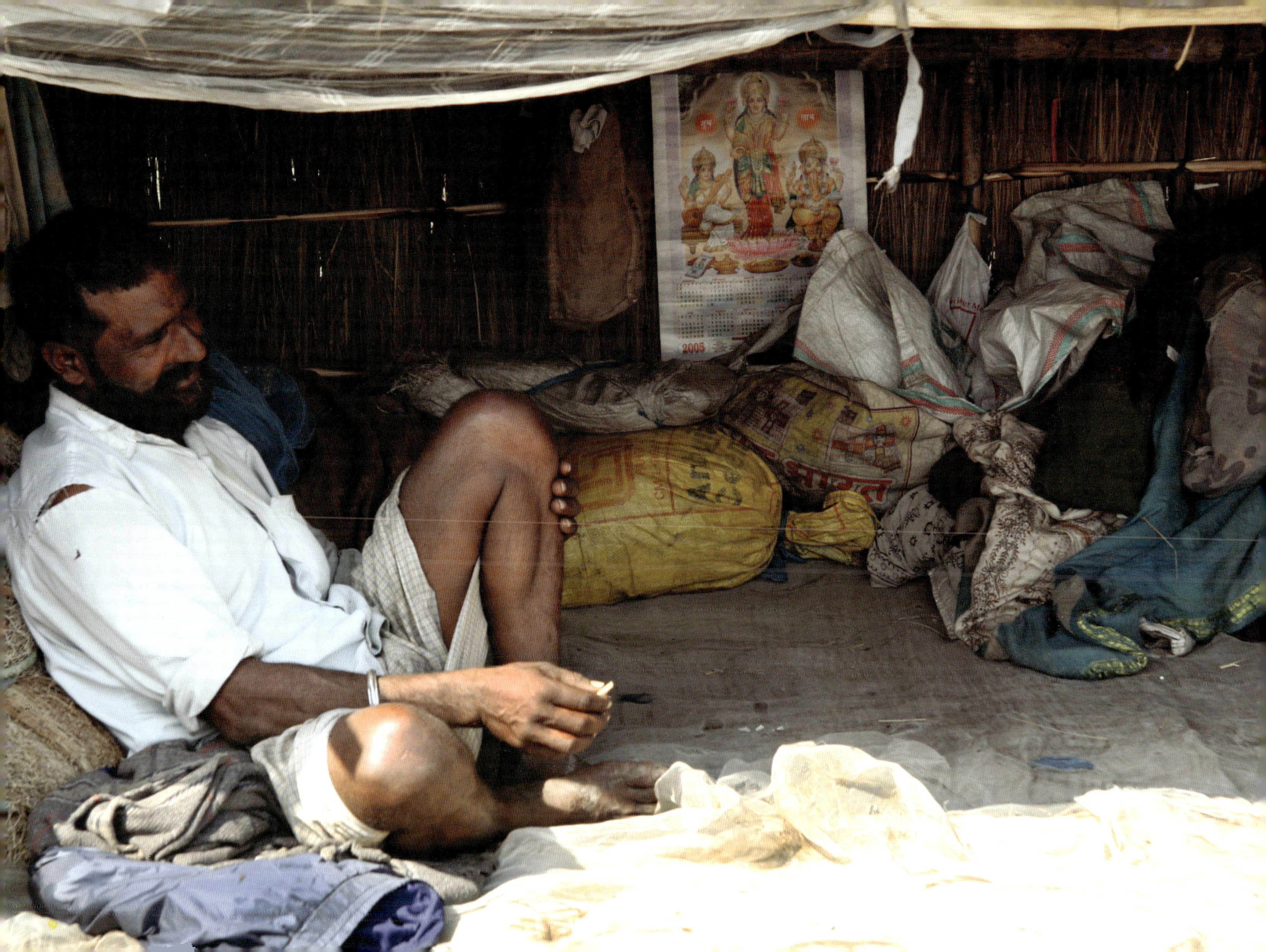
2005

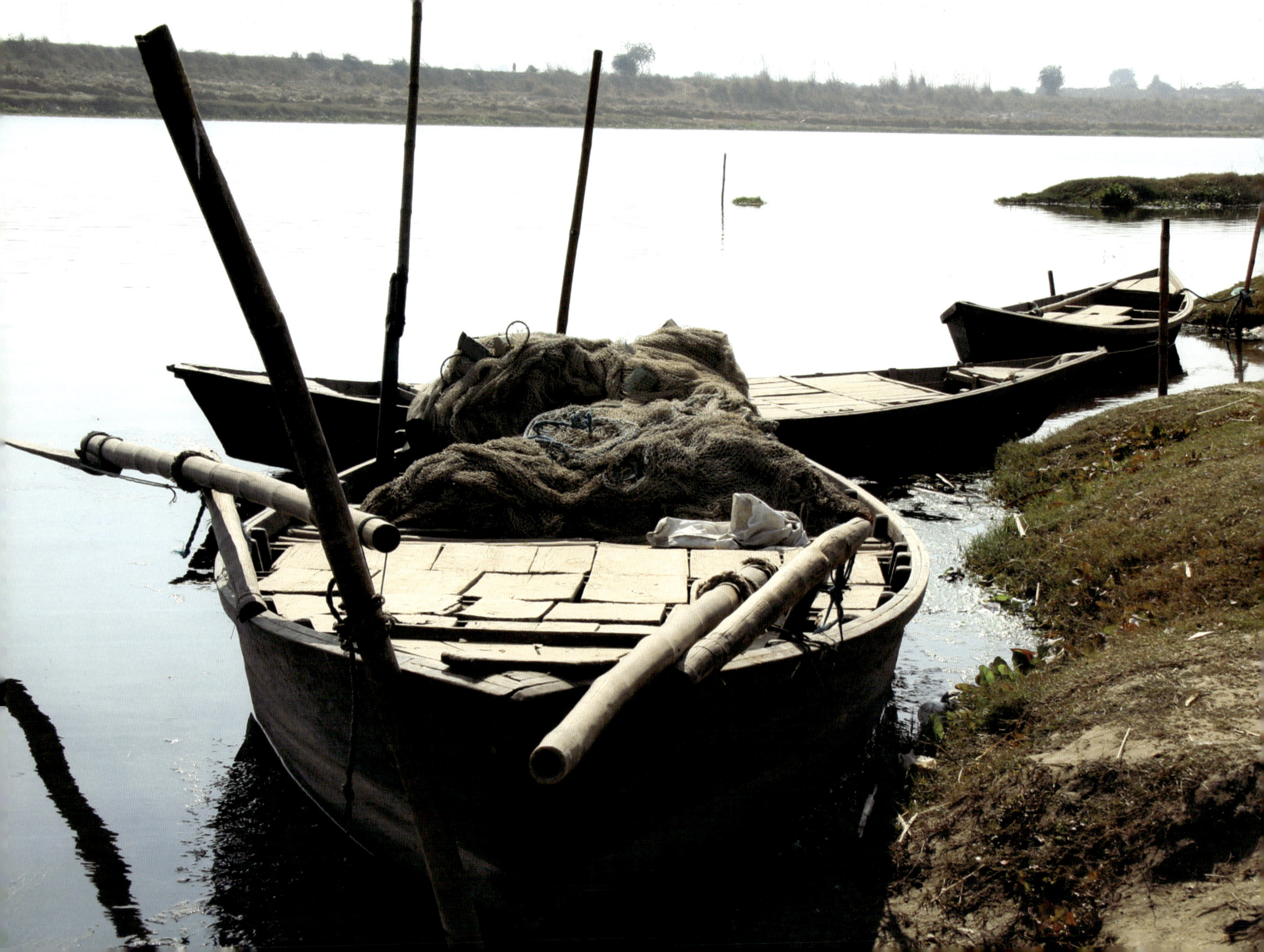

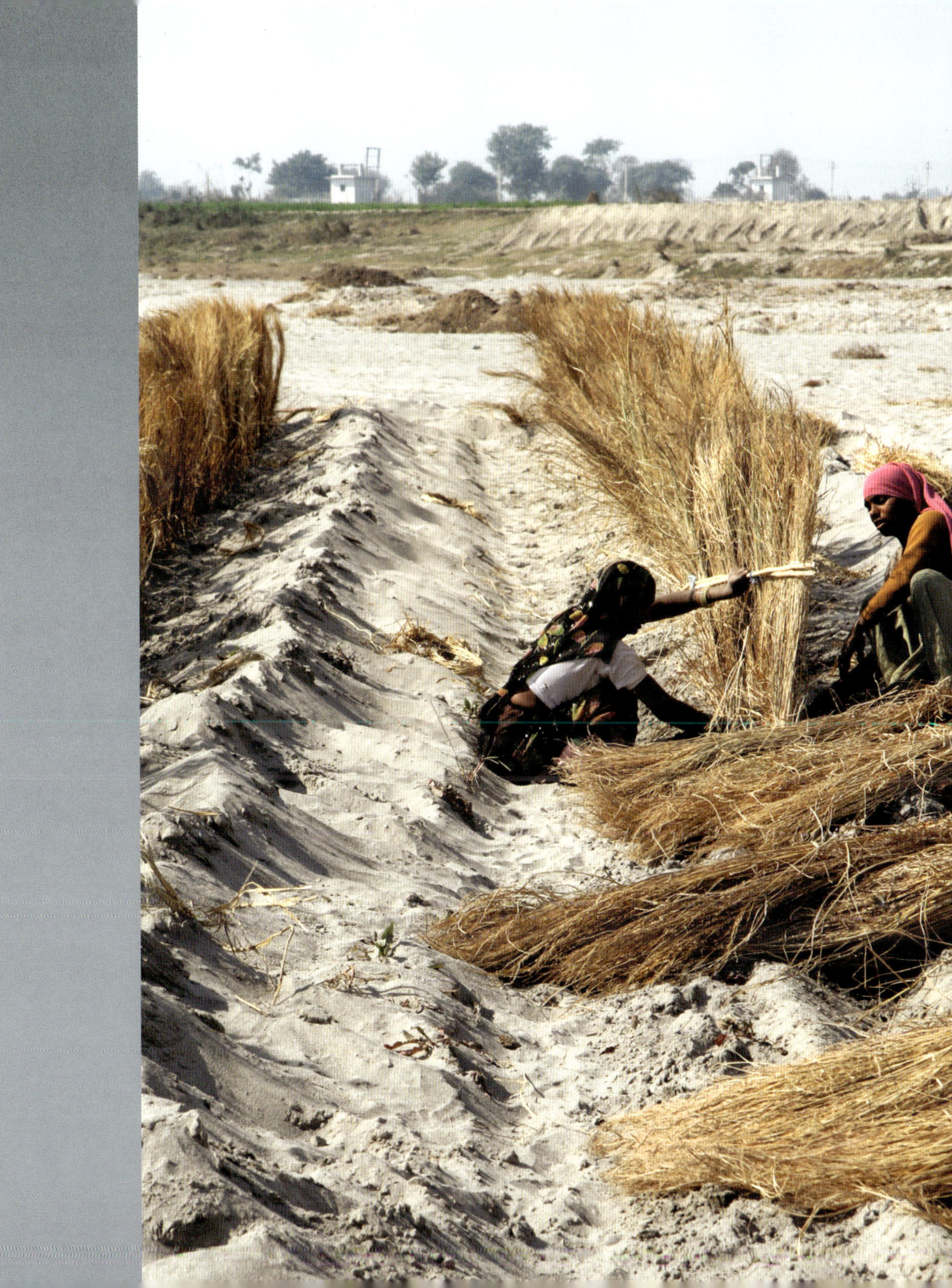

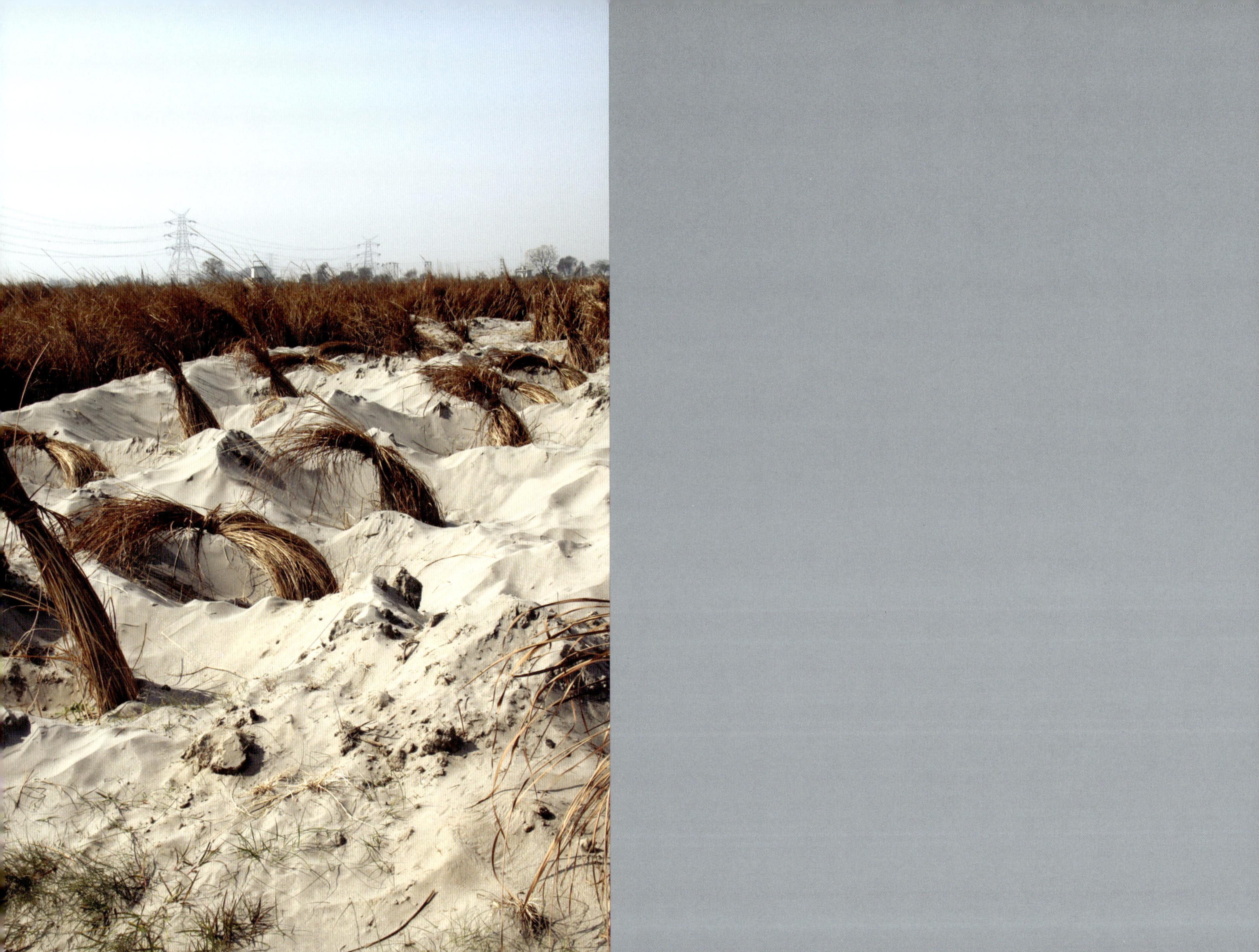

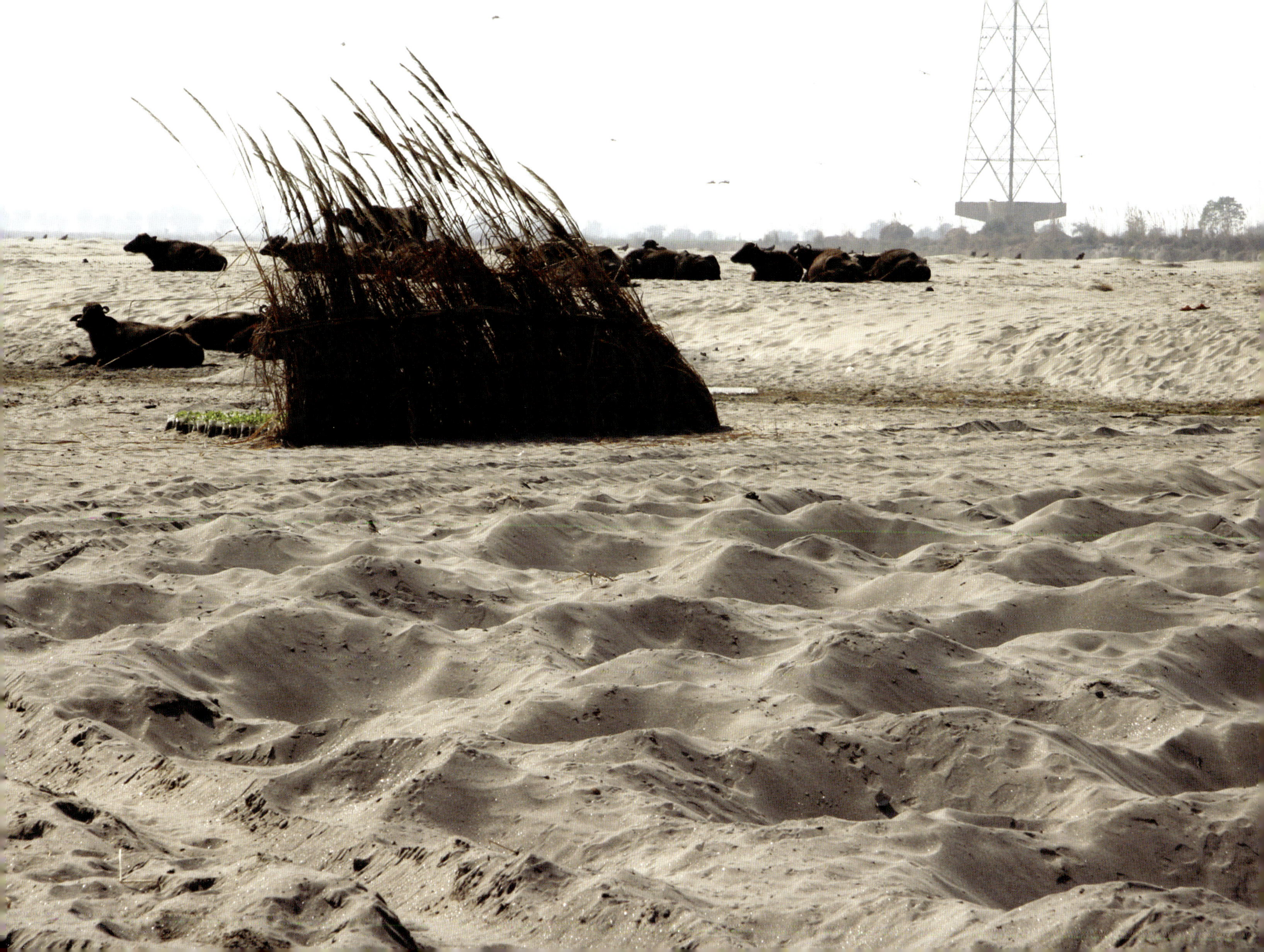

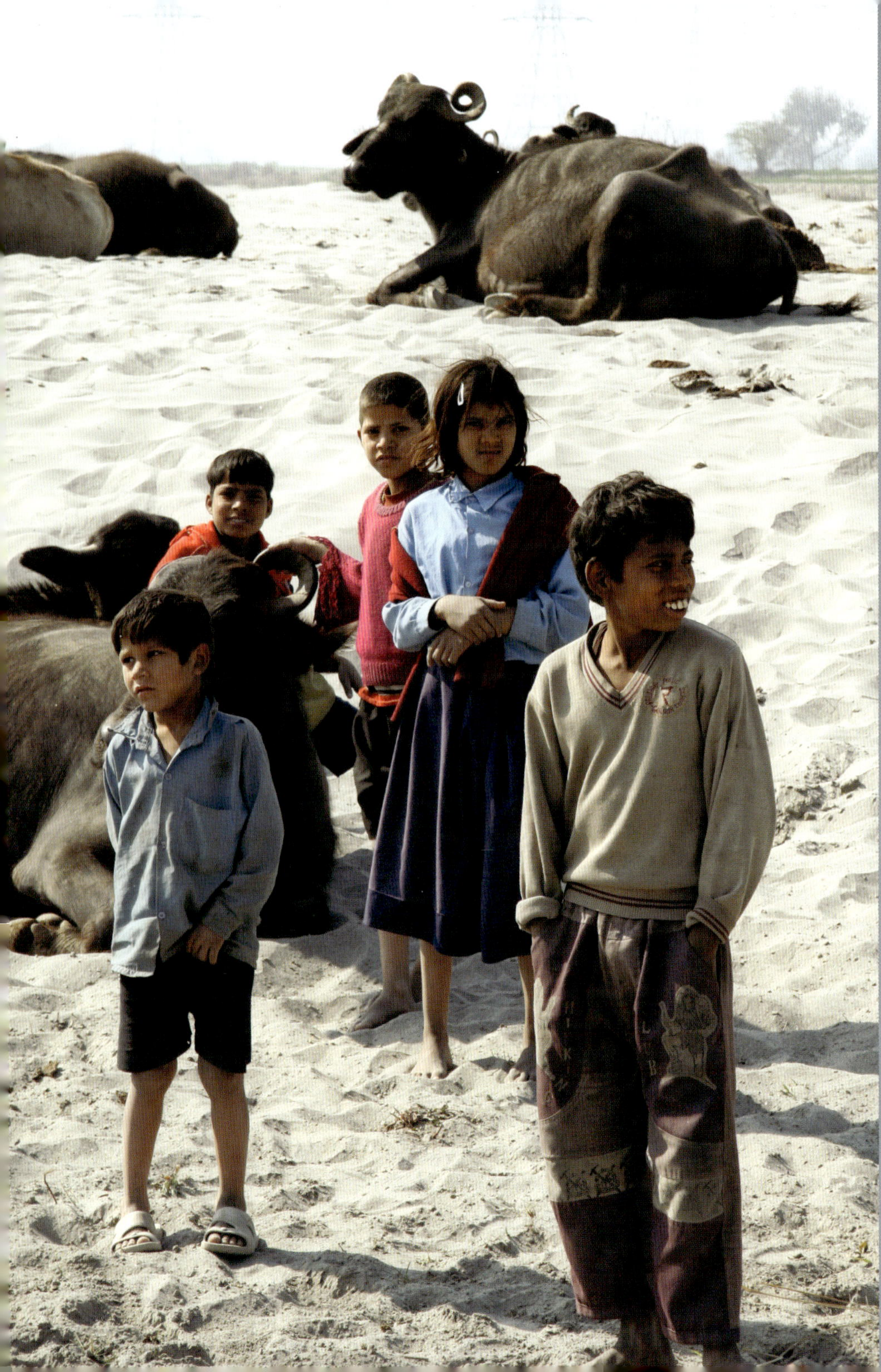

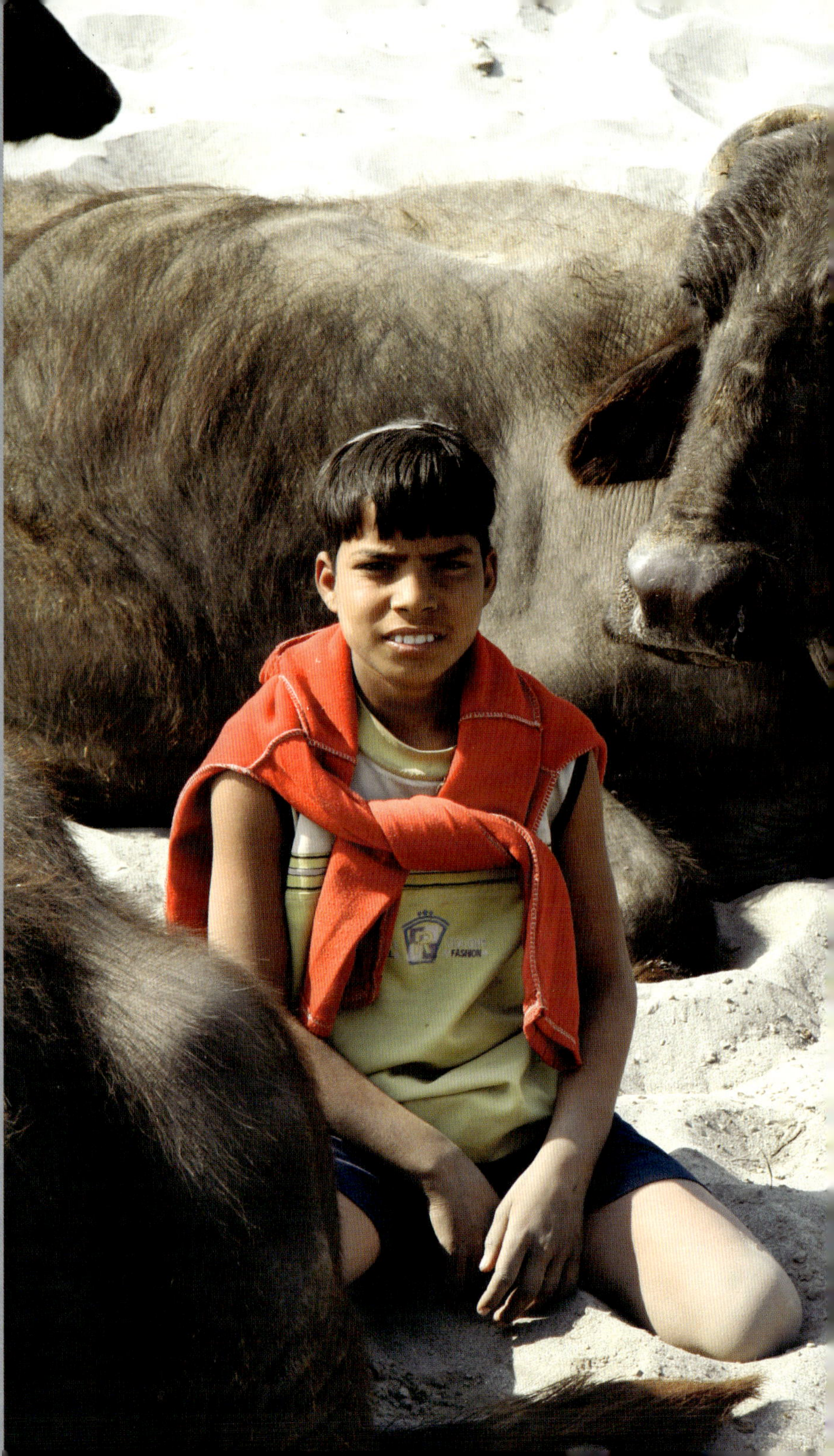

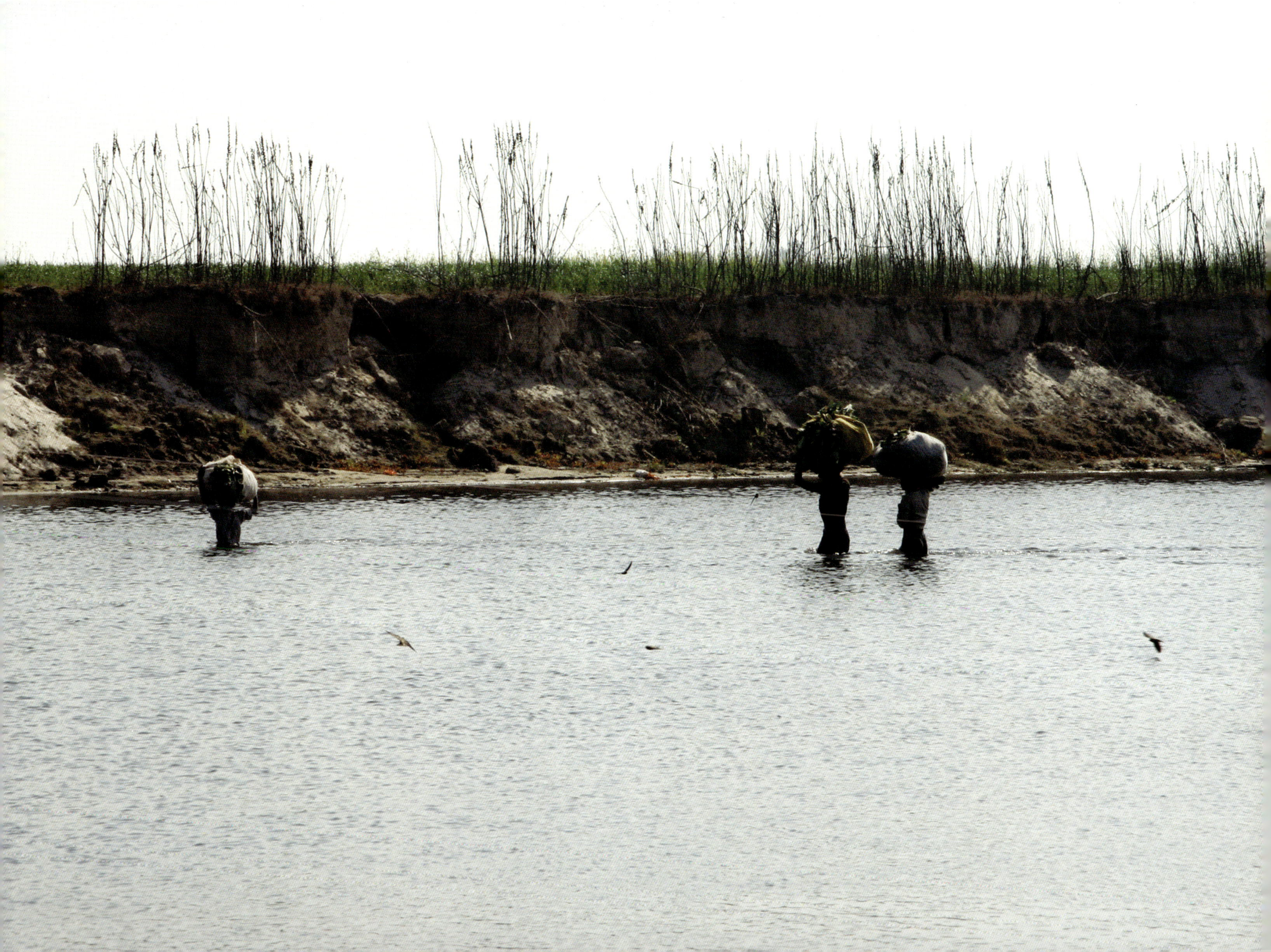

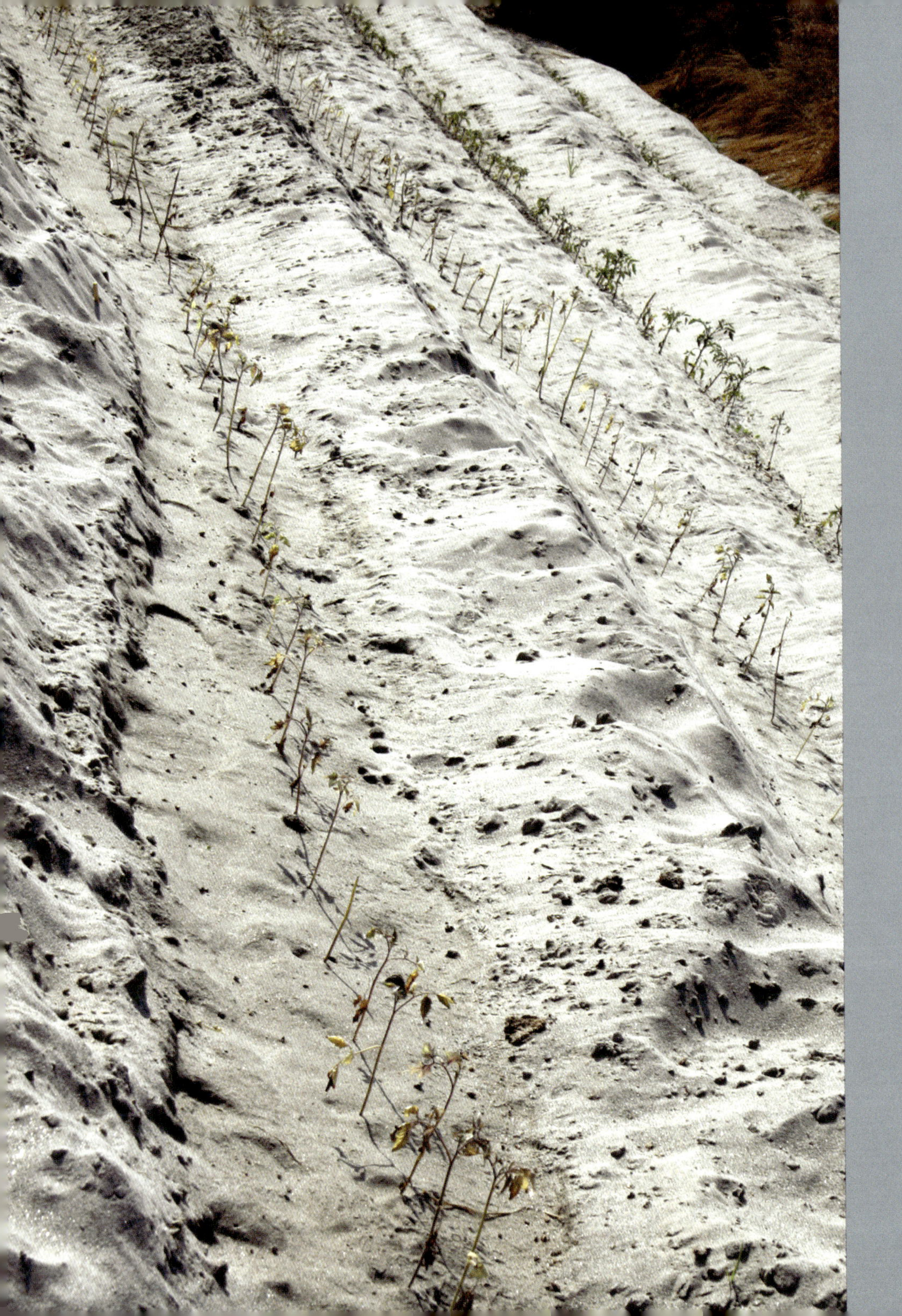

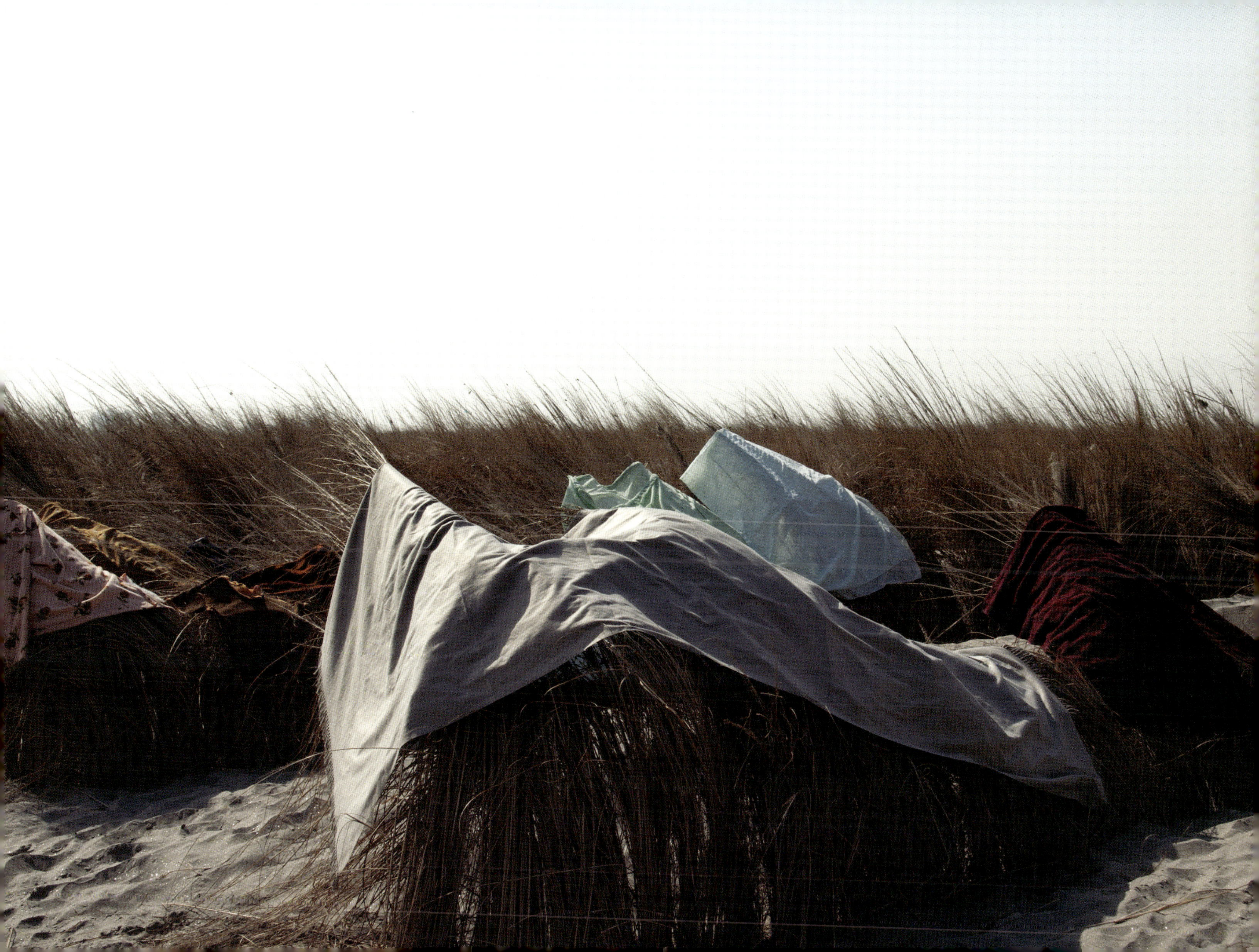

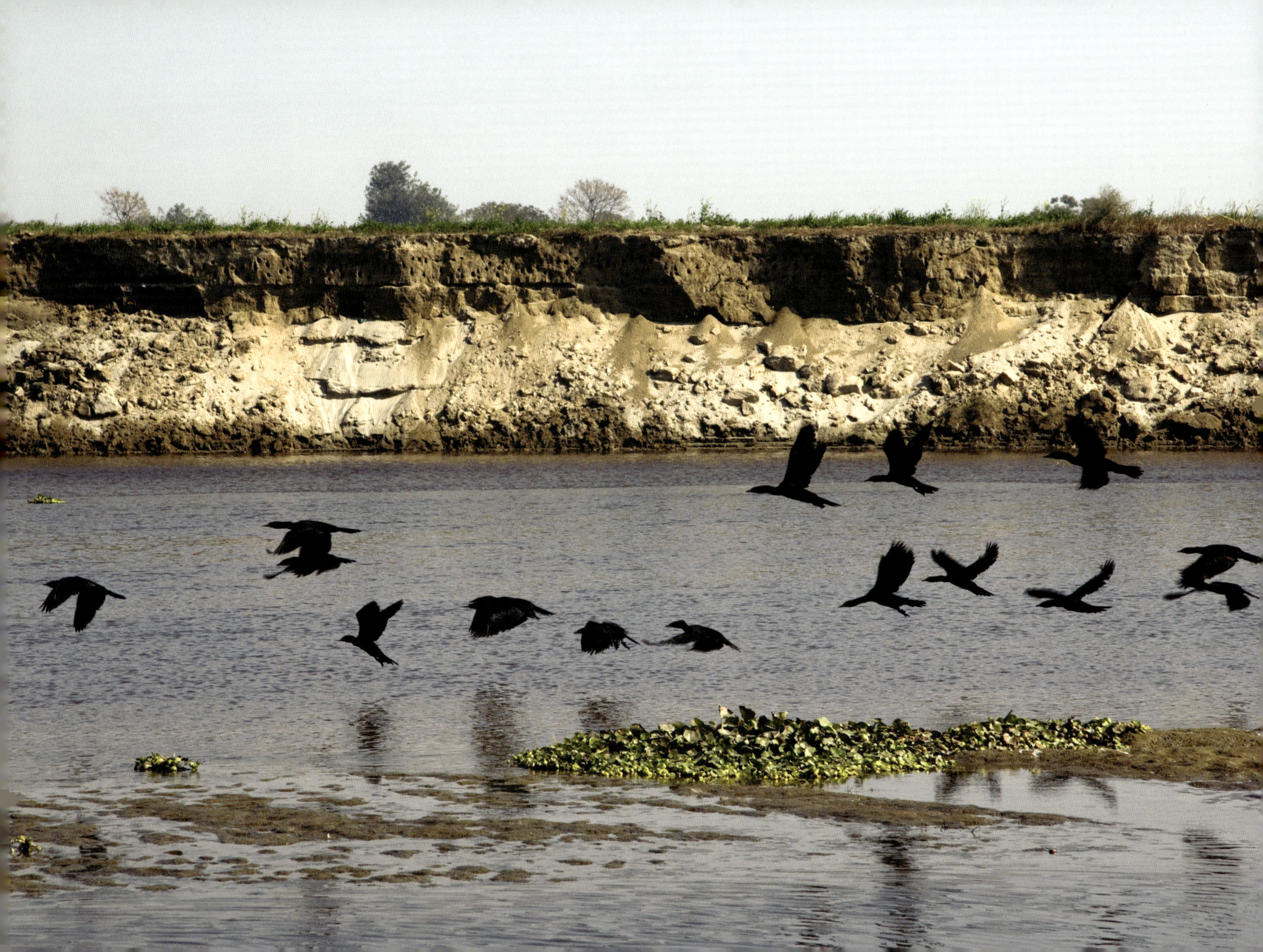

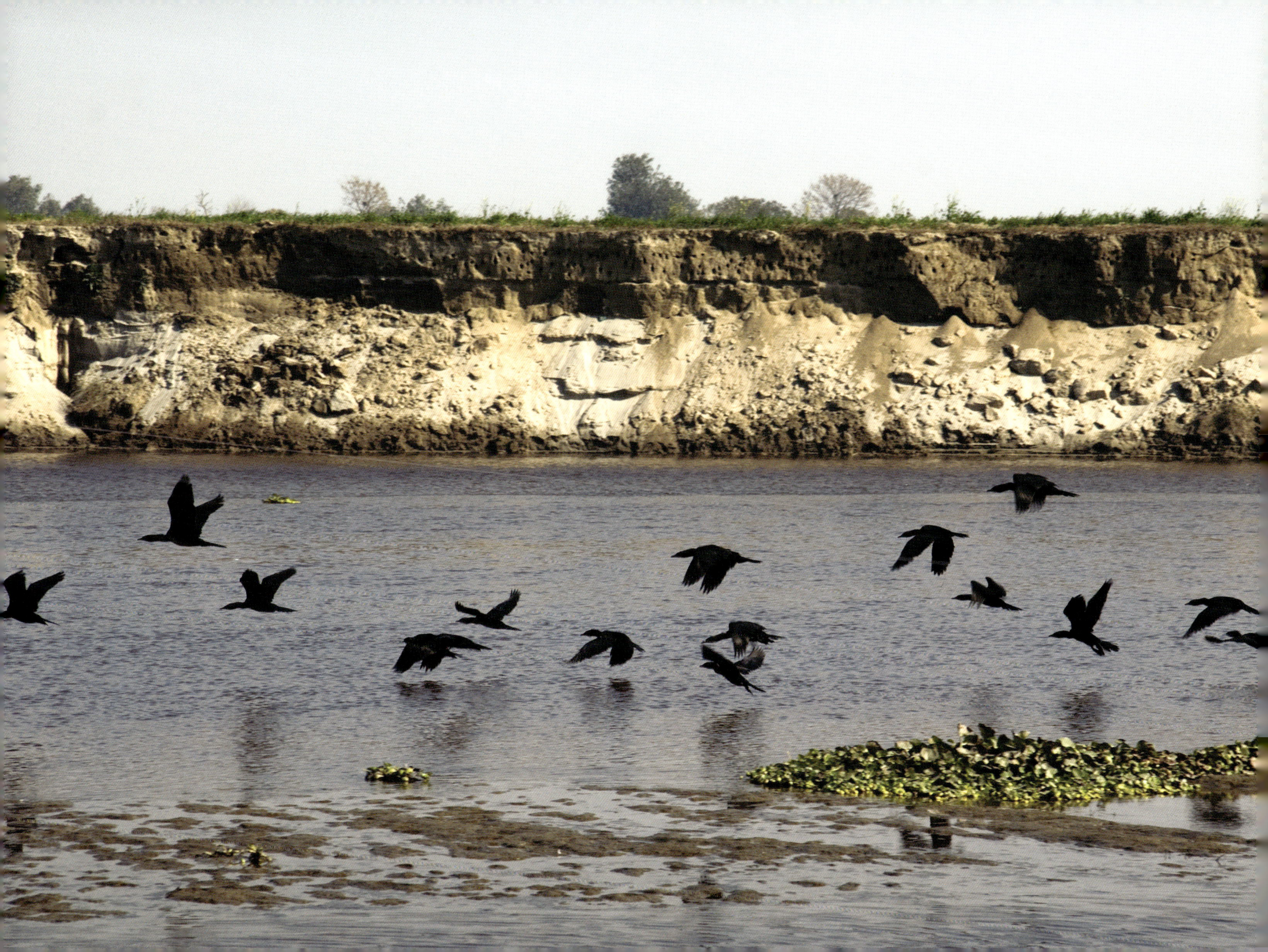

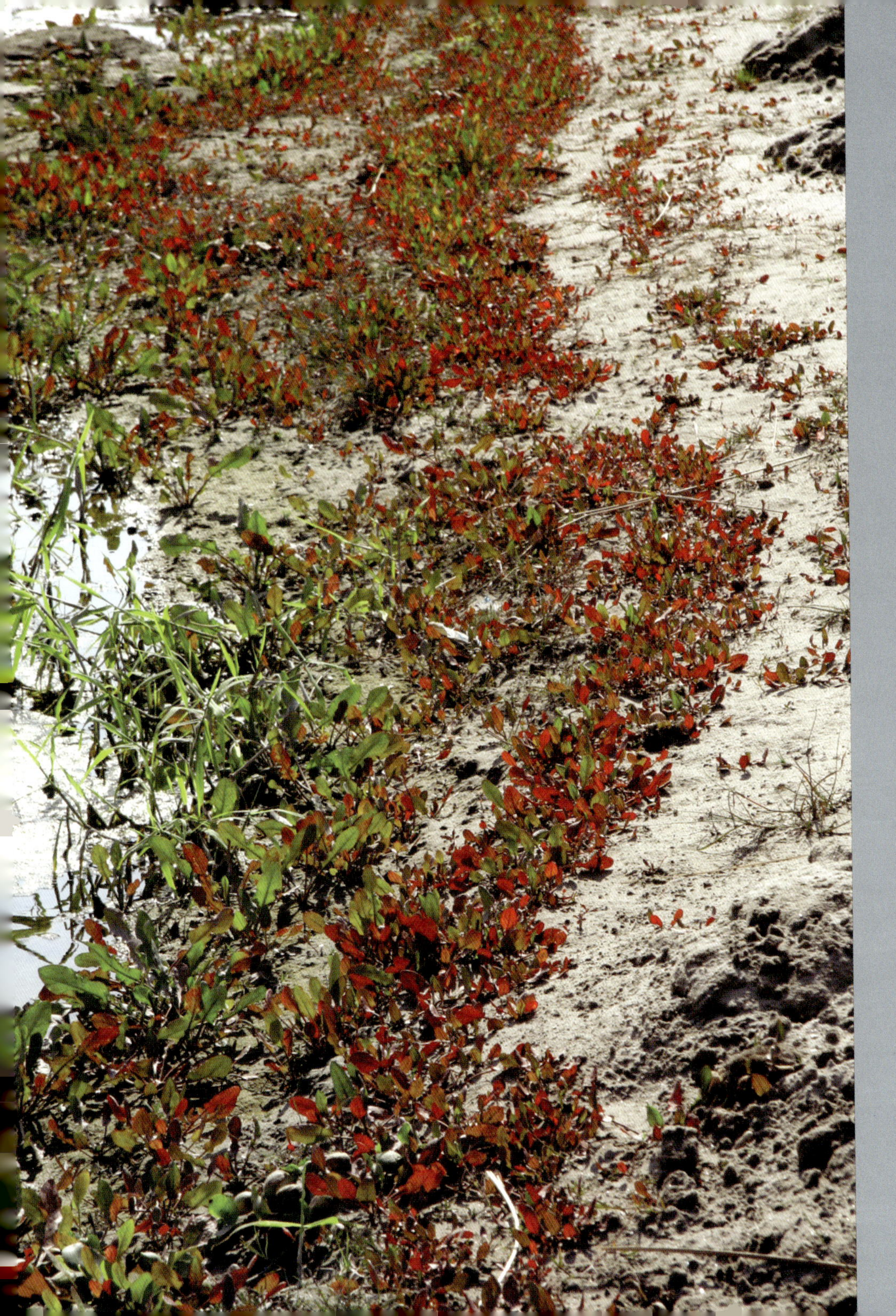

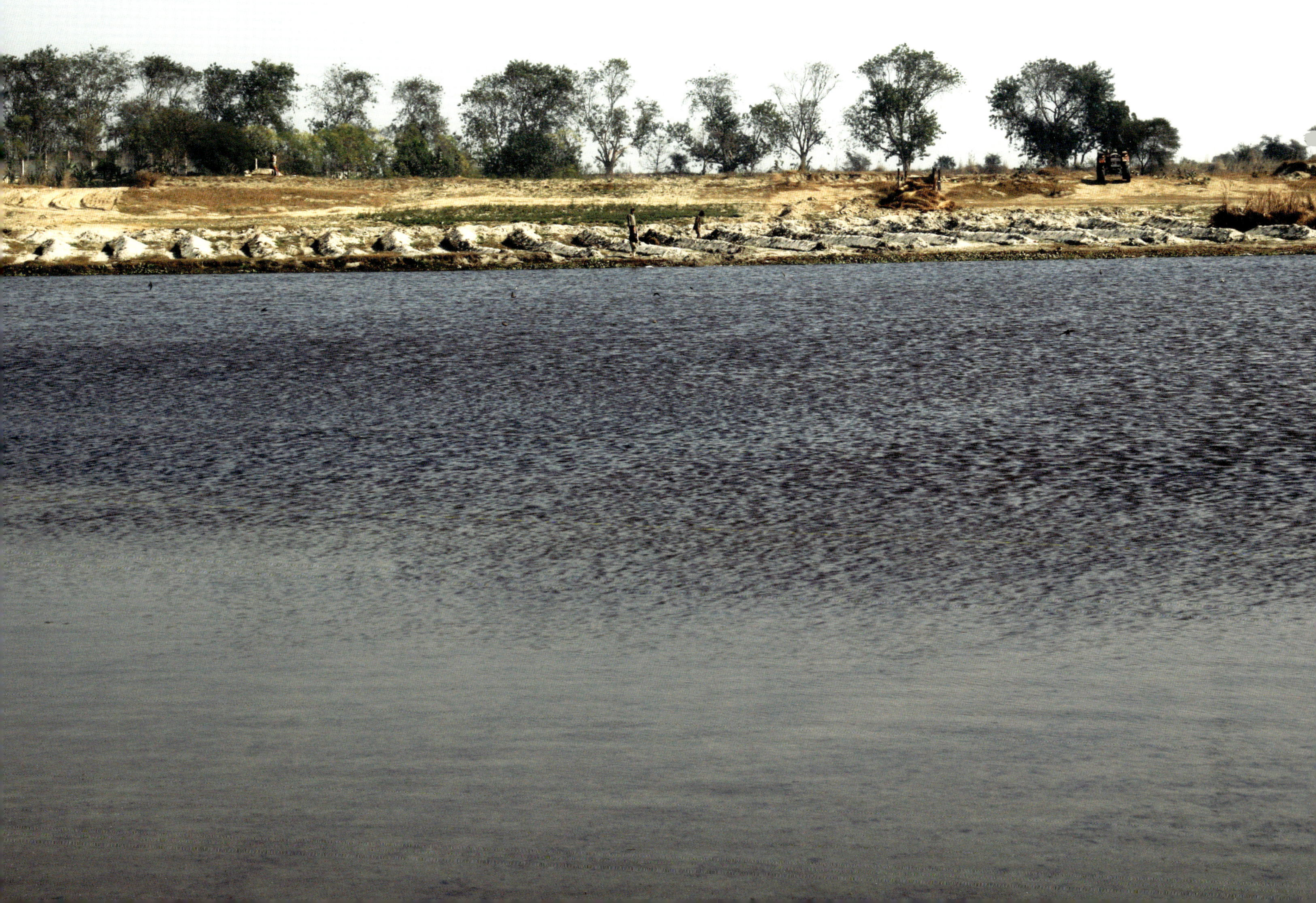

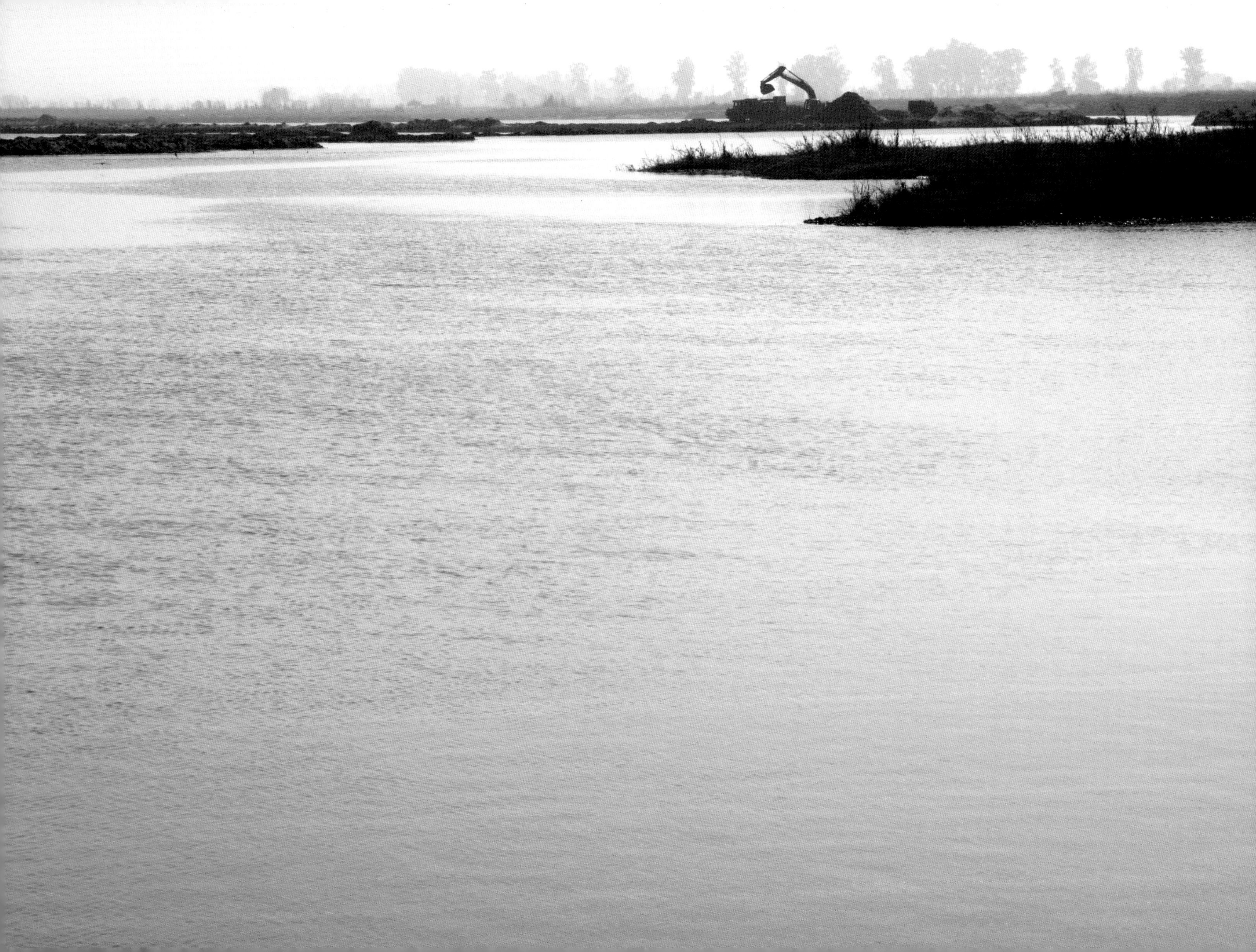

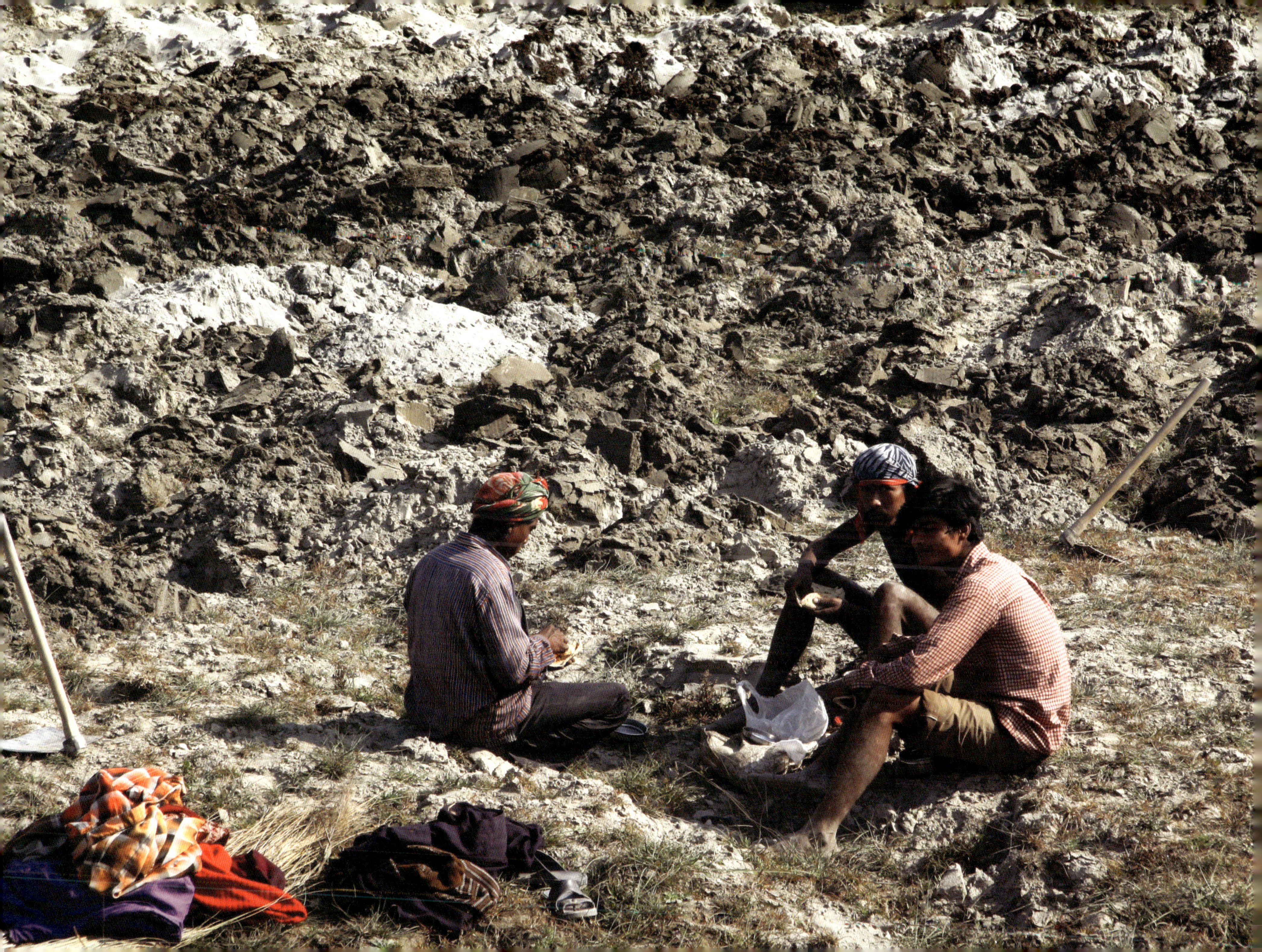

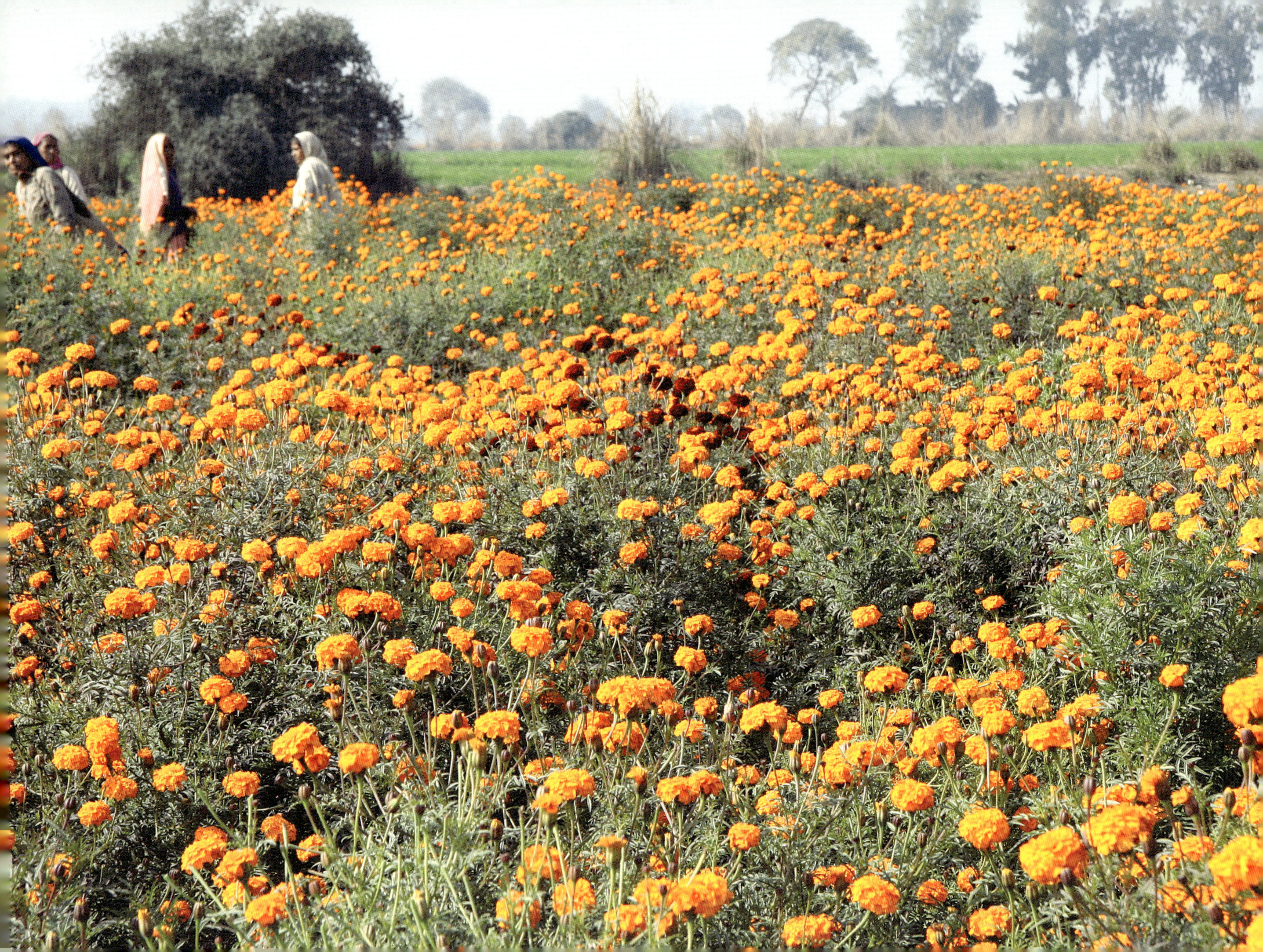

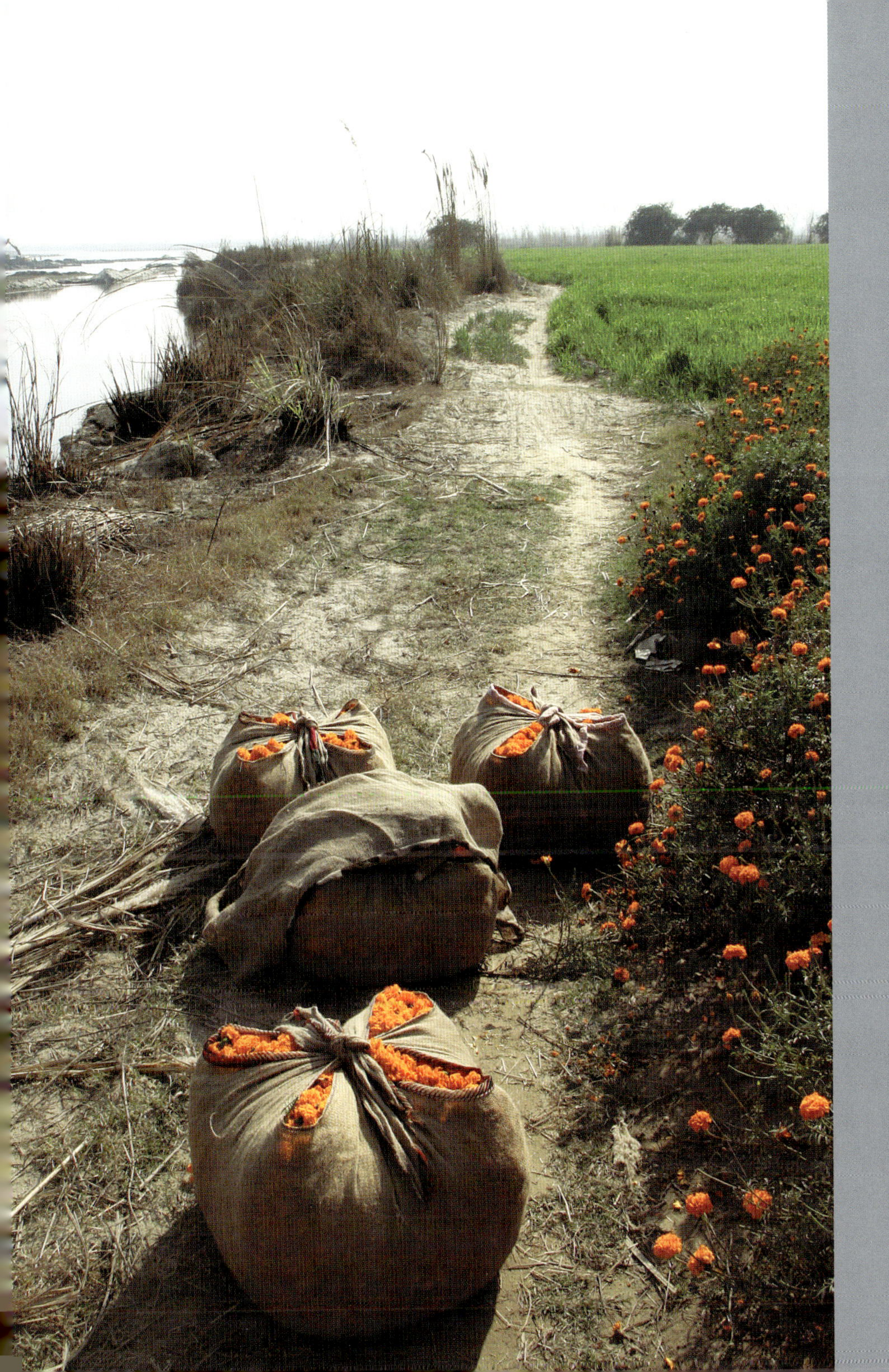

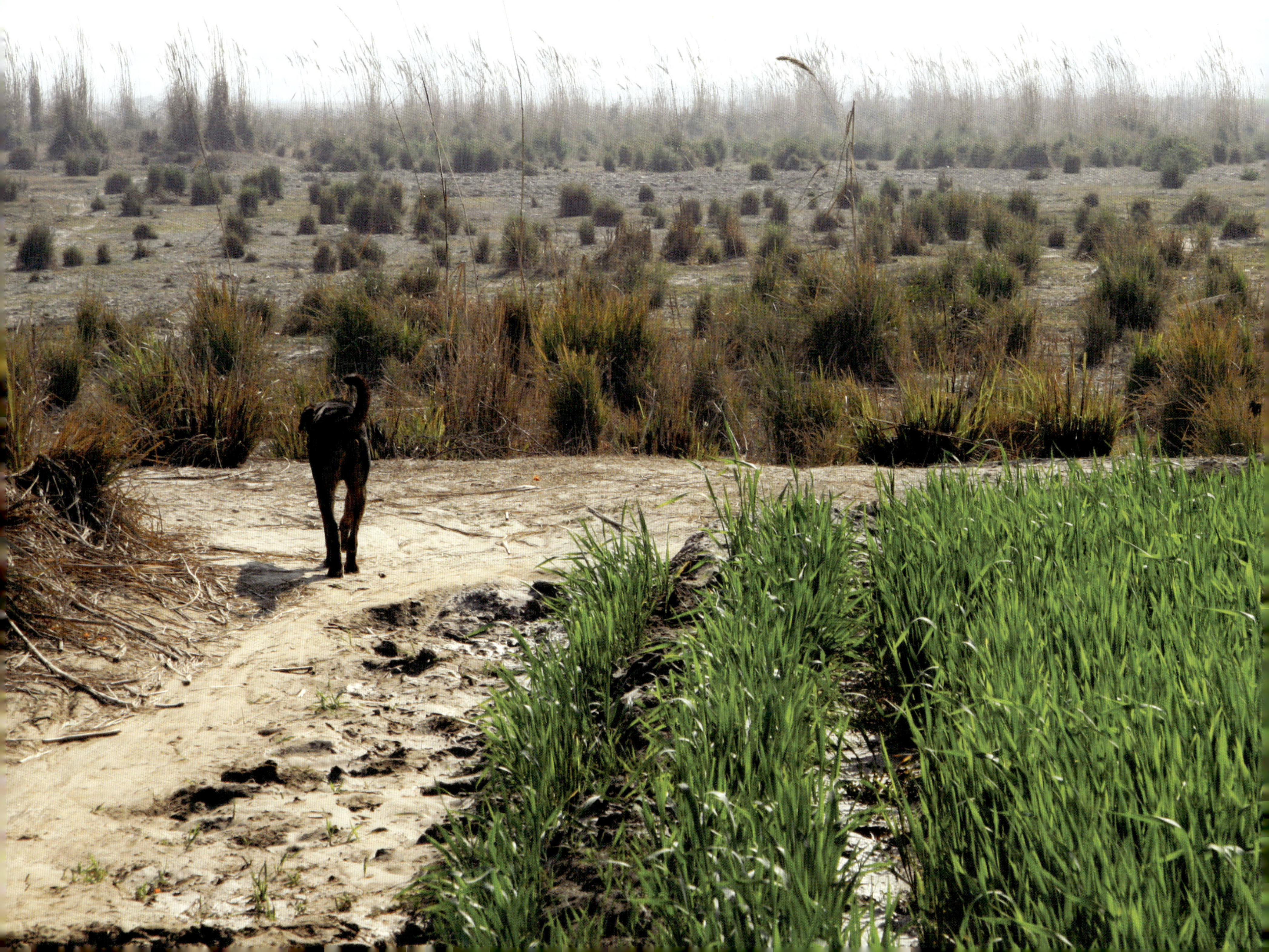

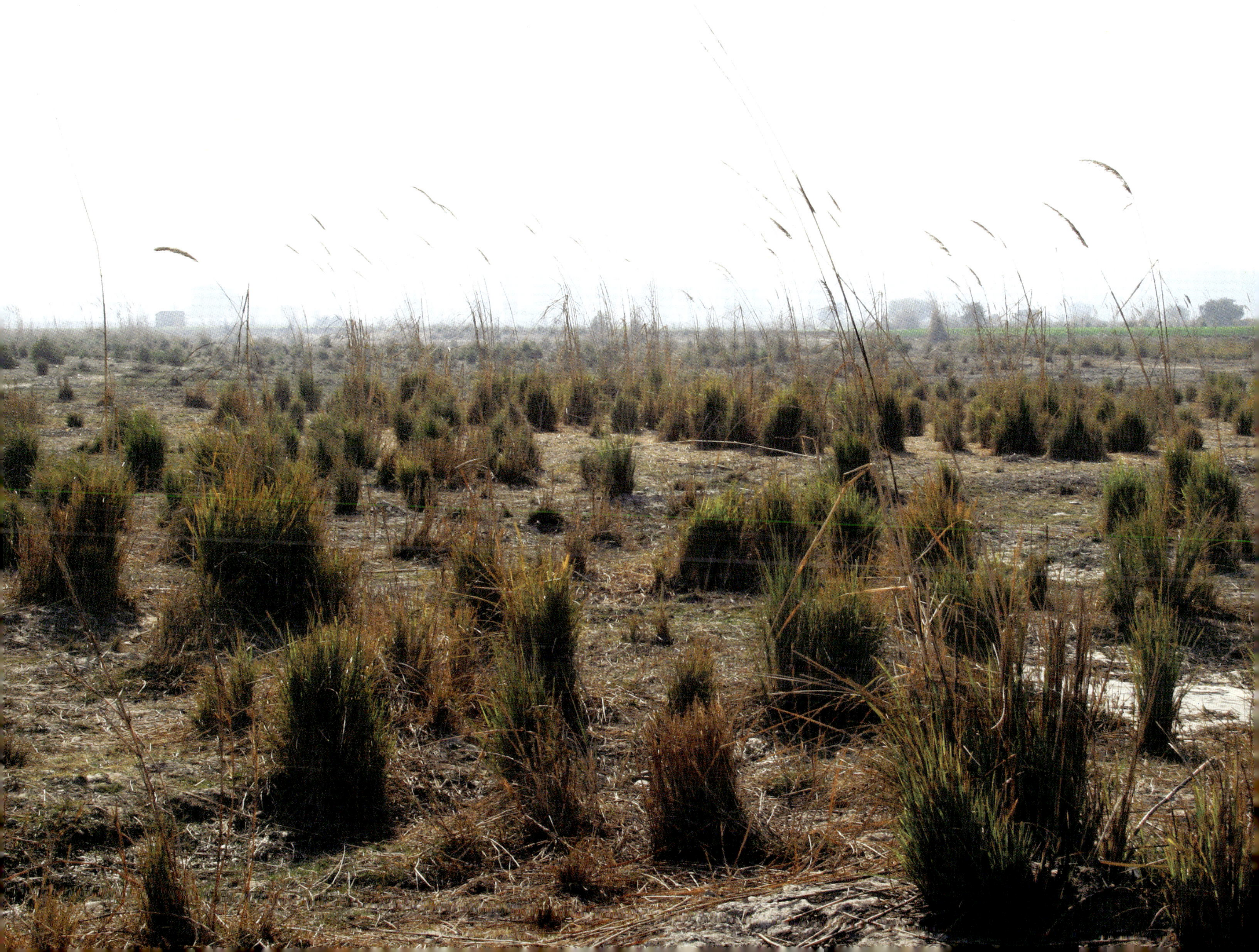

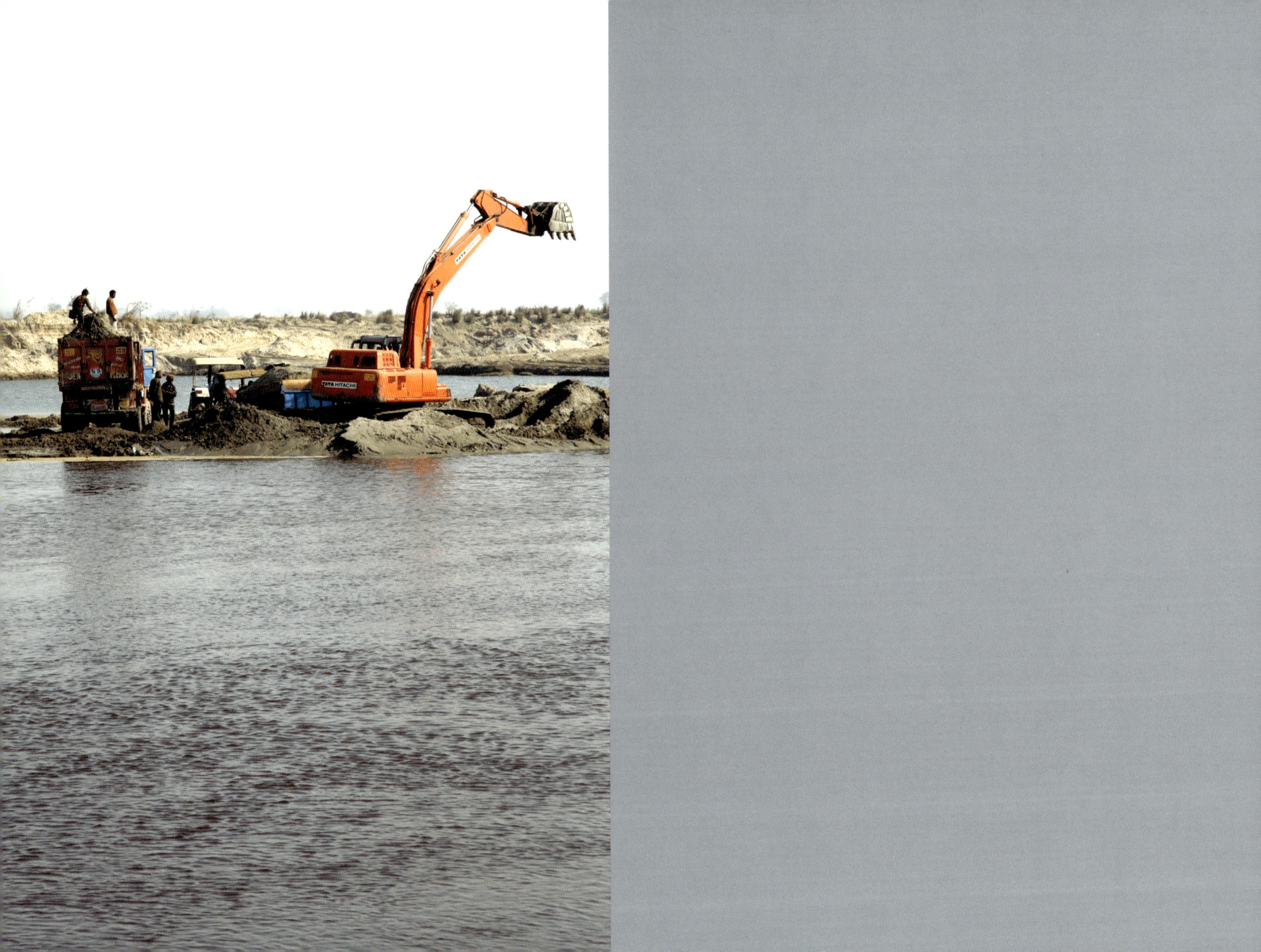
TATA HITACHI

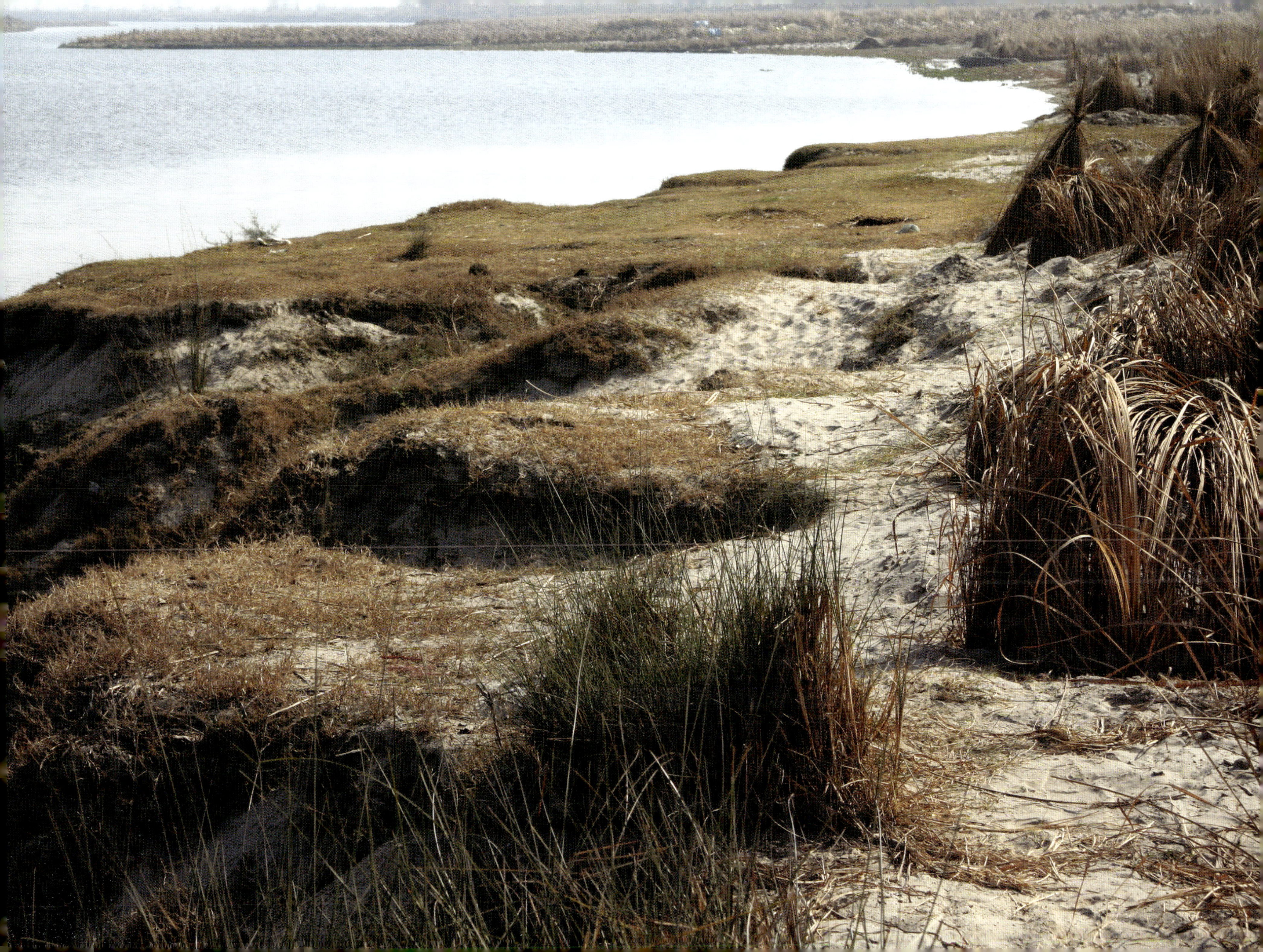

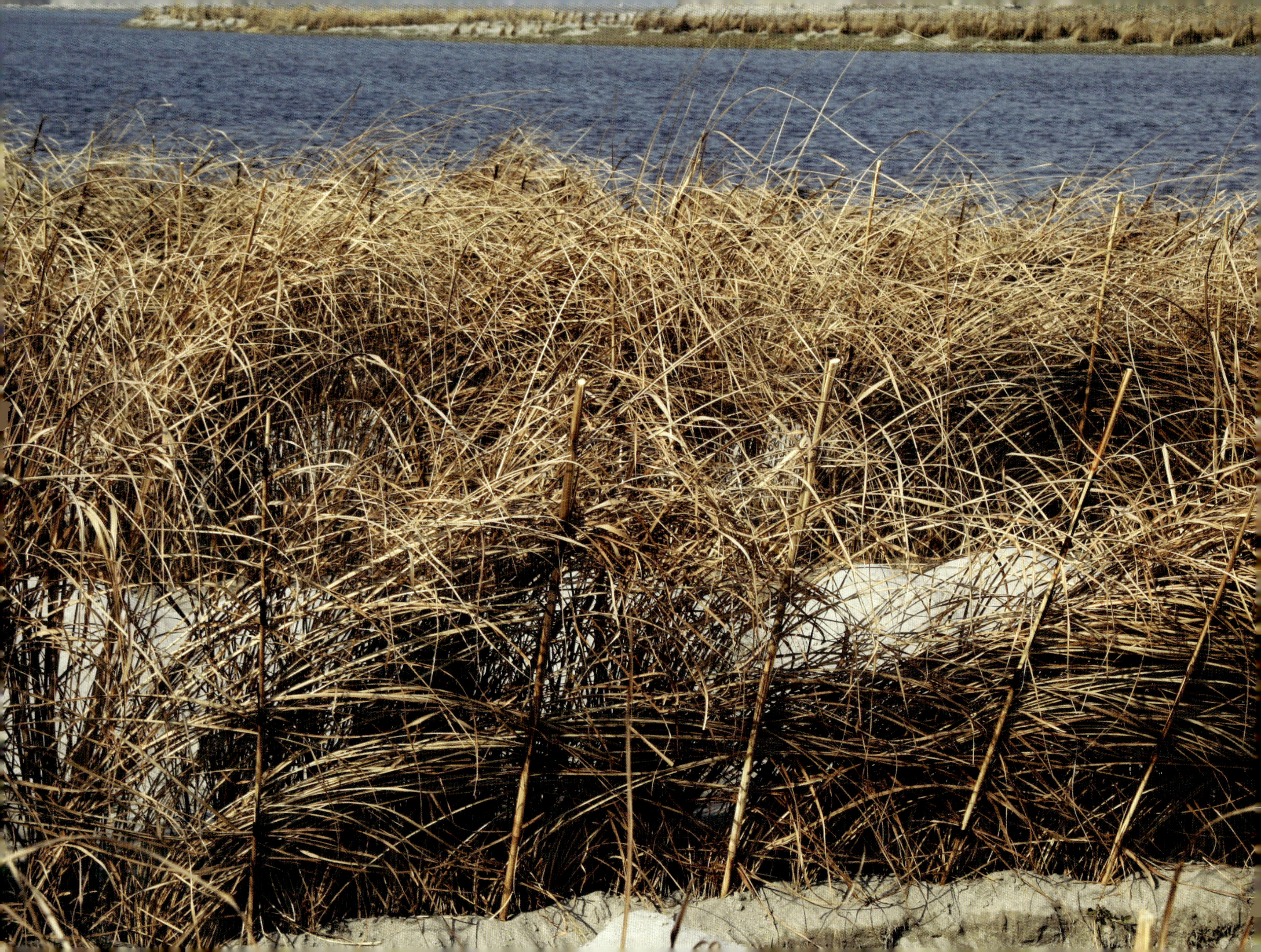

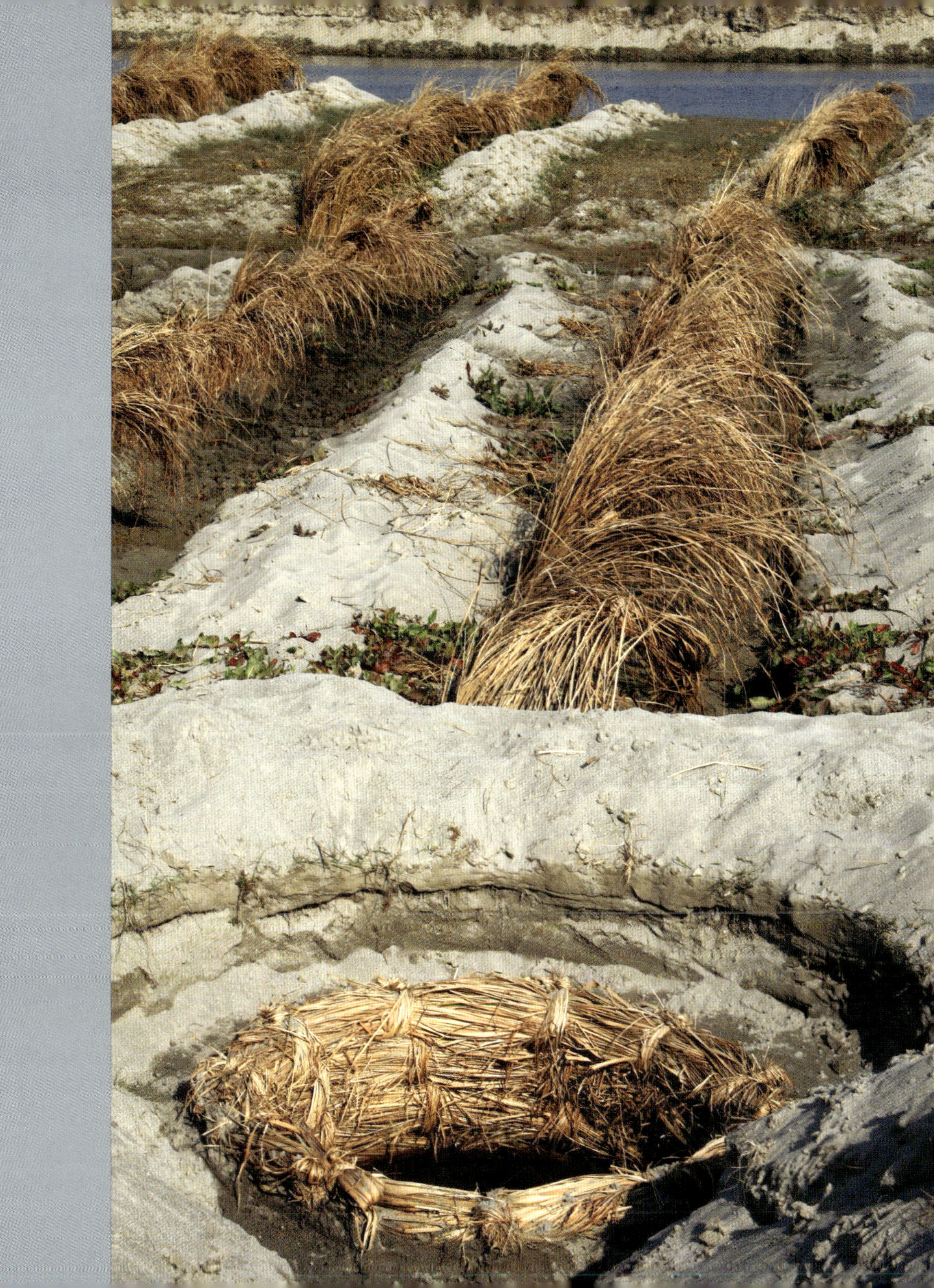

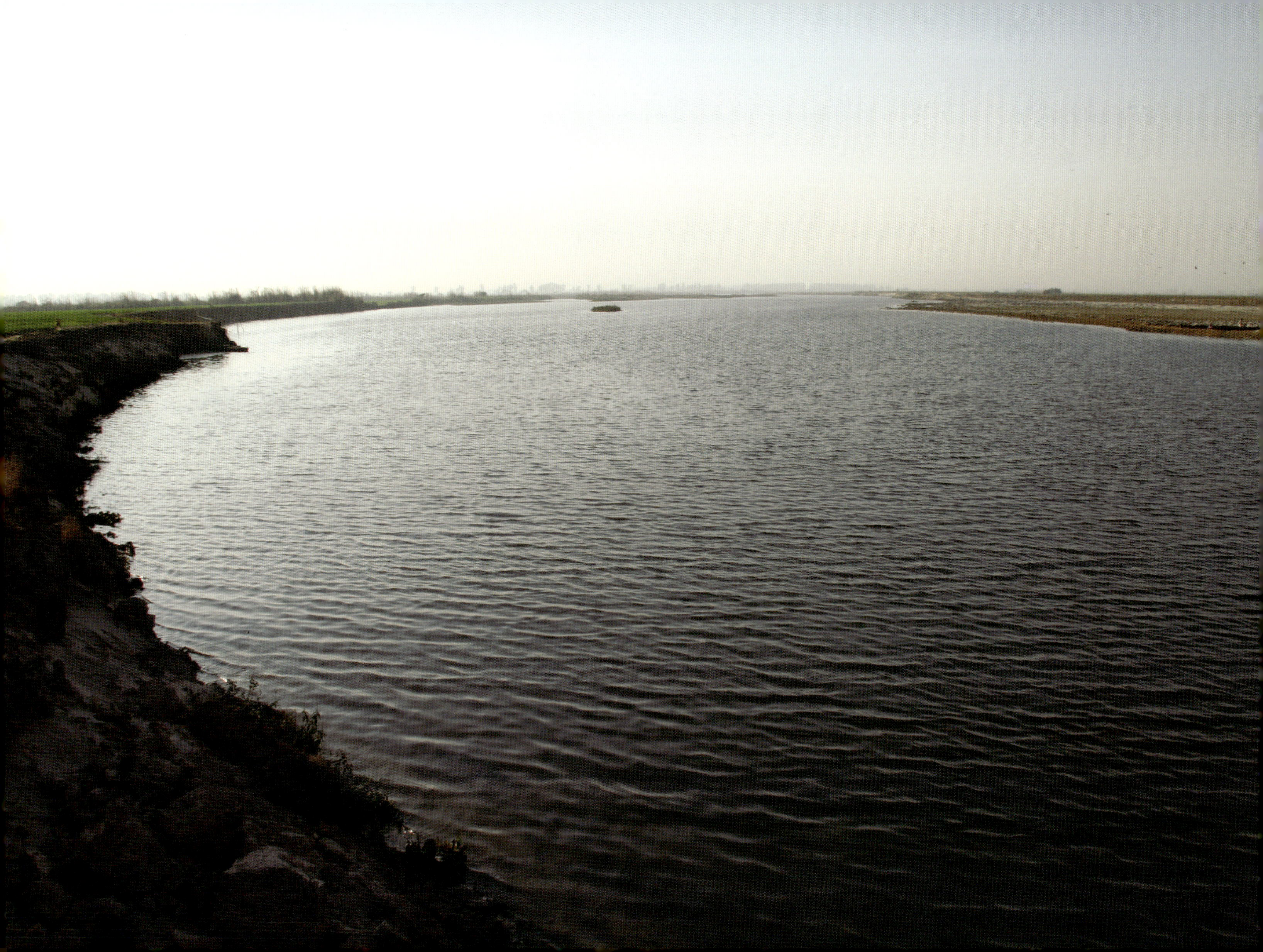

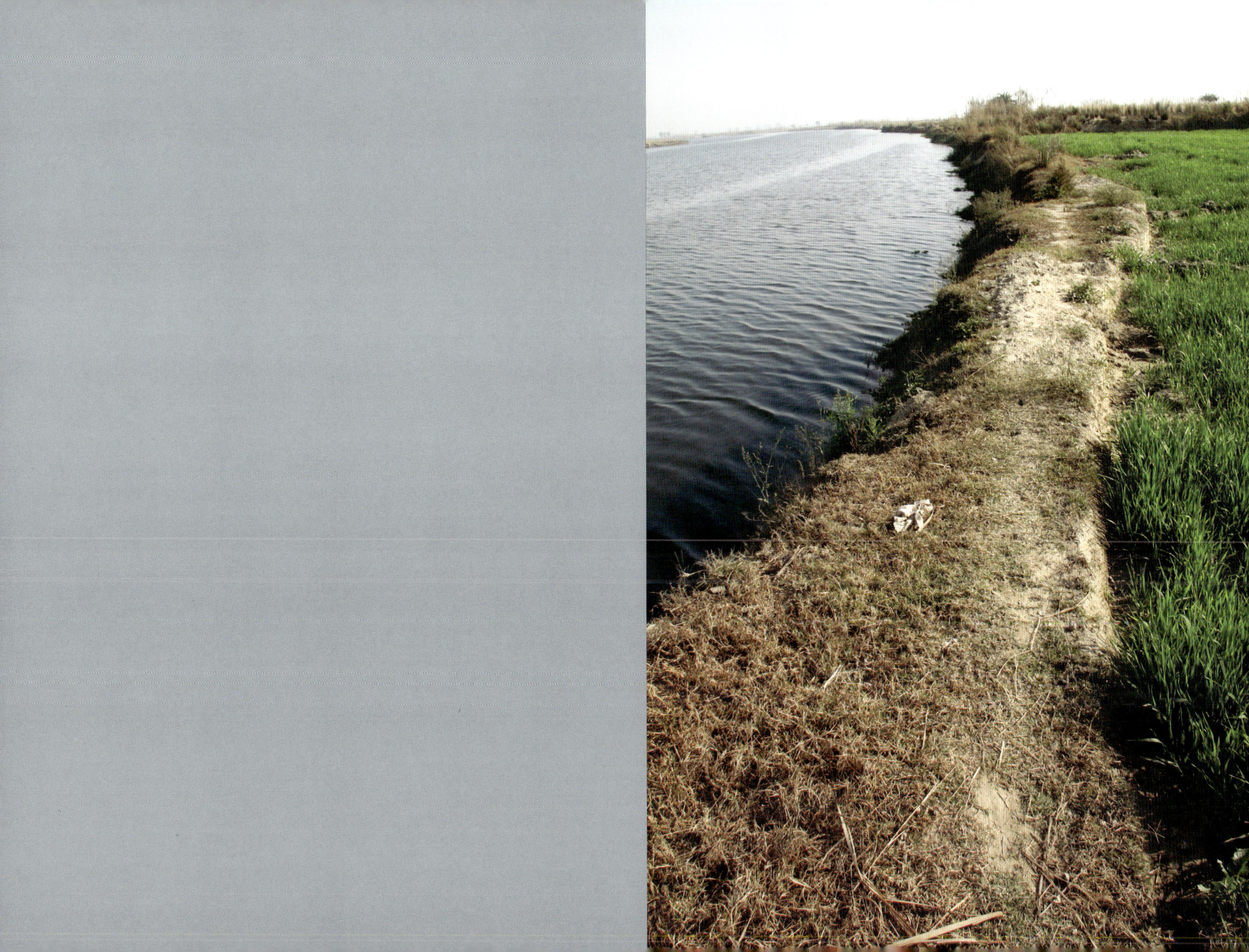

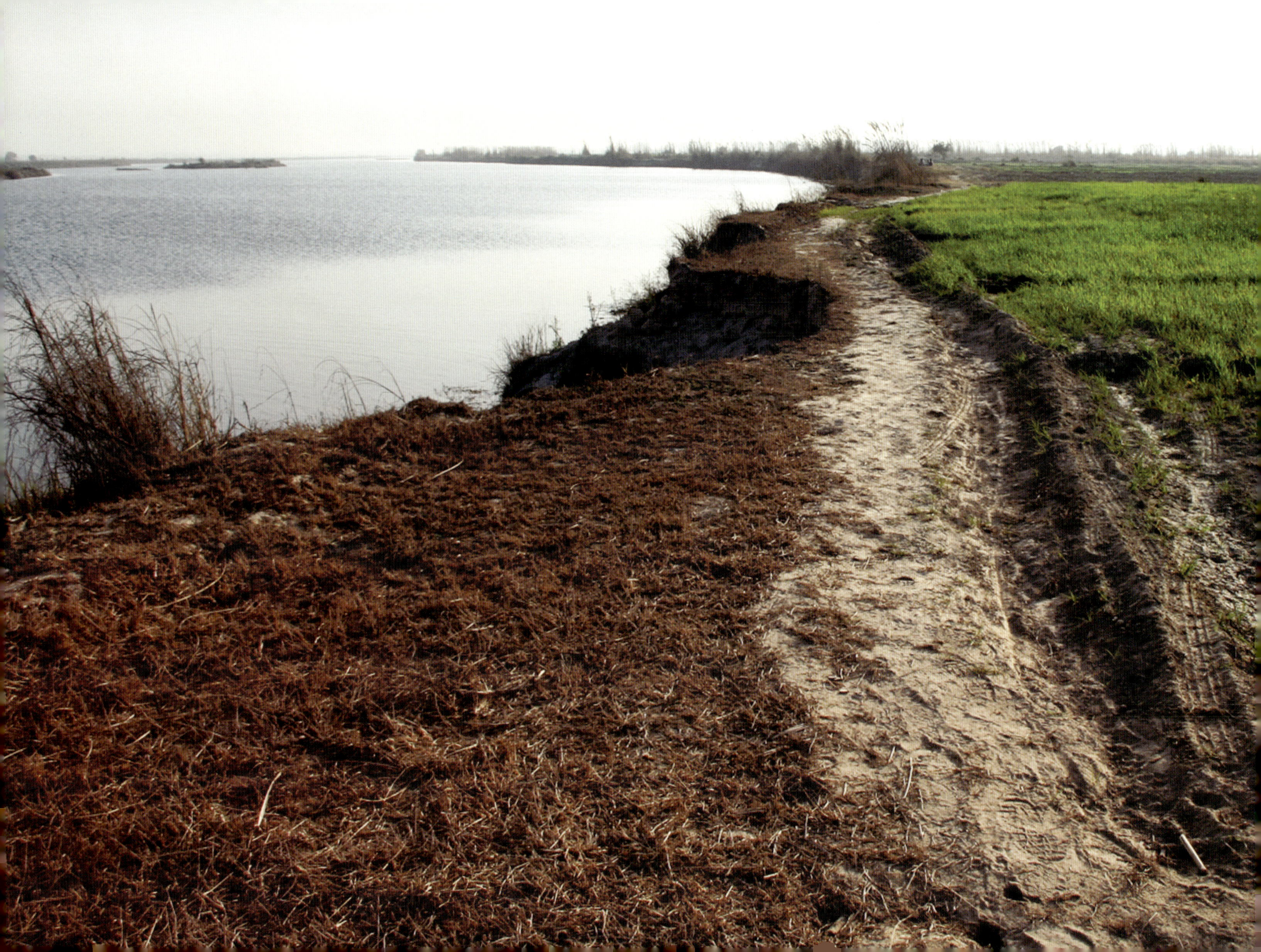

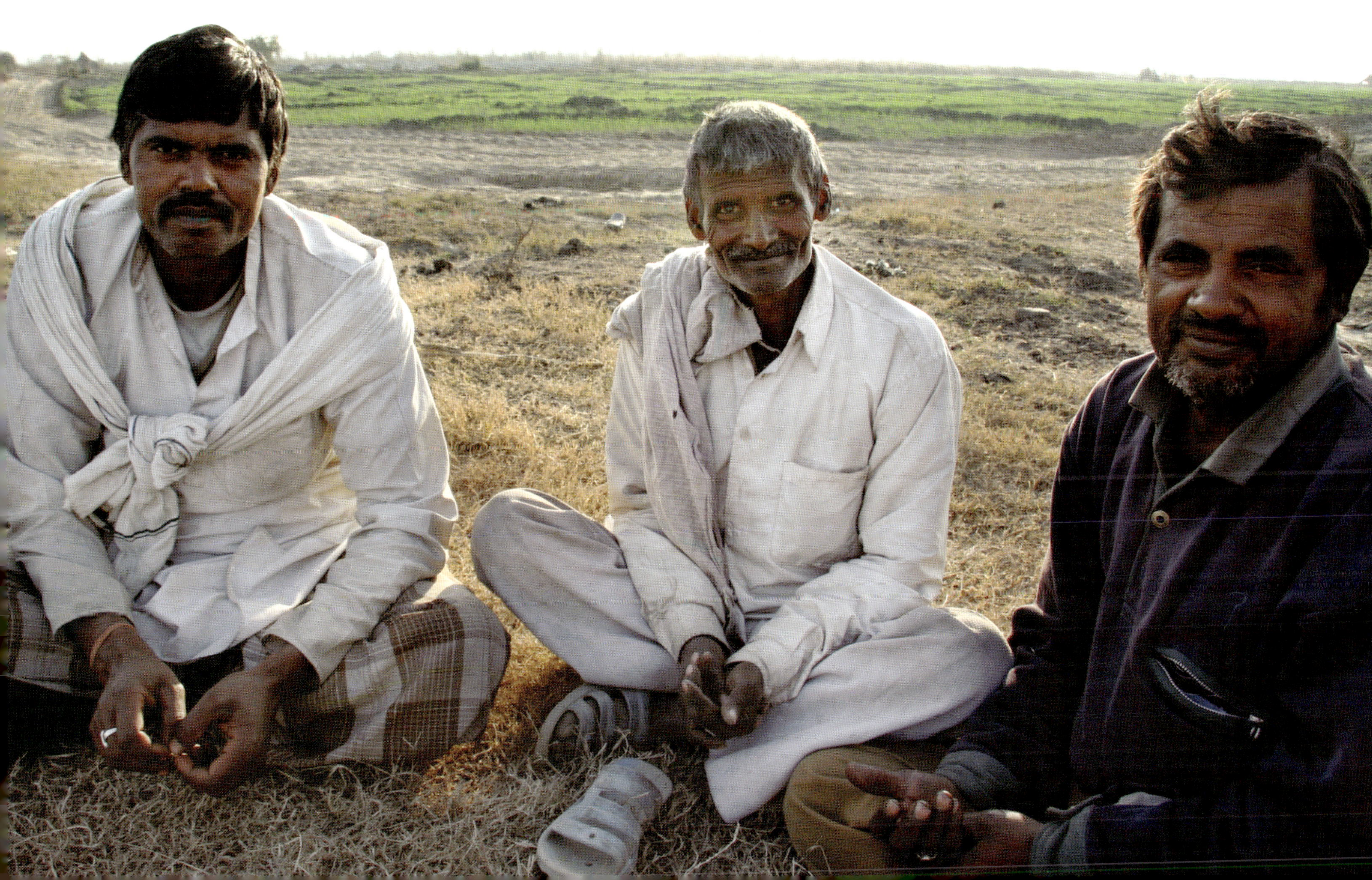

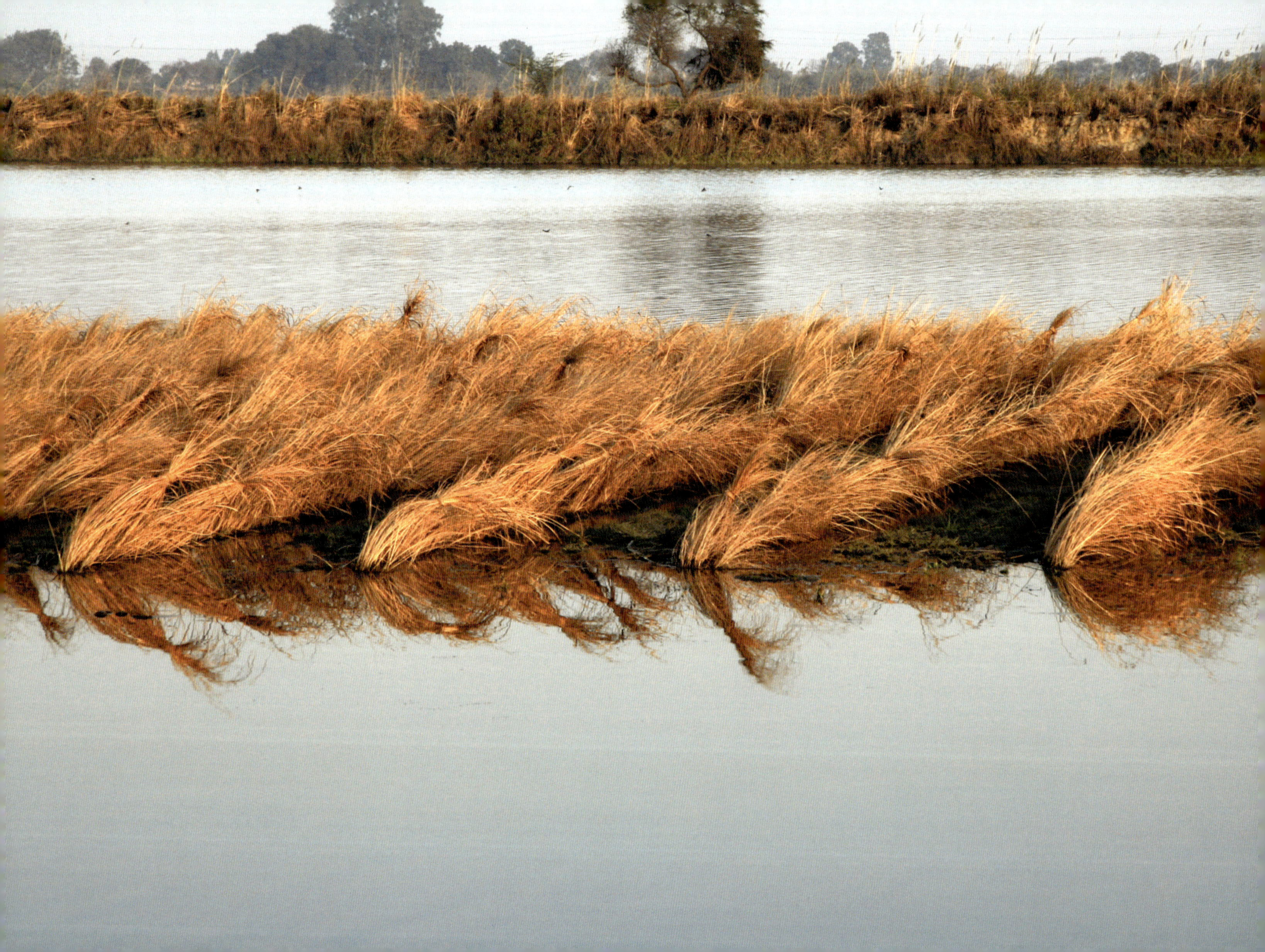

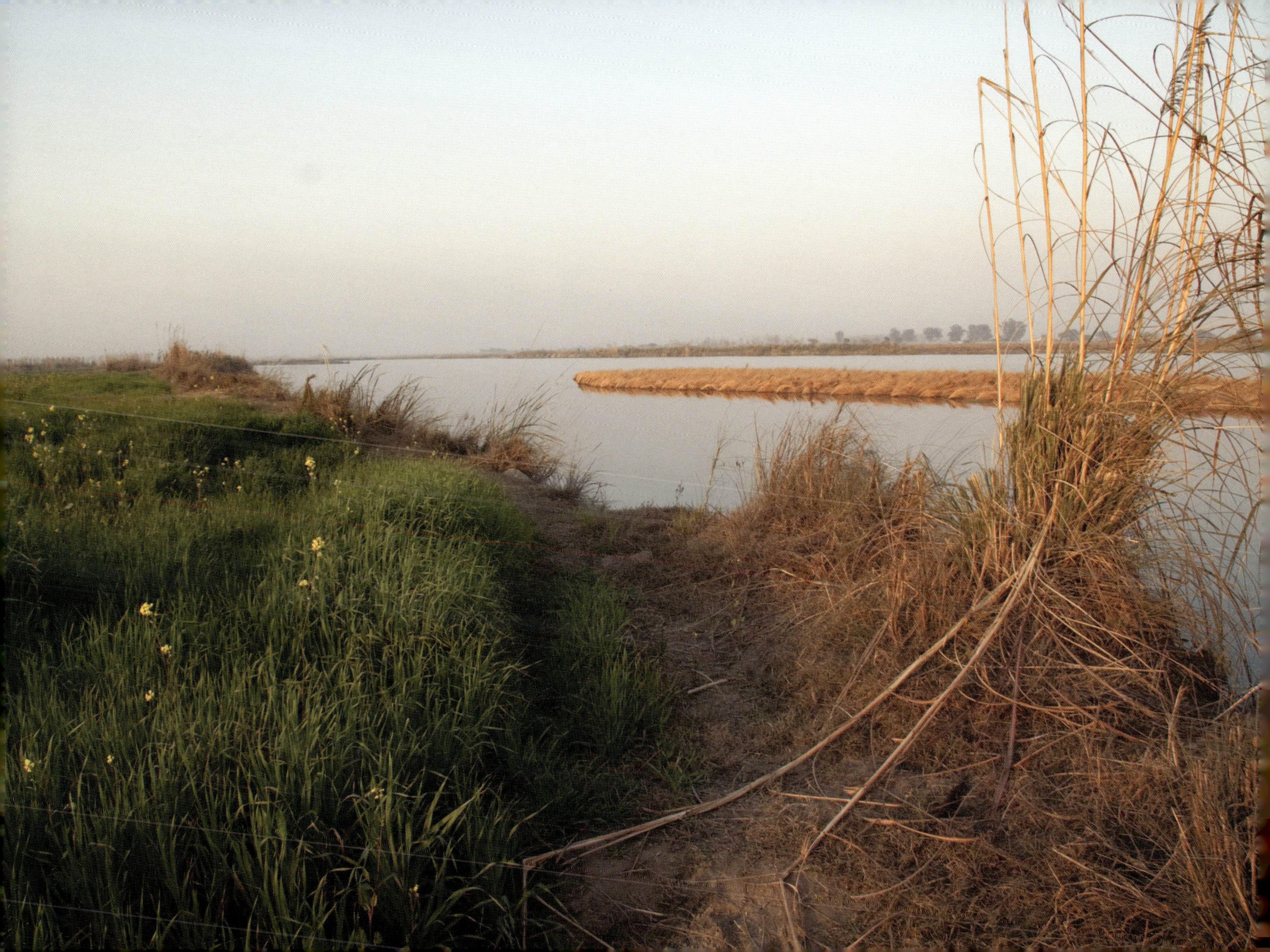

24 JANUARY 2007

9:30AM

jagatpur
labour
men women
fields
fog
birds
ferry across
touch
just
there
paths
across
through grass
marshes
wazirabad
breakfast lunch?
daal
on dung cakes
boat
across
sonia bihar
pipes
sucking
leaking
water
rest
tea
on the road
the barrage
no photo
no standing
no waiting
walk
sur ghat
wall
drain
gushes rushes
spills
the yamuna
stare
walk
up
to the road
down again
up again
millennium
bridge?
peer baba
gurudwara
mandir
stink
madness
forgotten
way
climb up
the road
down
the yamuna
access
denied.
Again,
and again,
every time
finish
the day's
walk
majnu ka tila

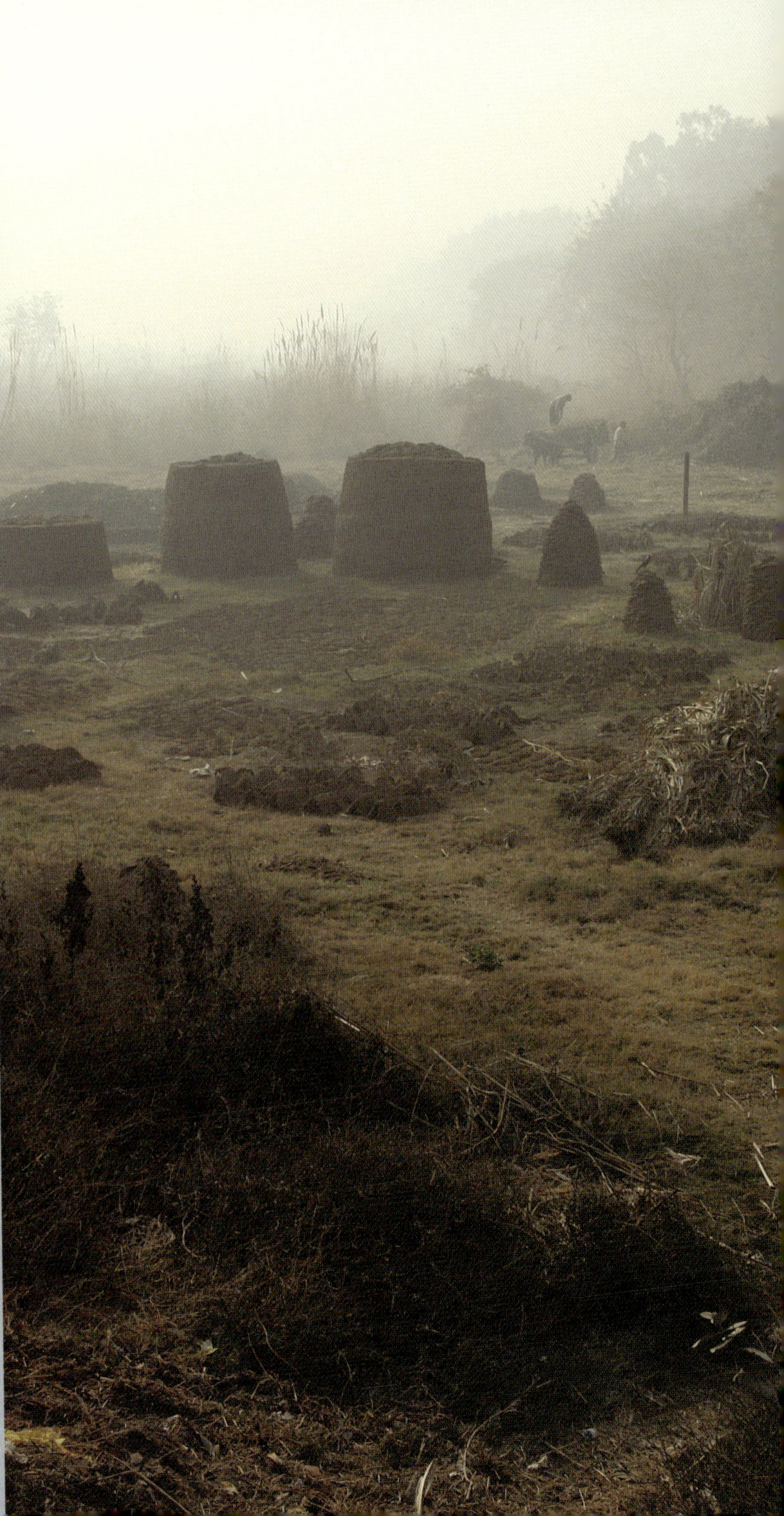

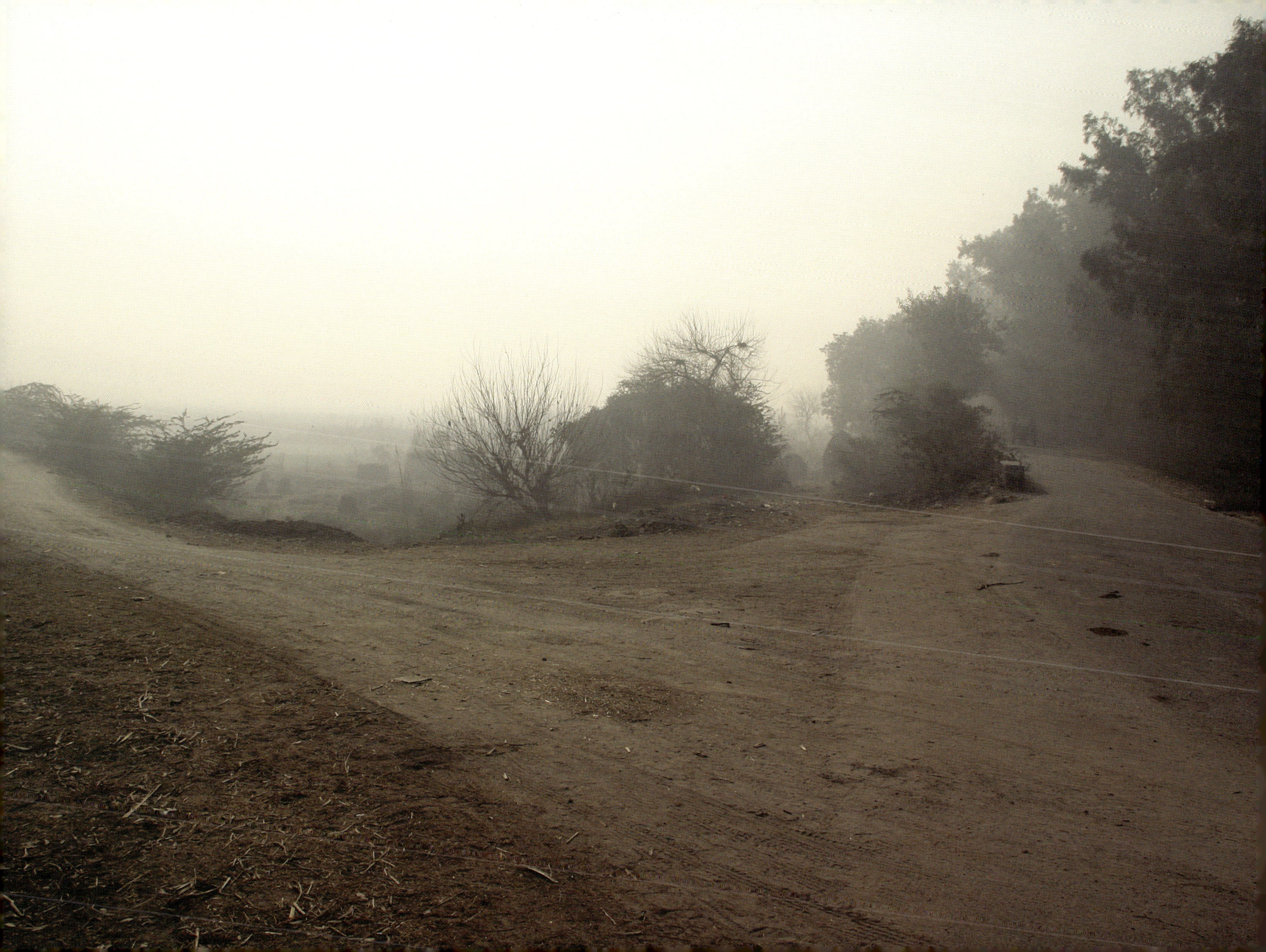

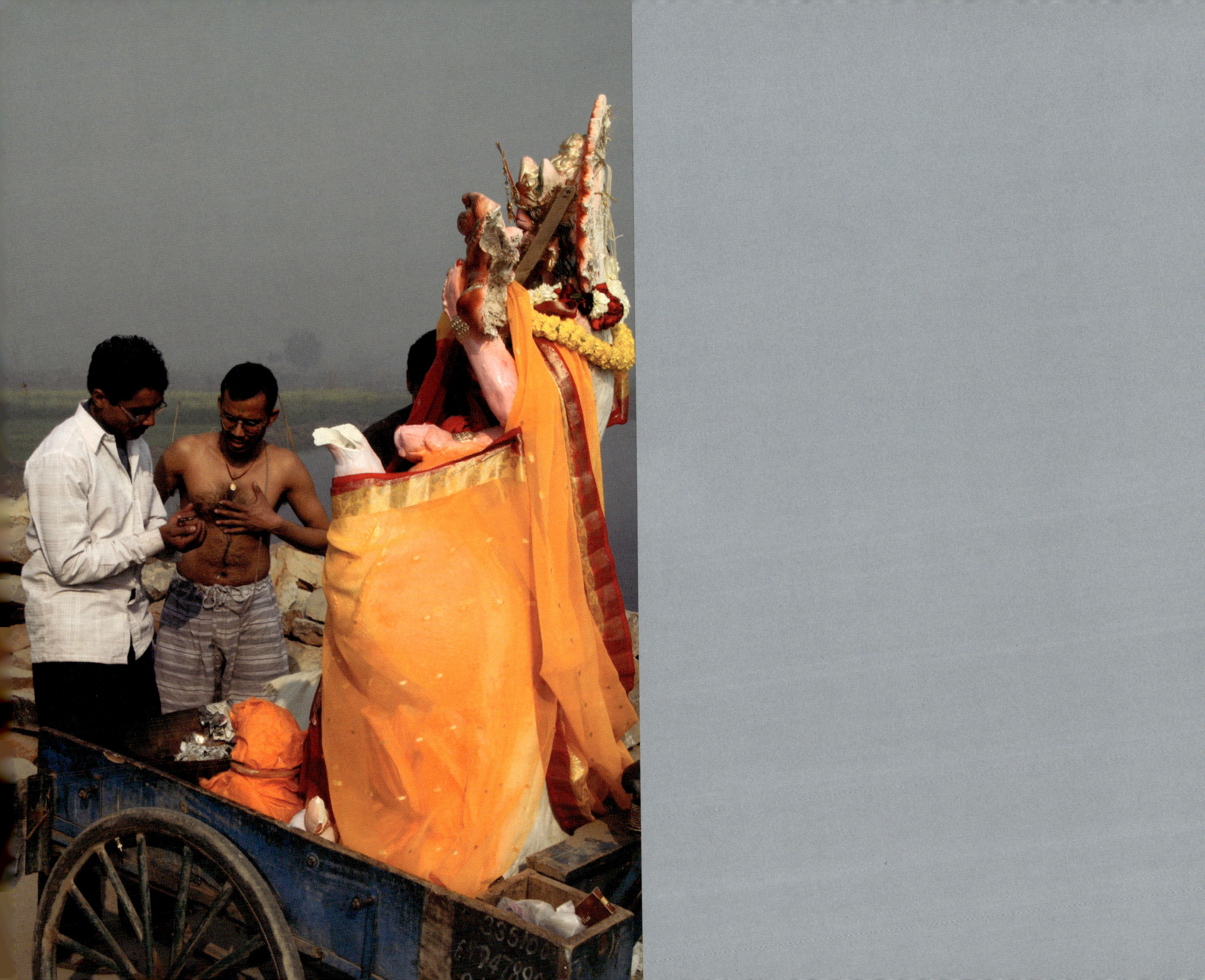

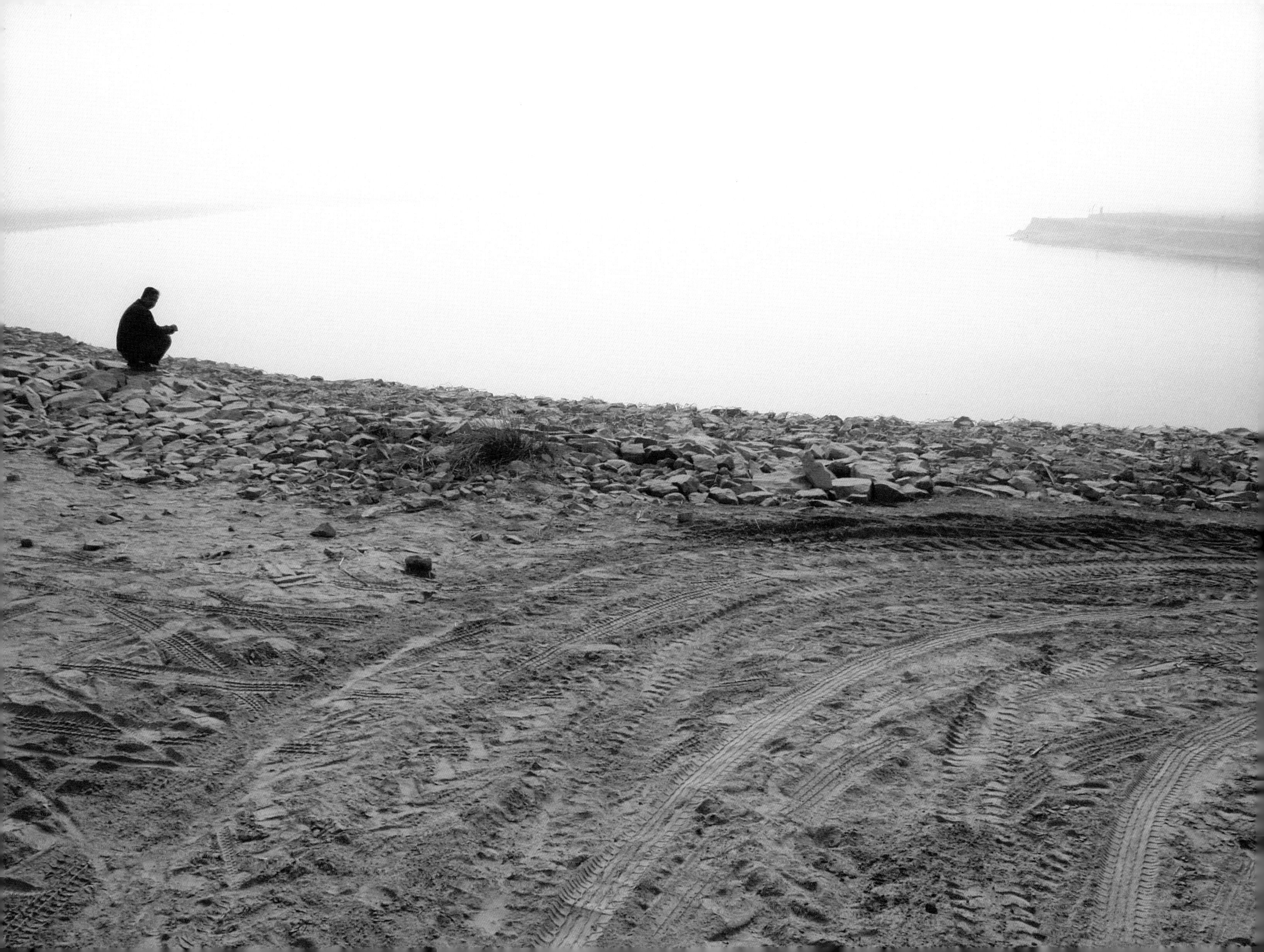

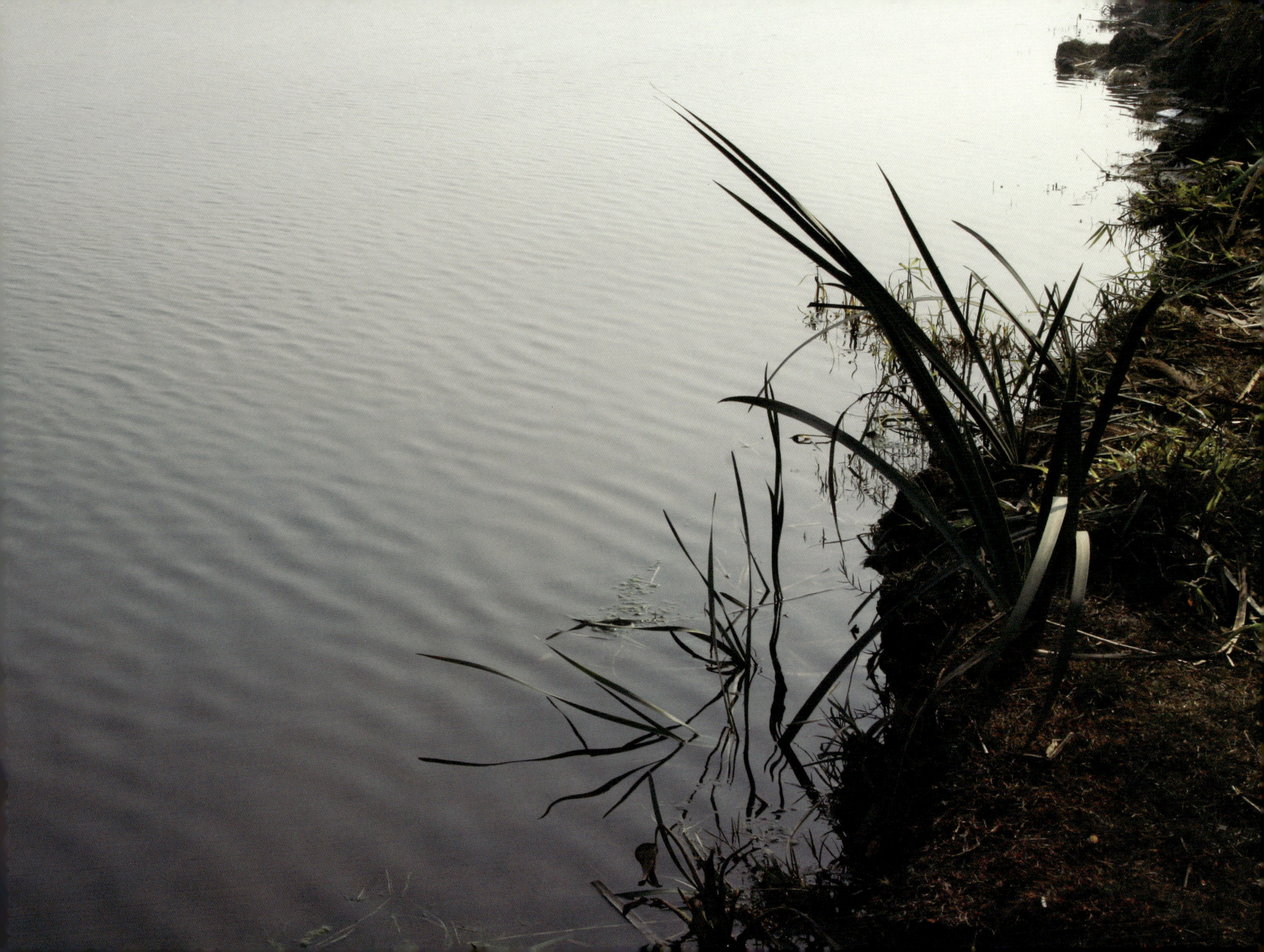

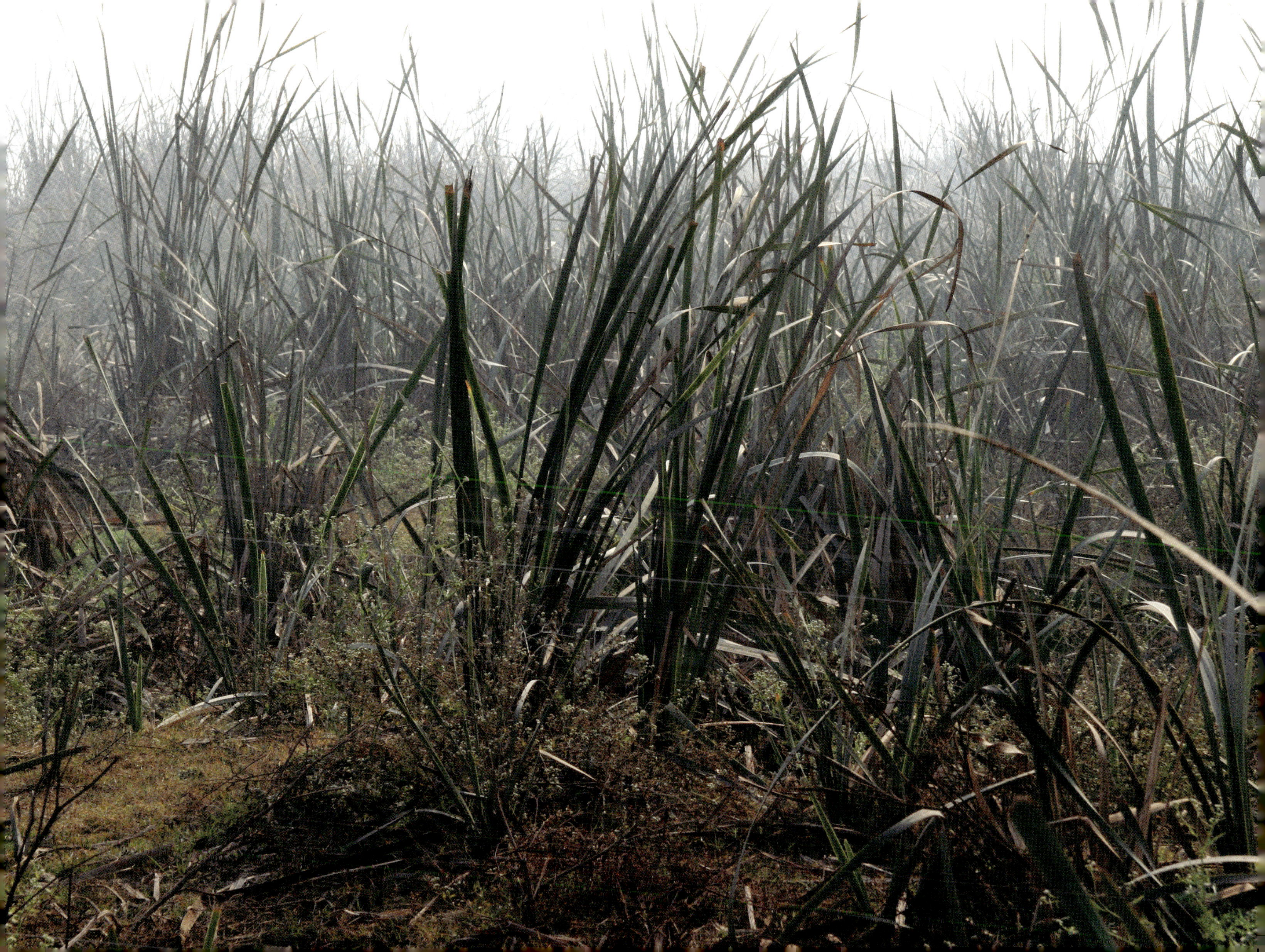

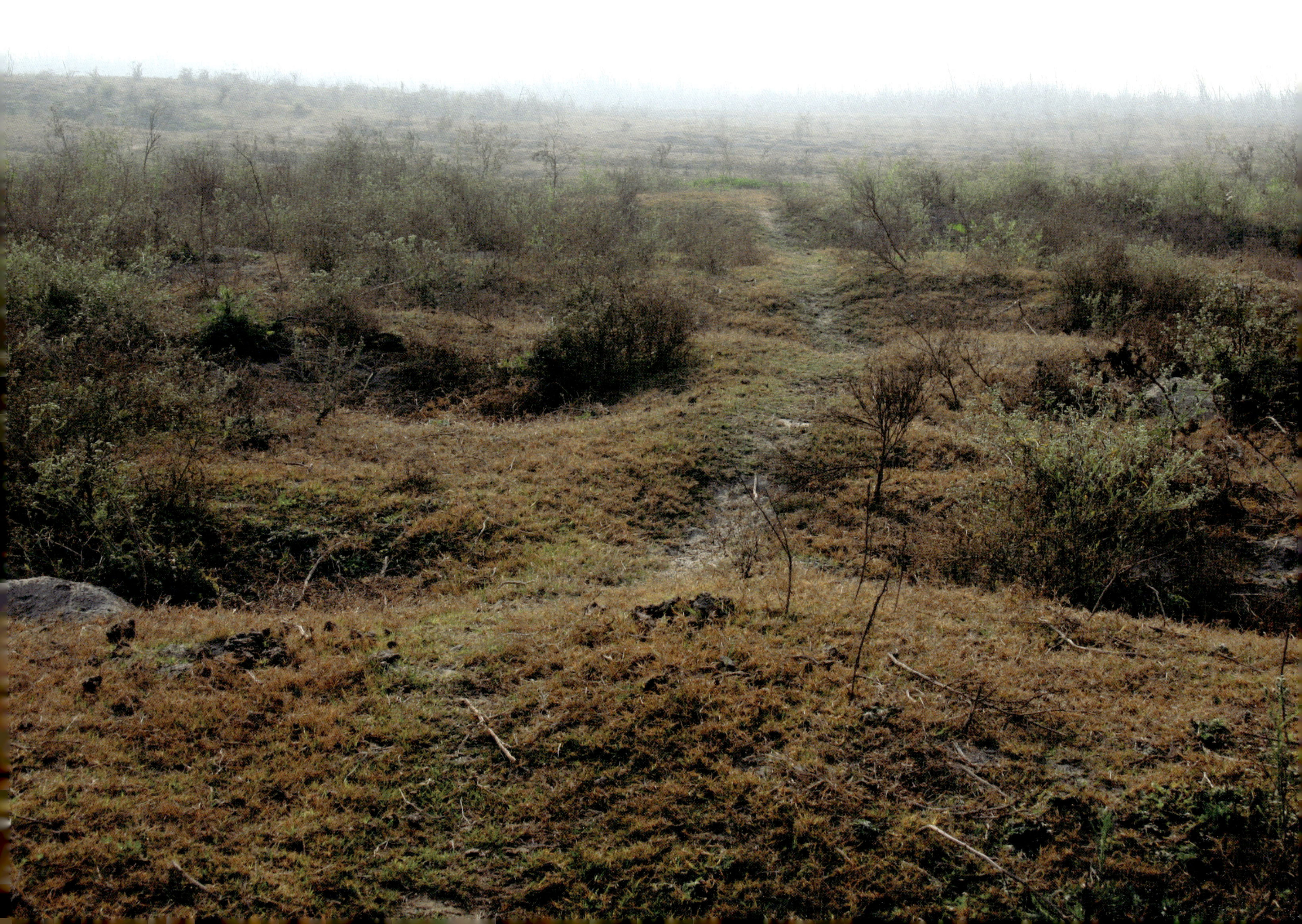

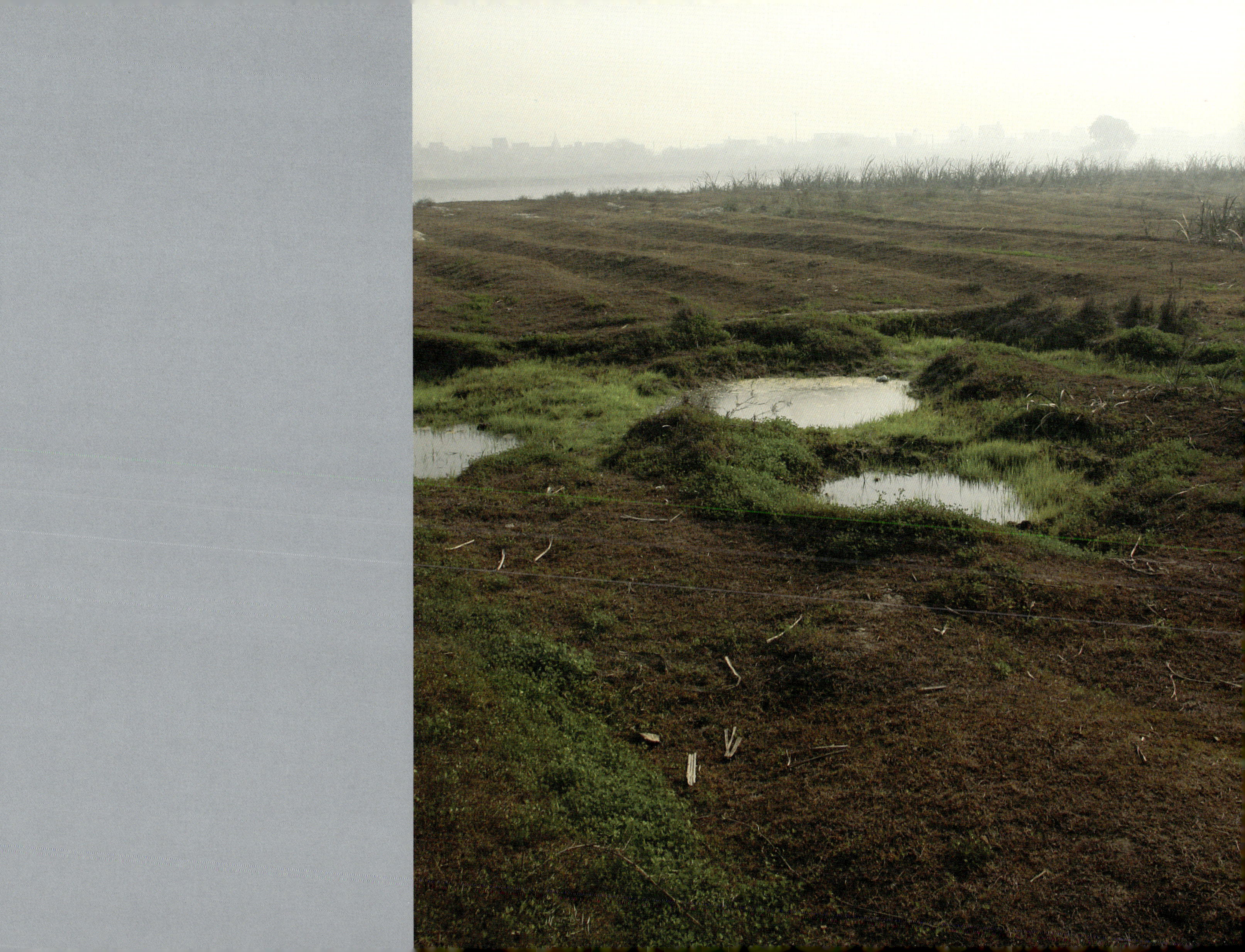

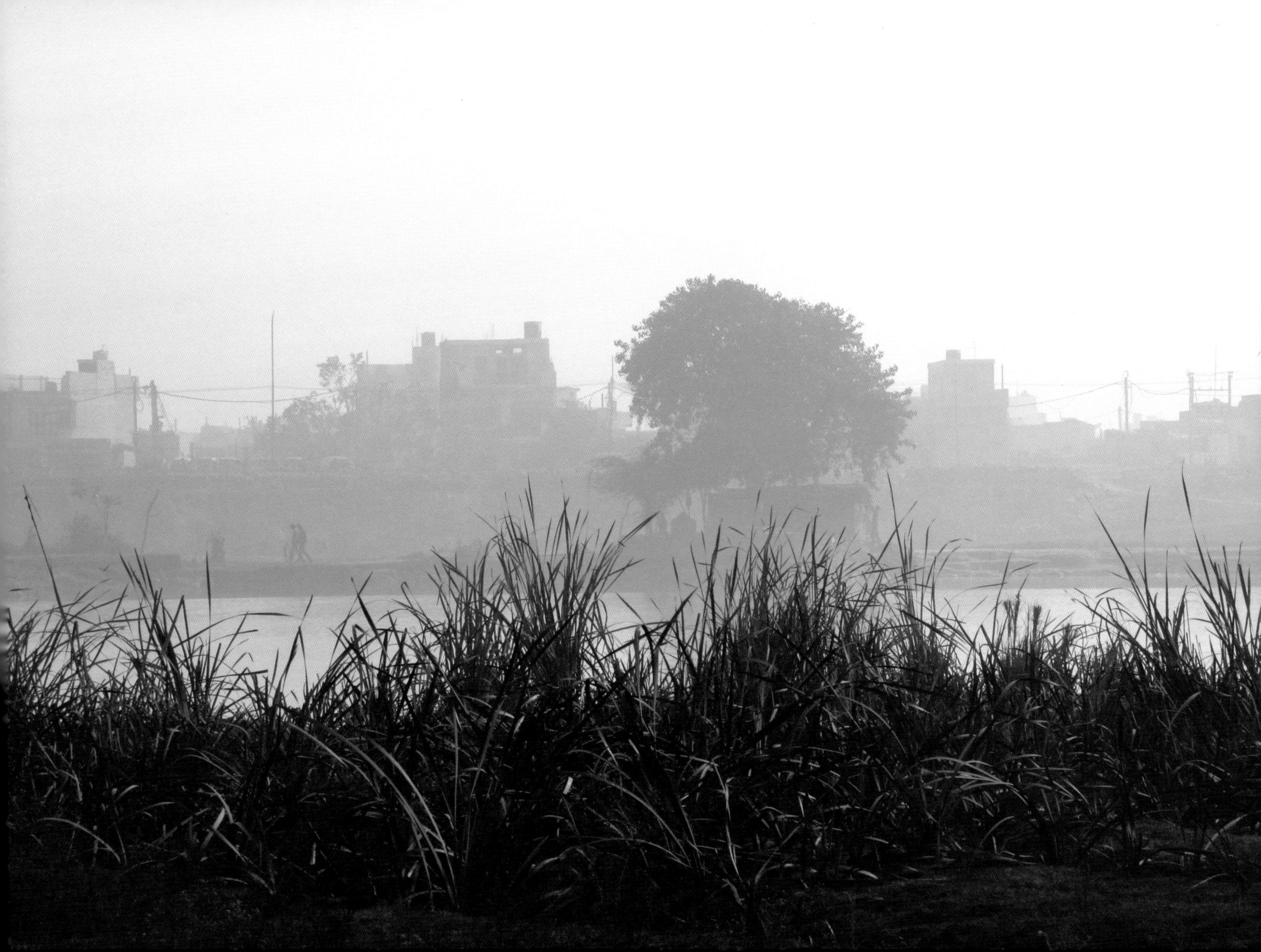

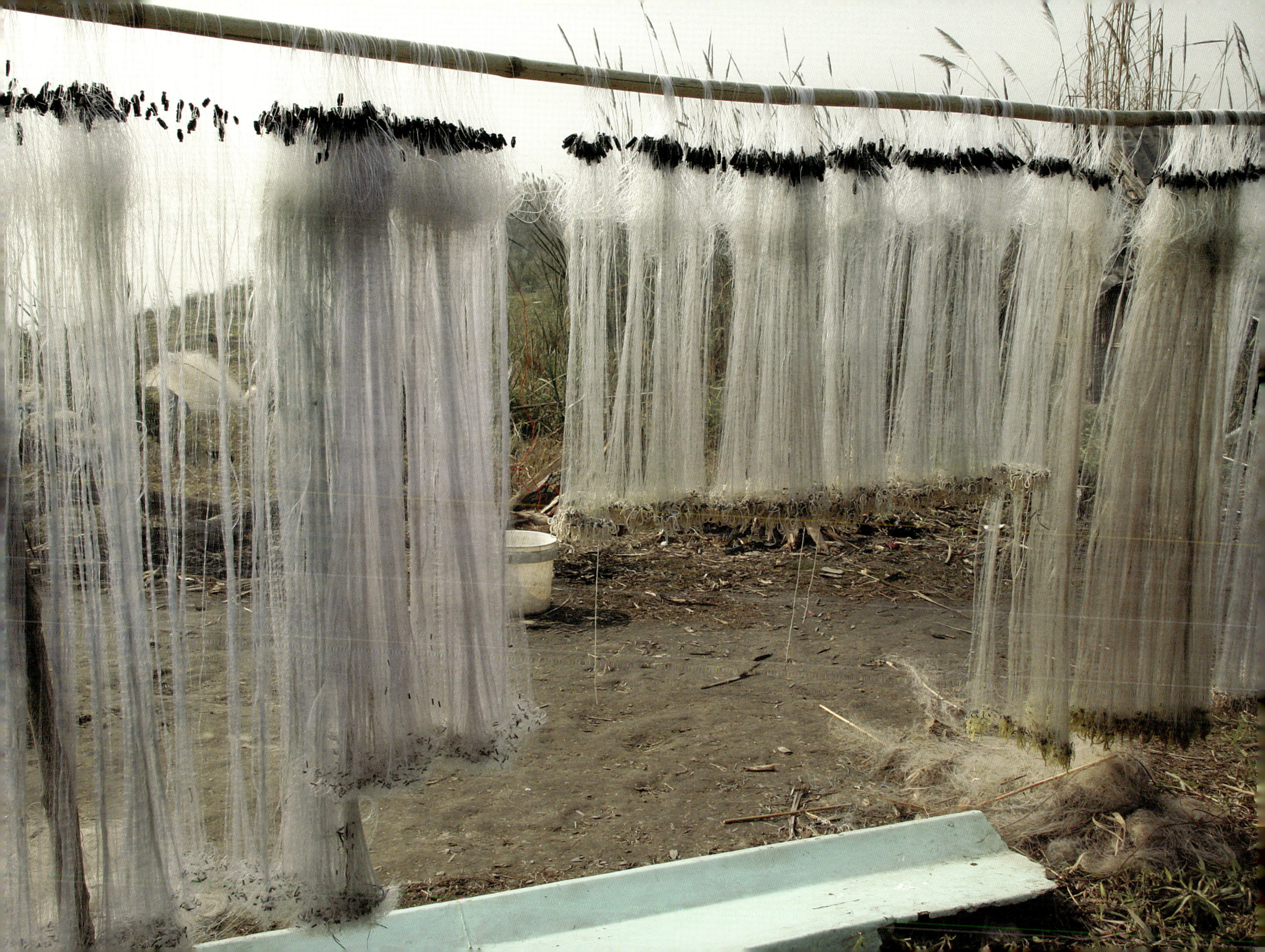

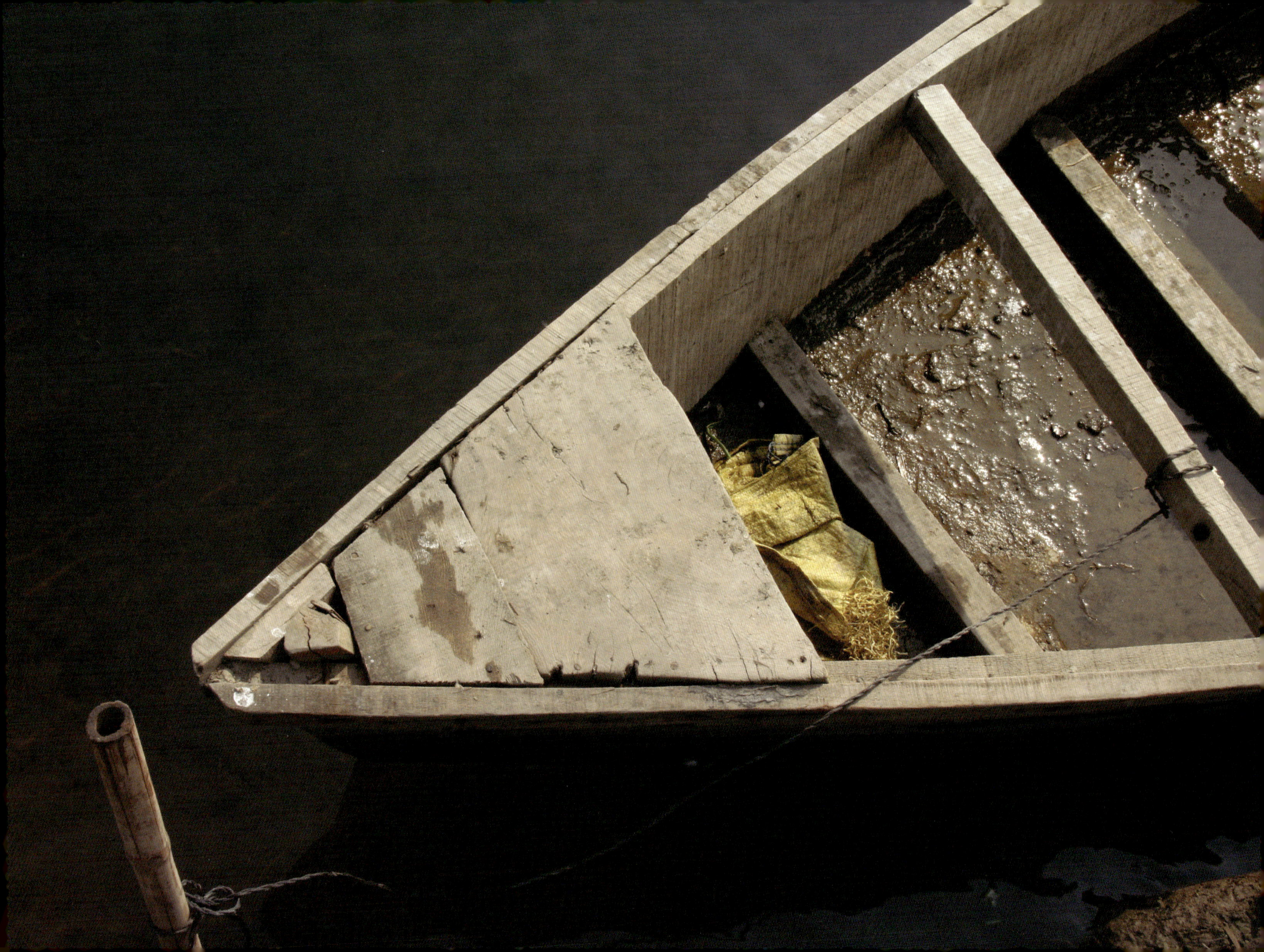

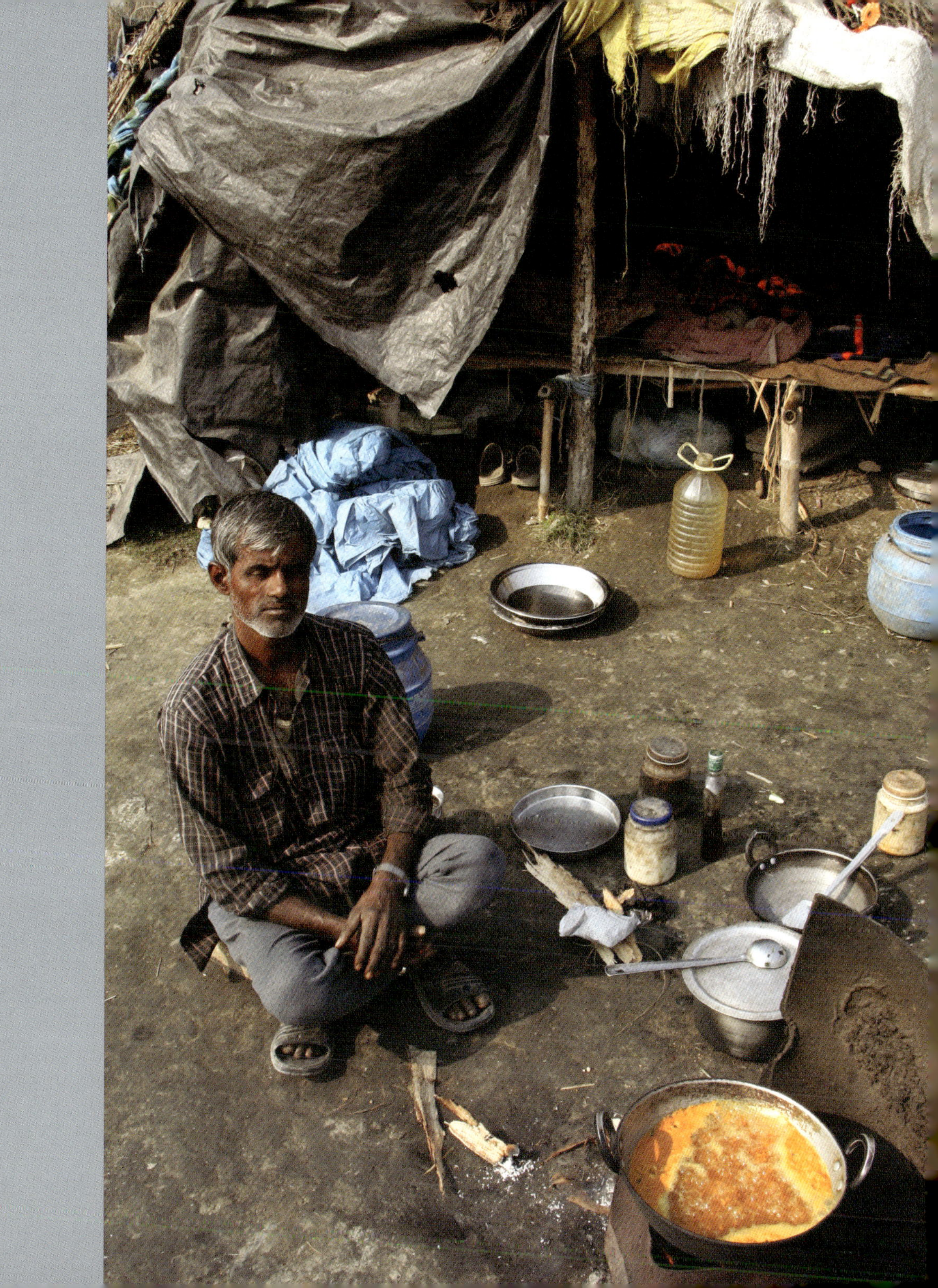

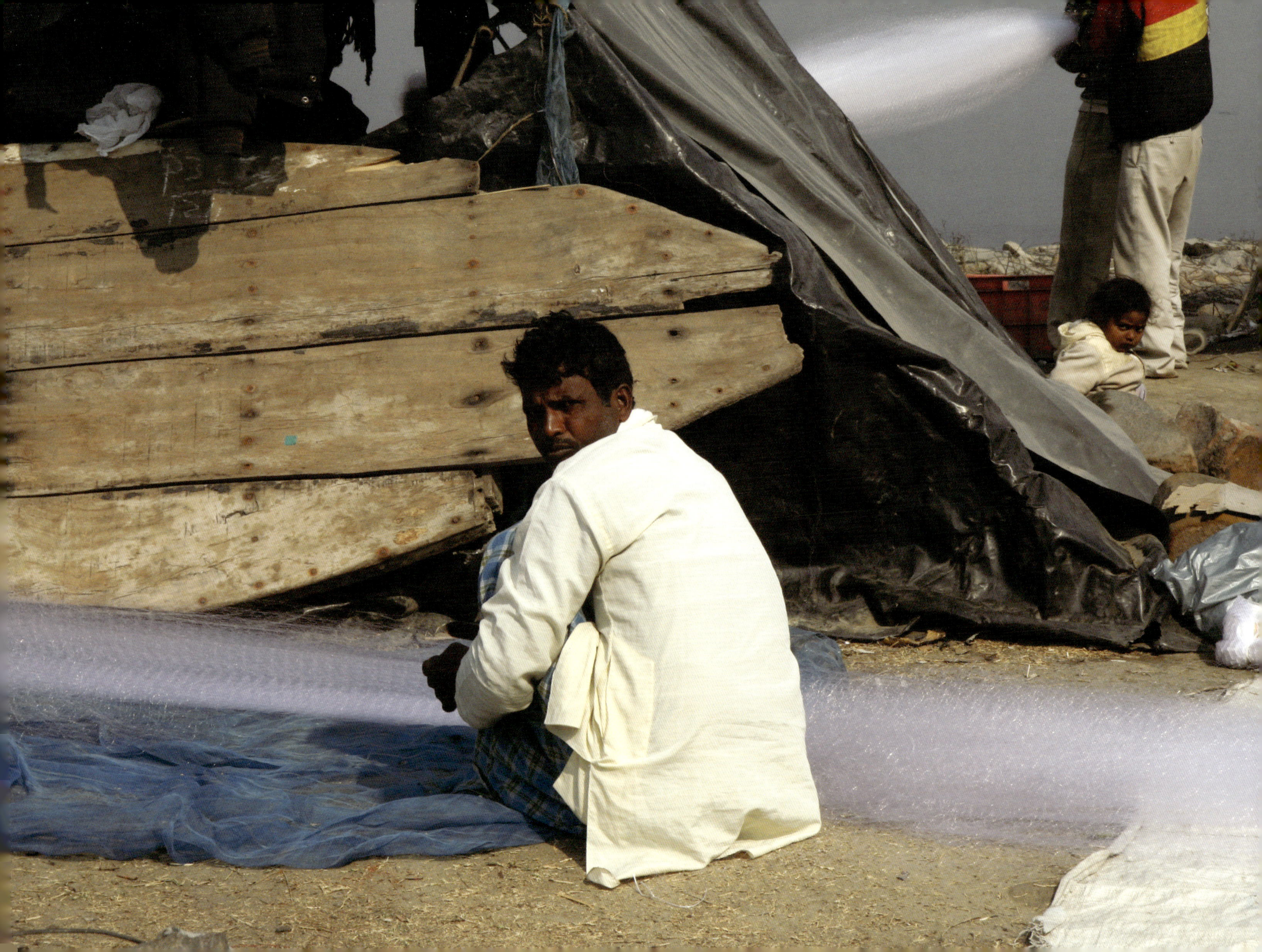

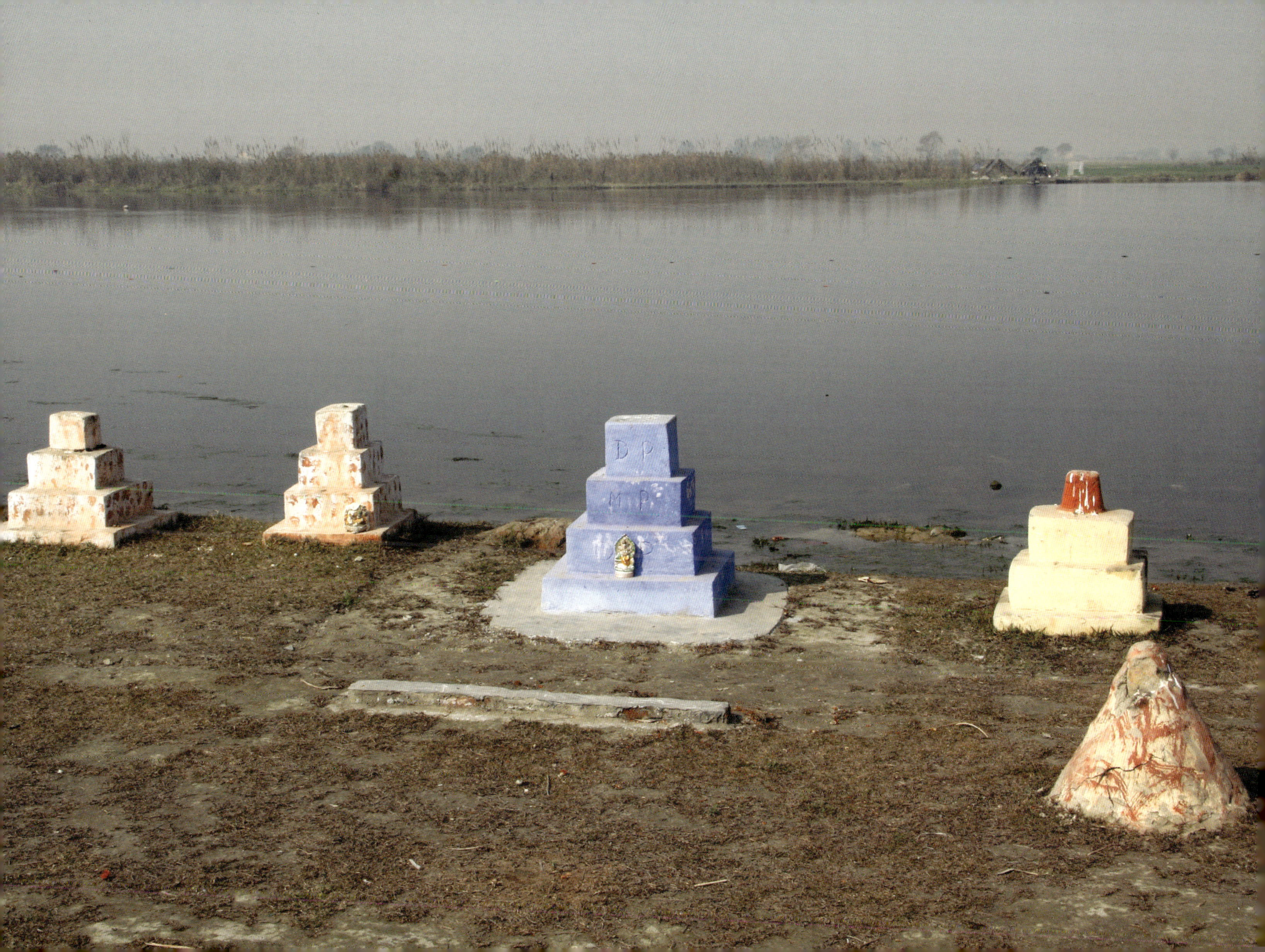
DP
MP

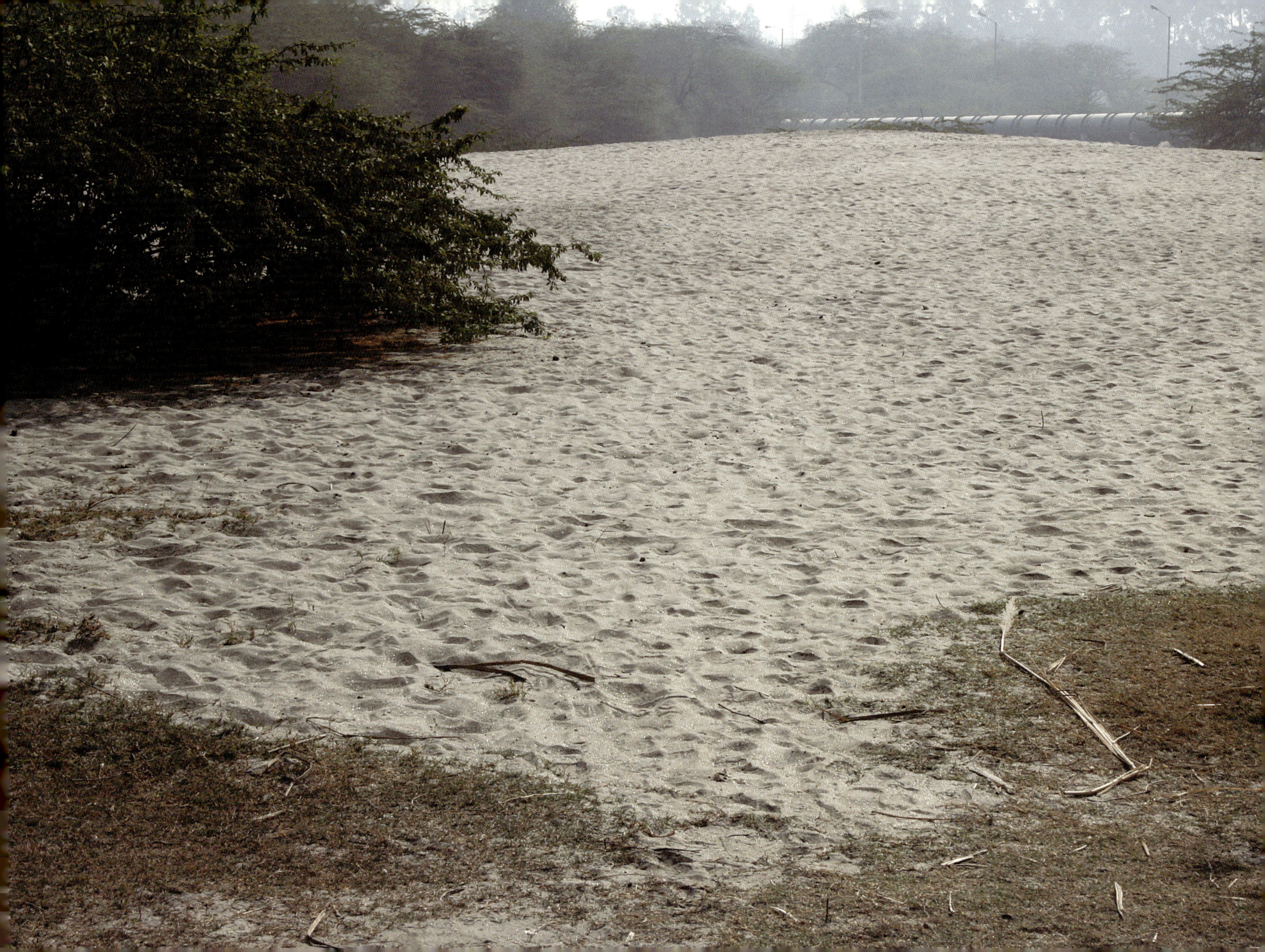

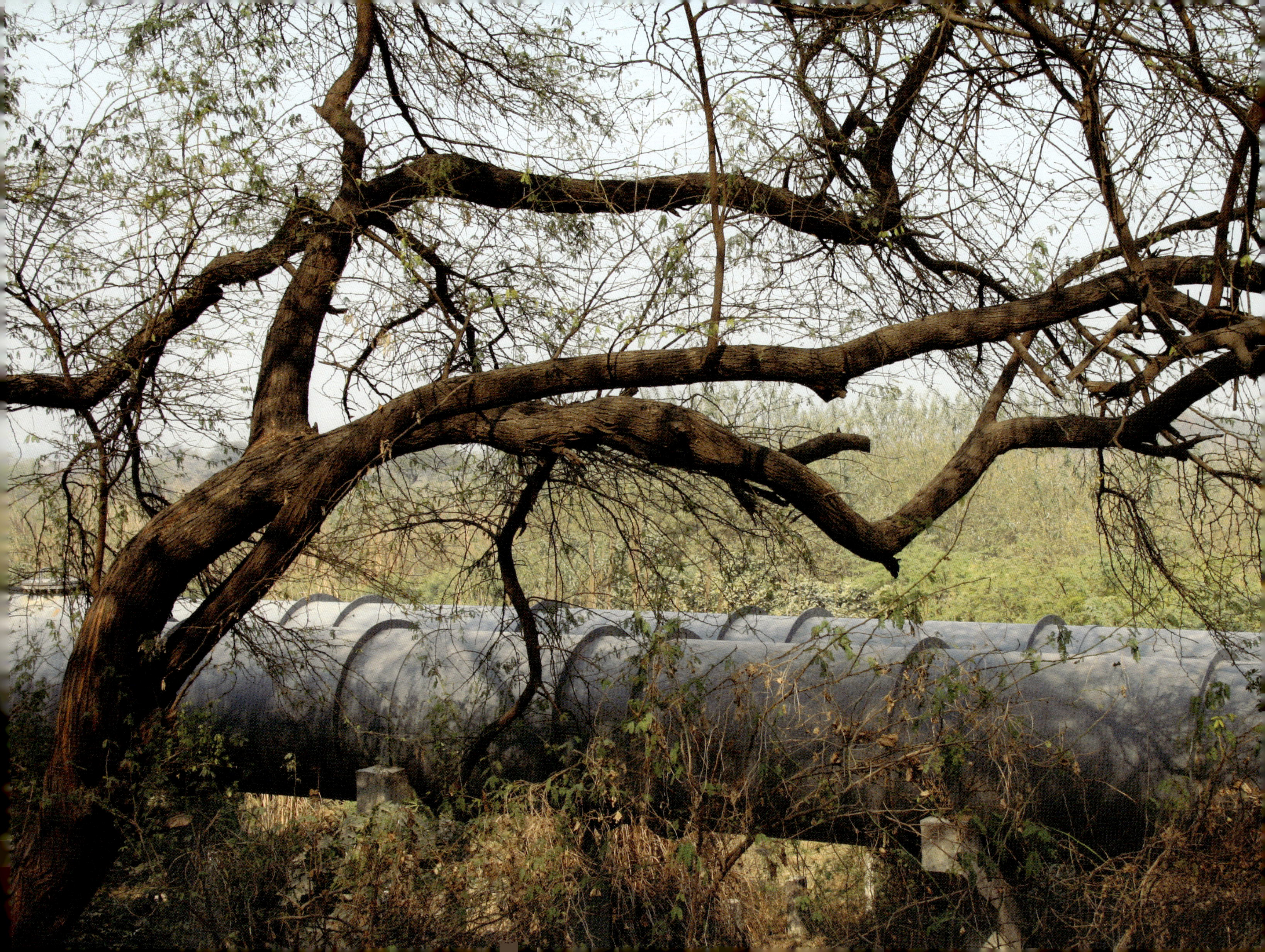

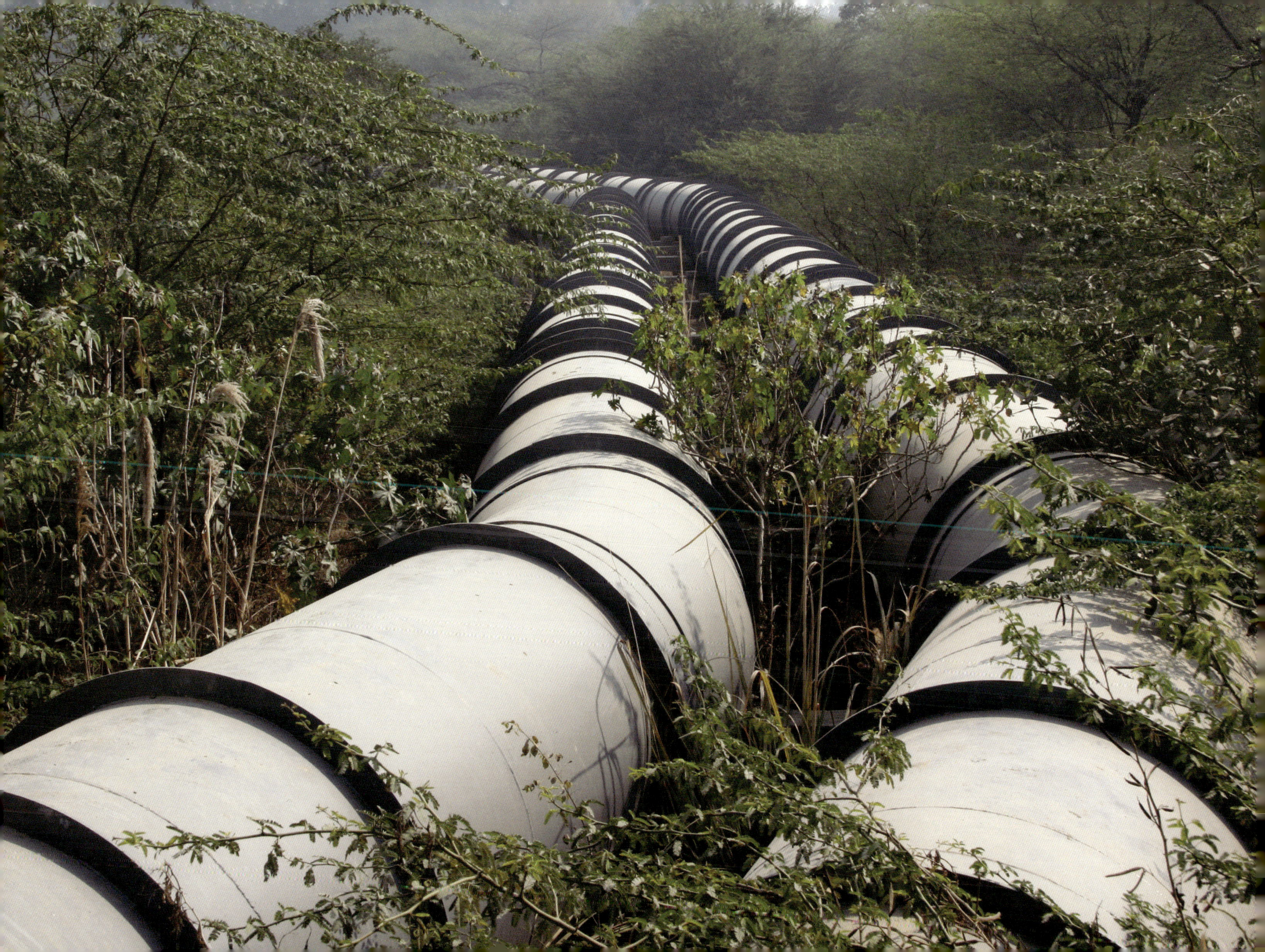

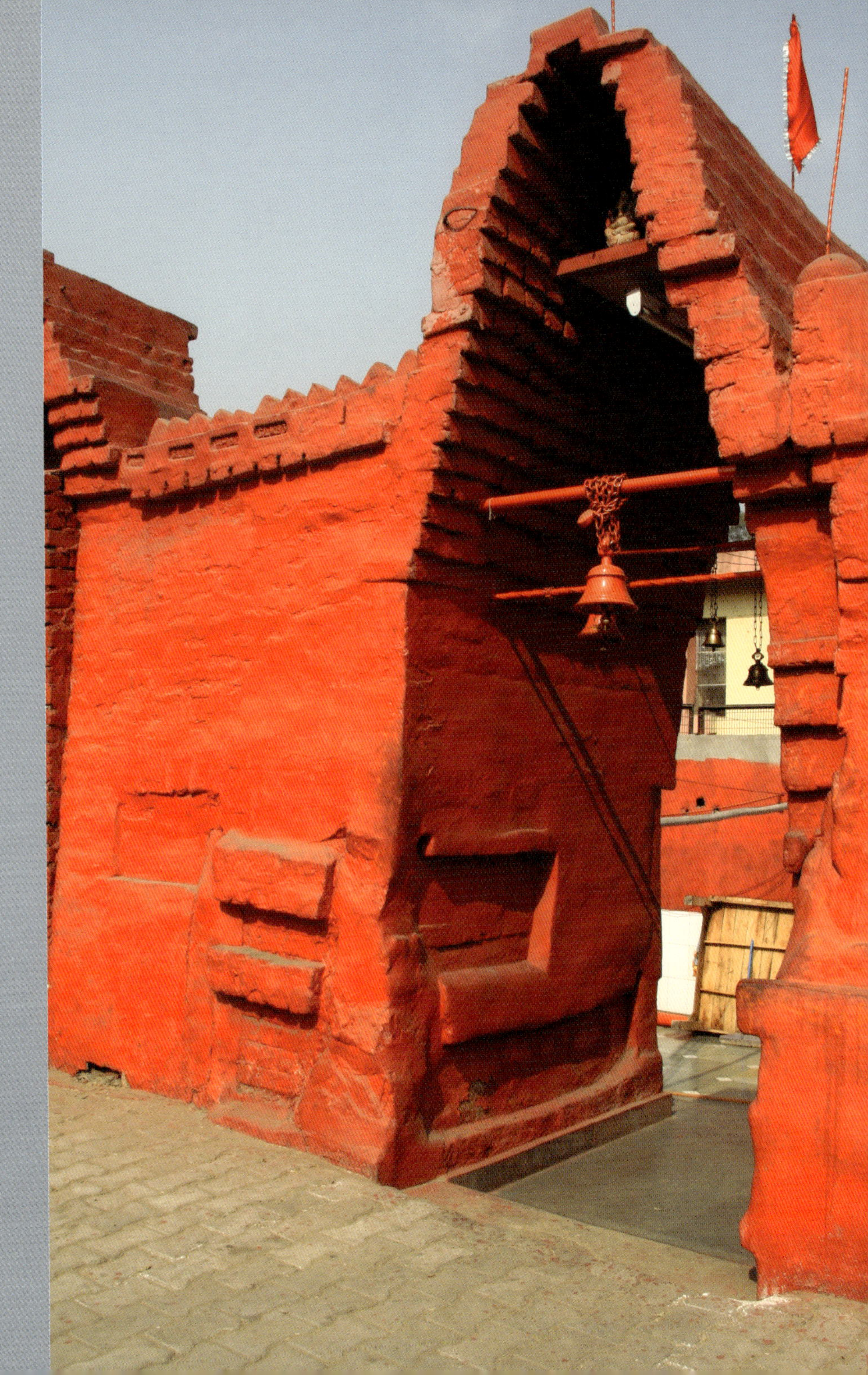

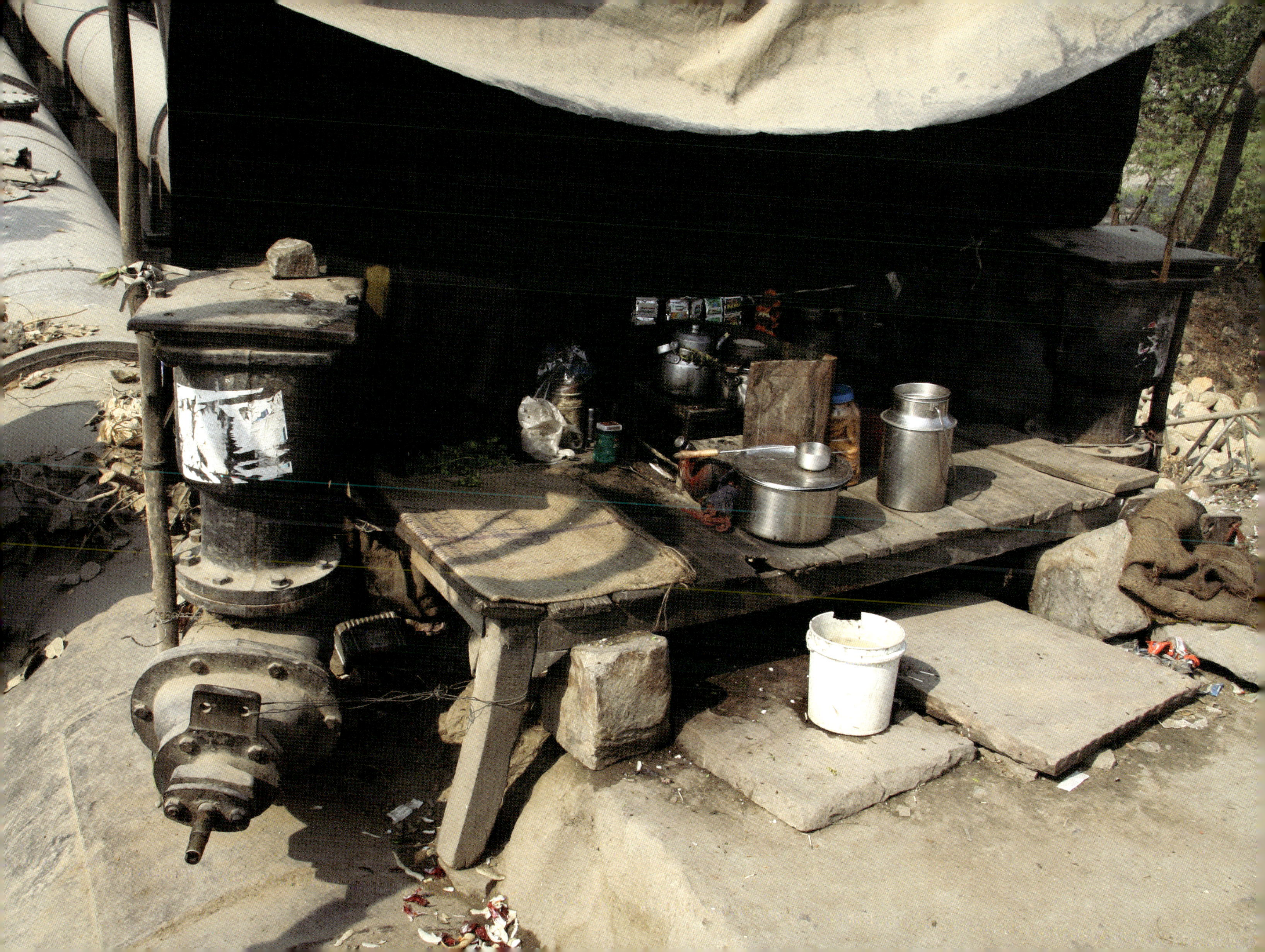

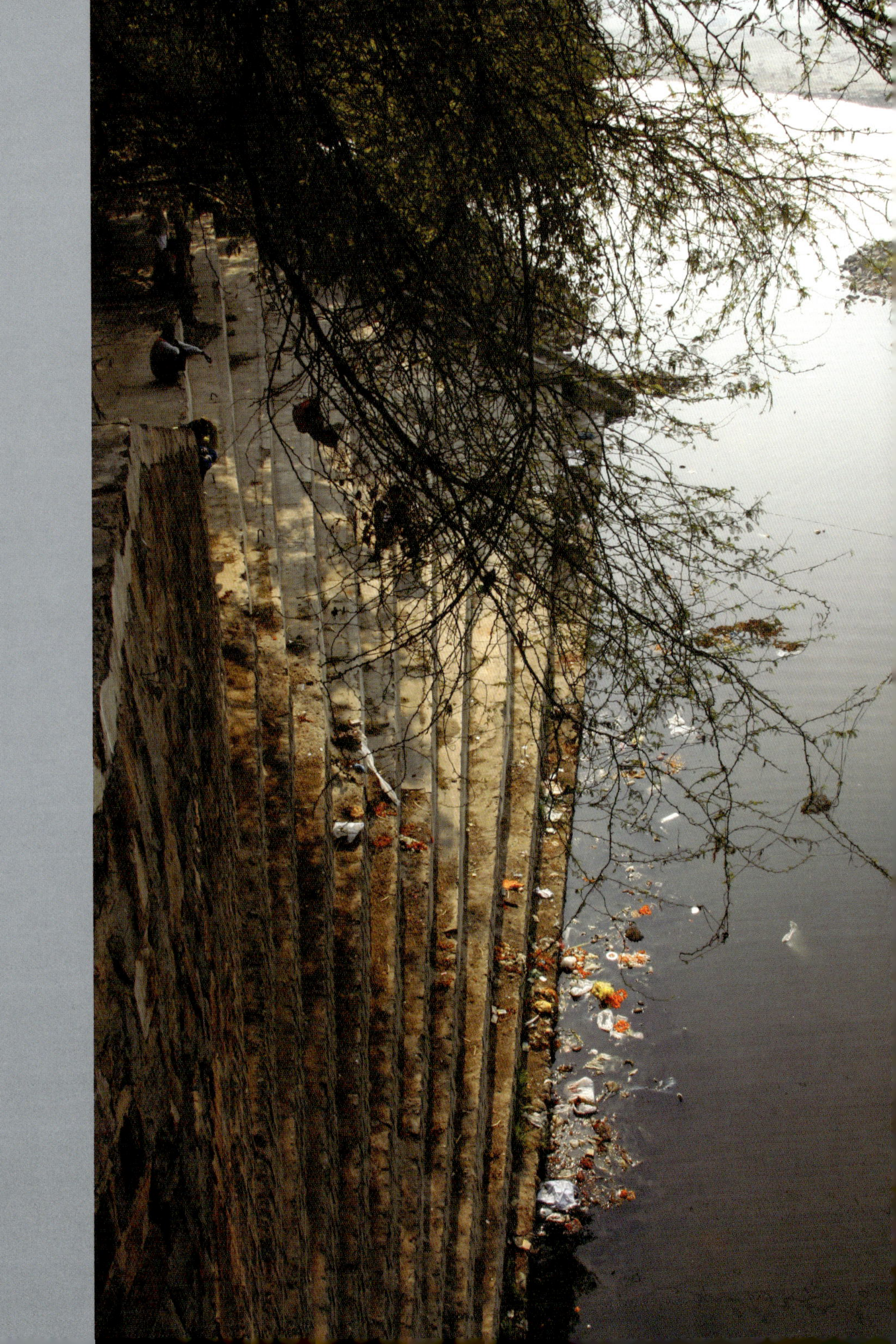

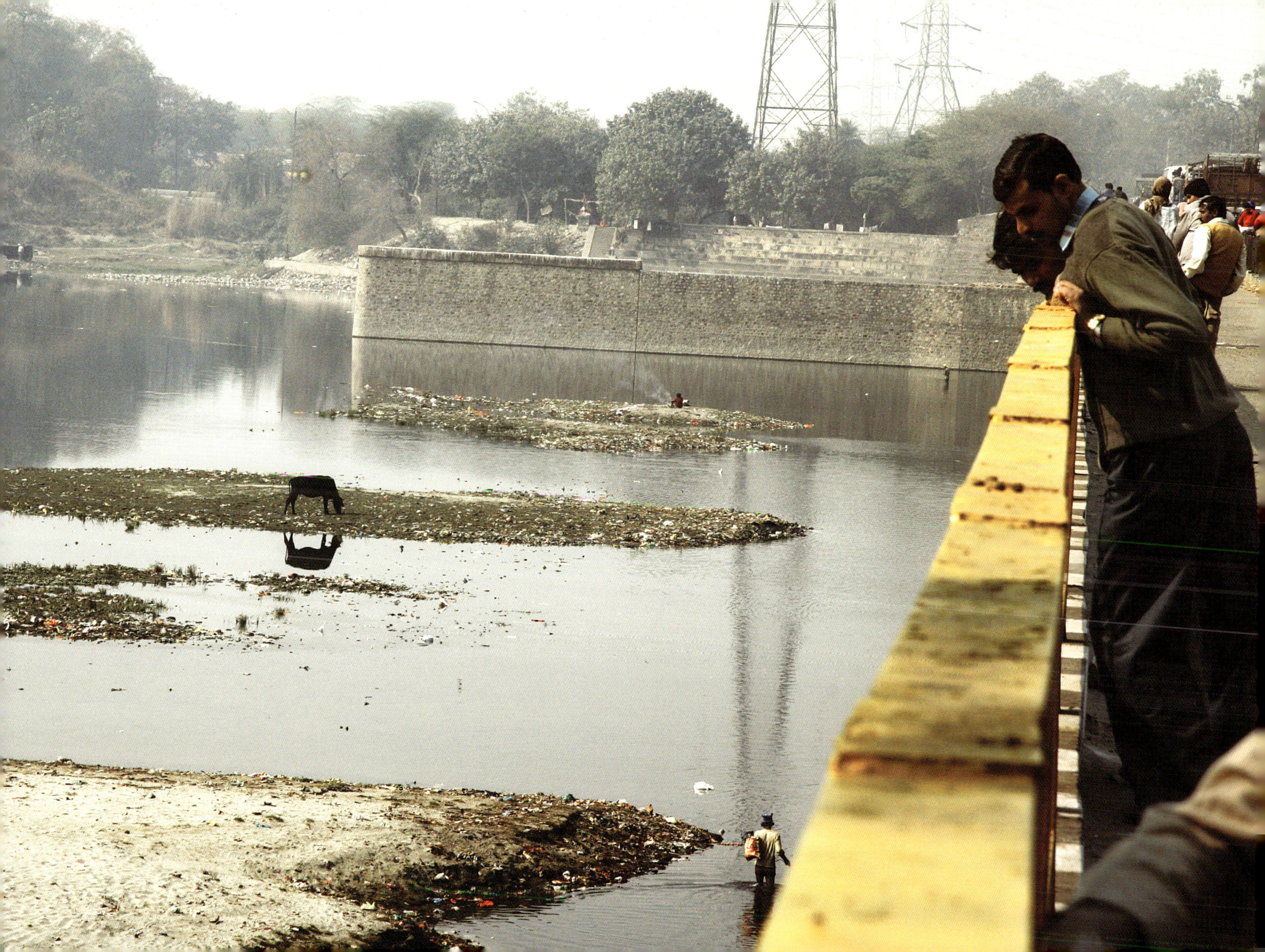

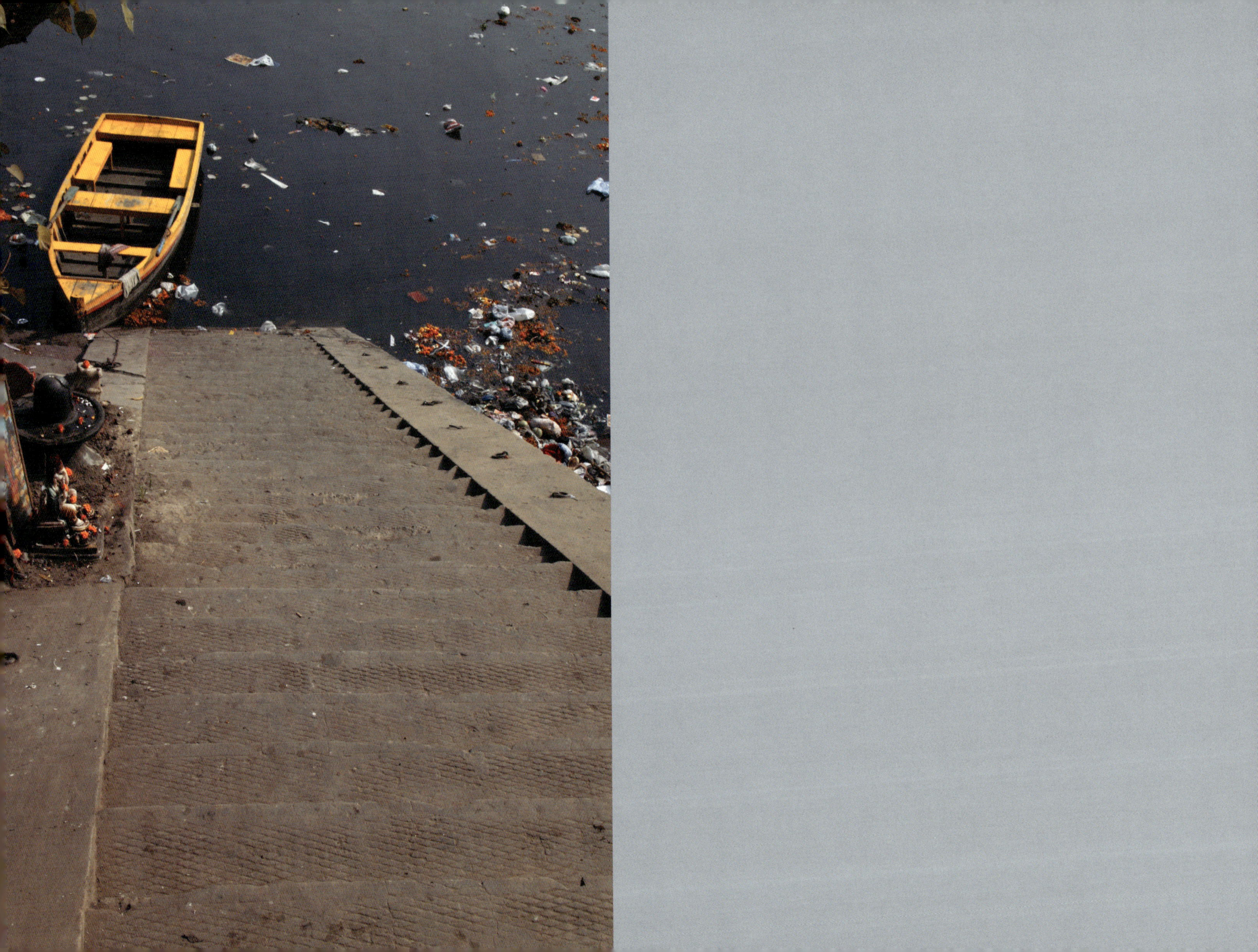

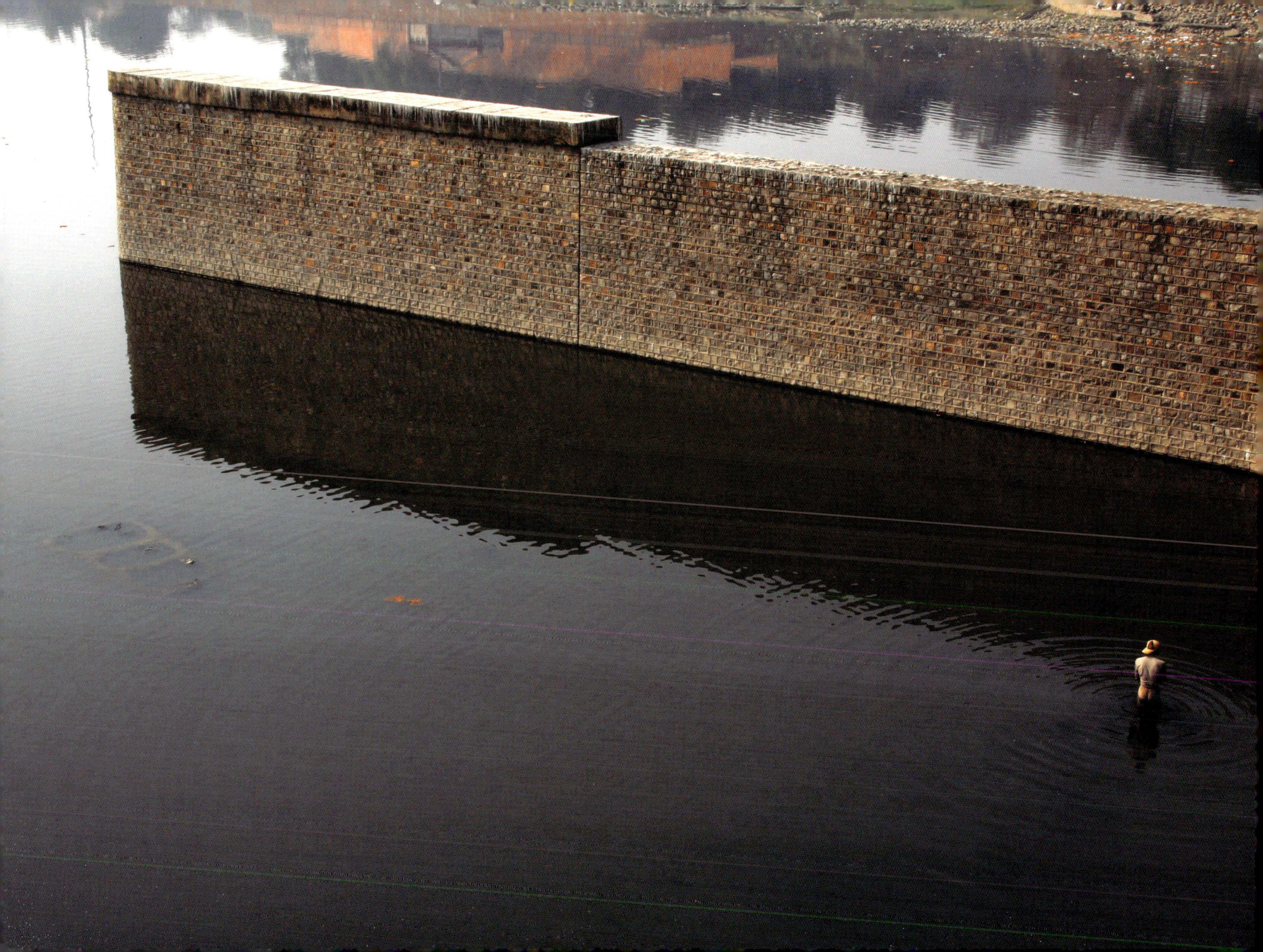

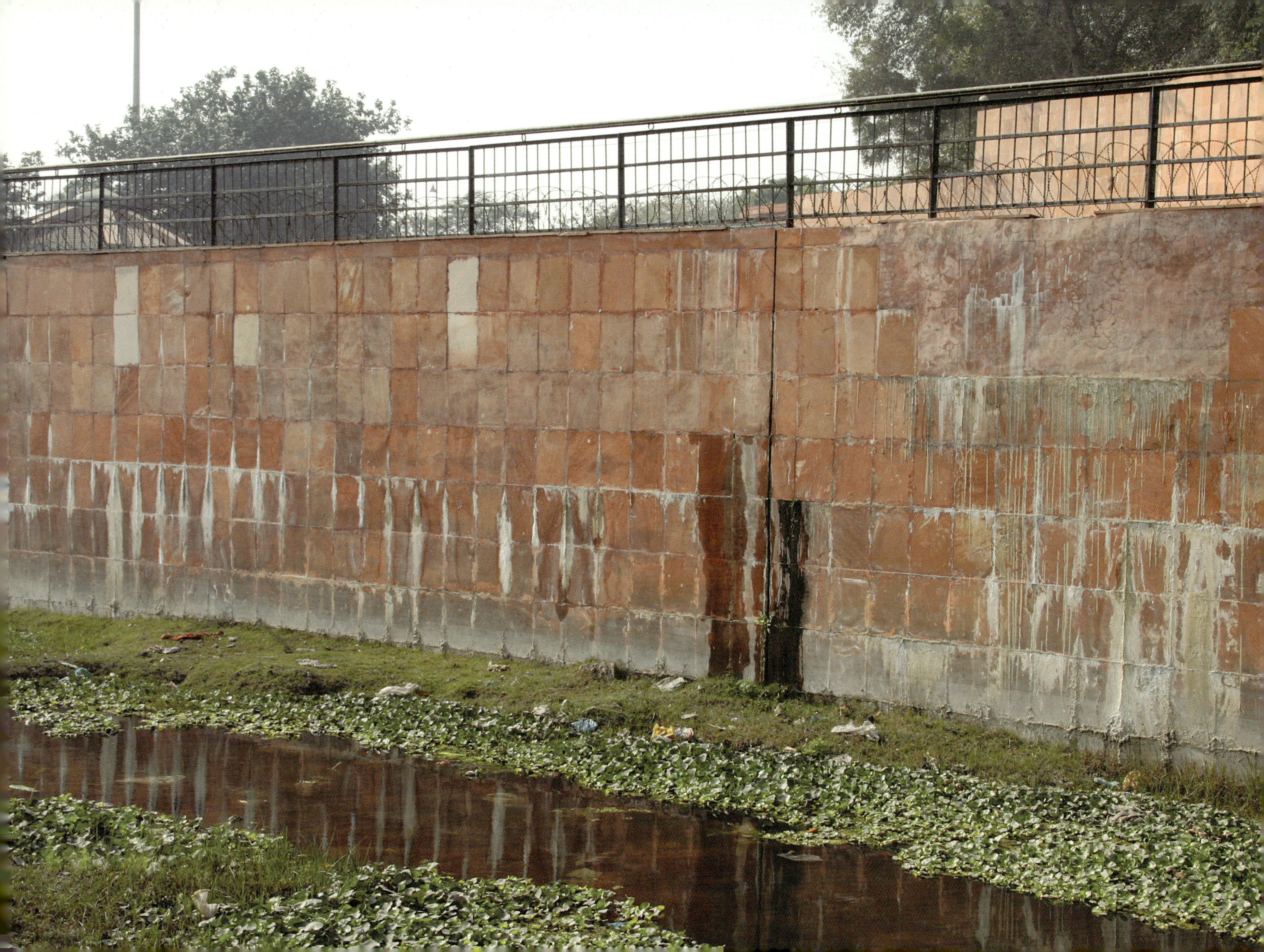

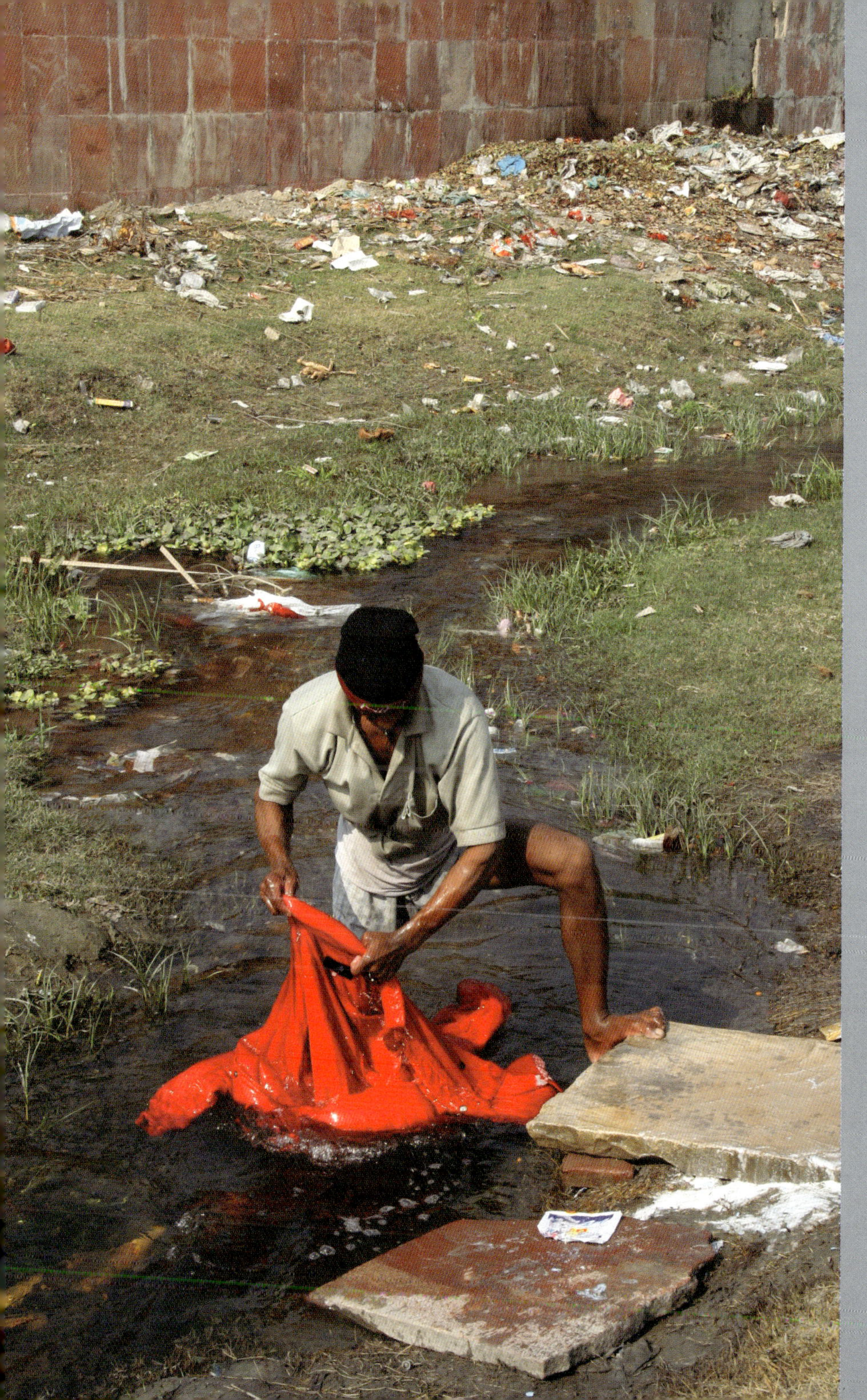

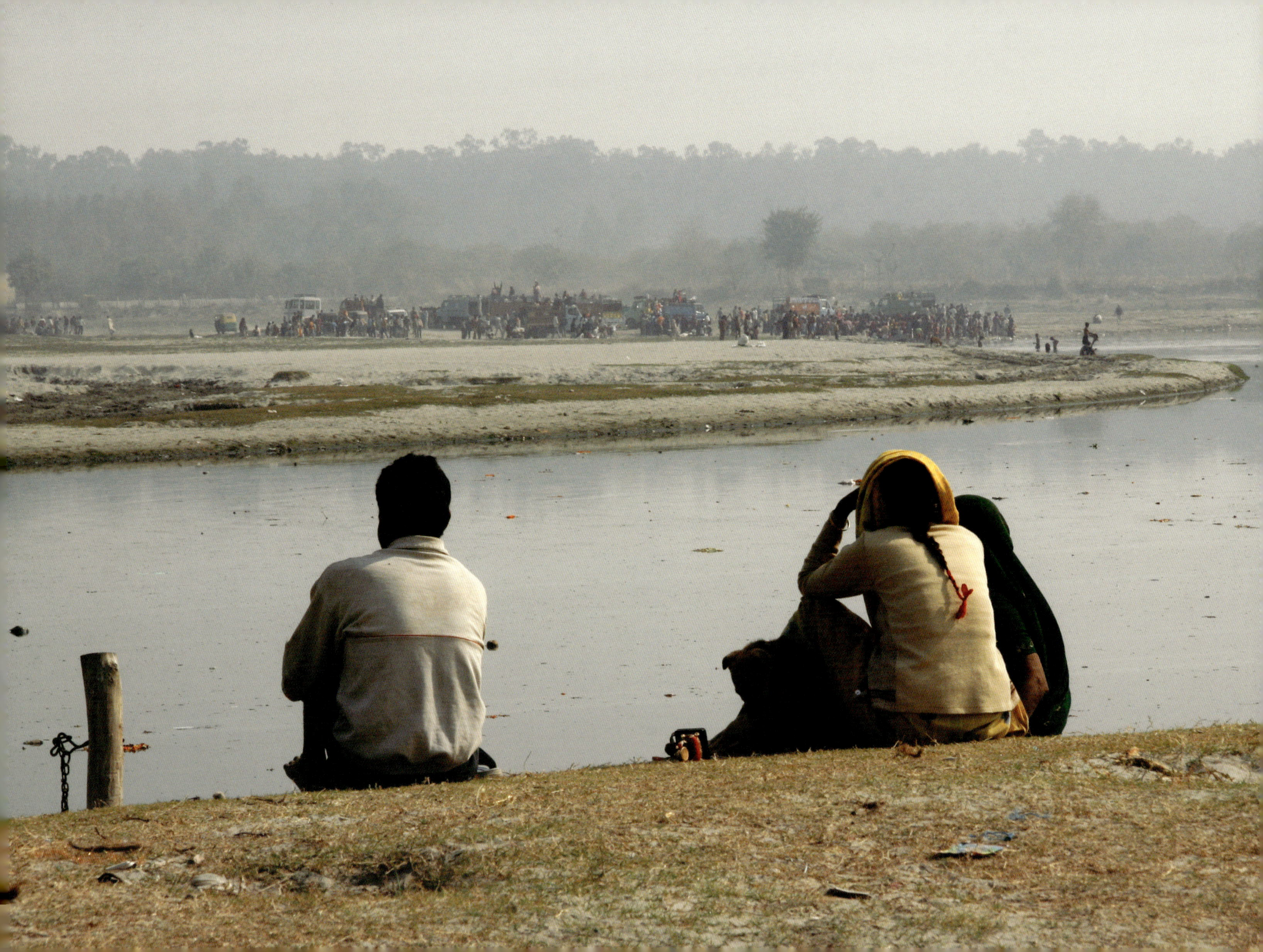

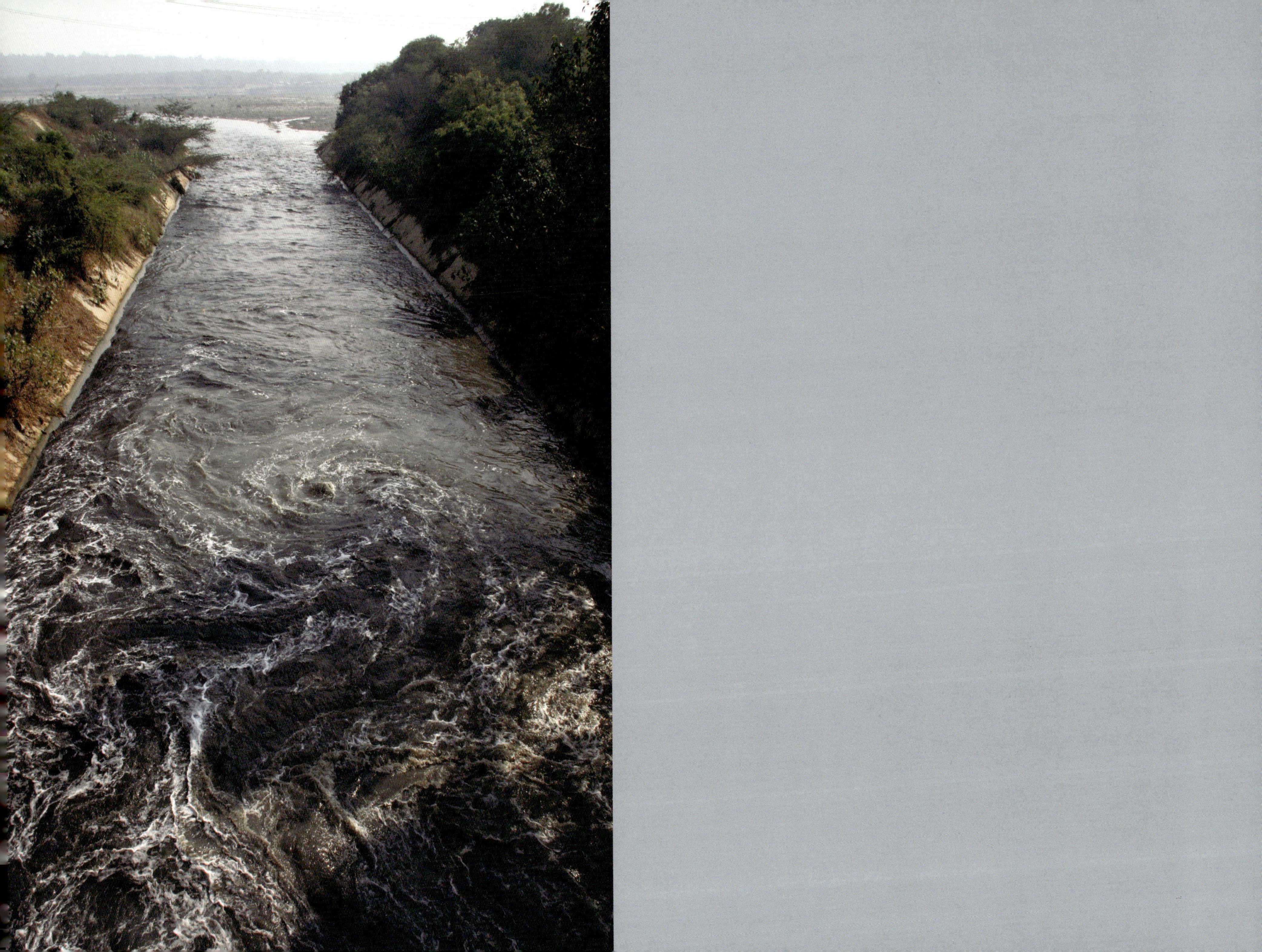

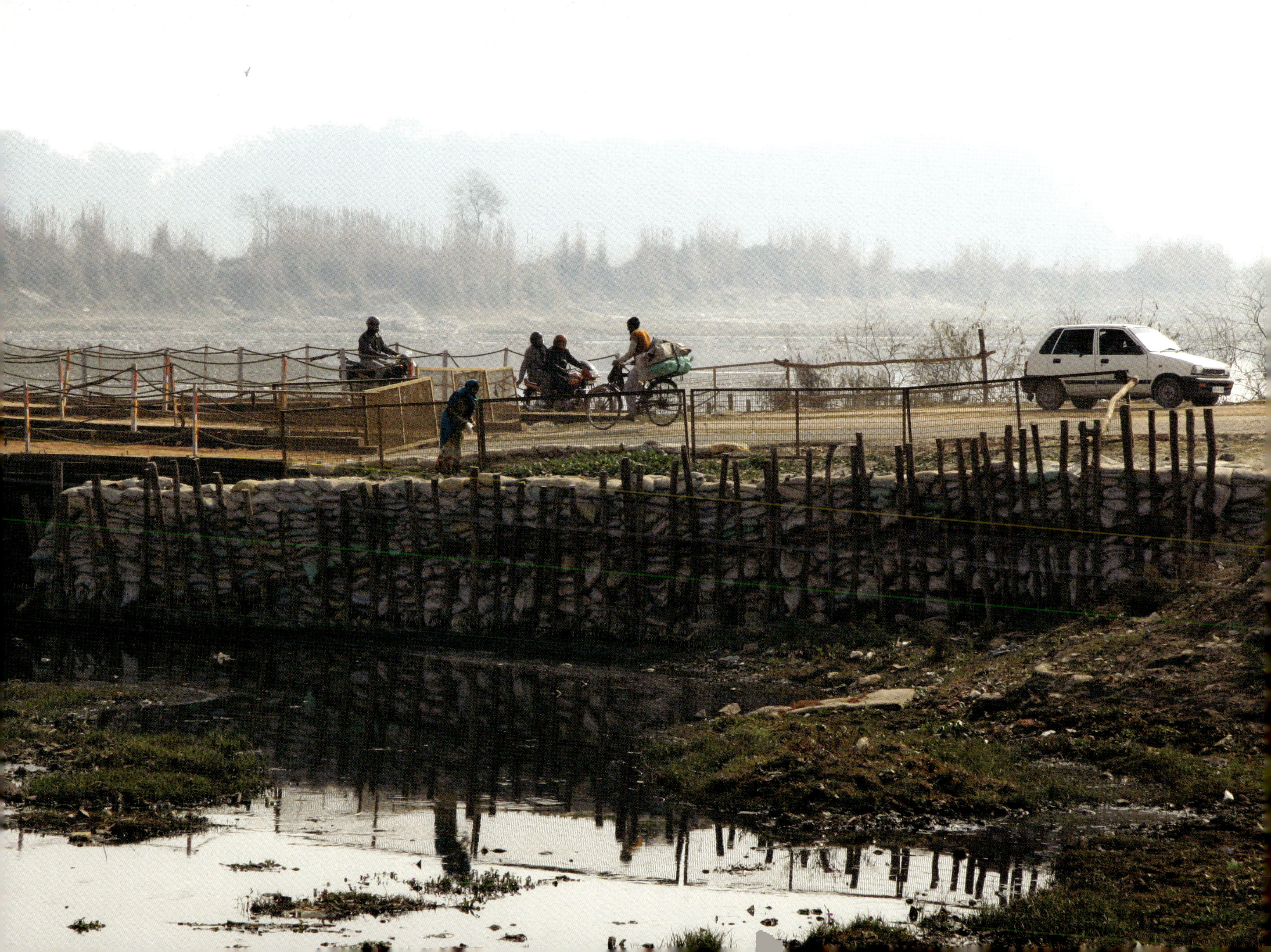

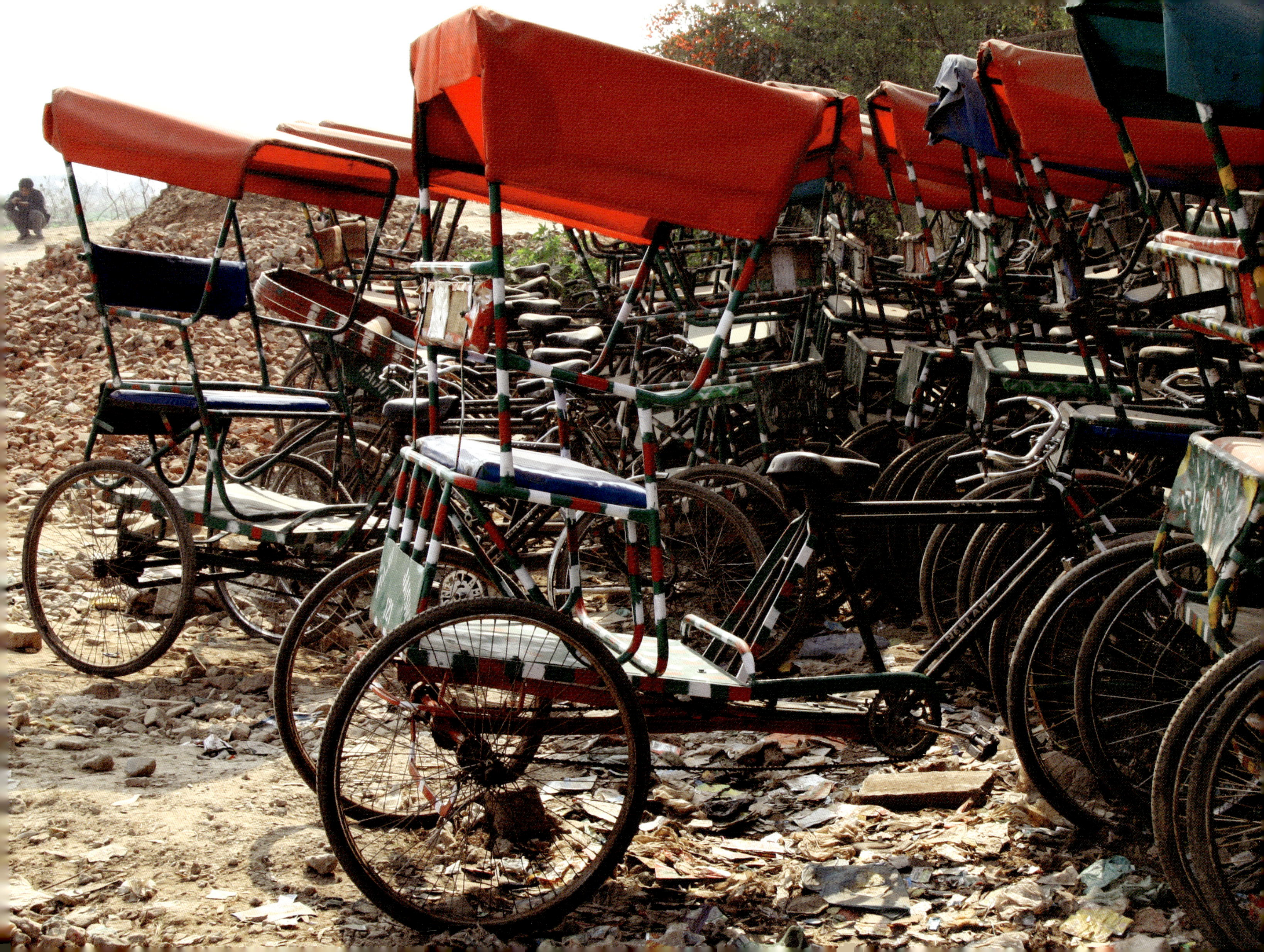

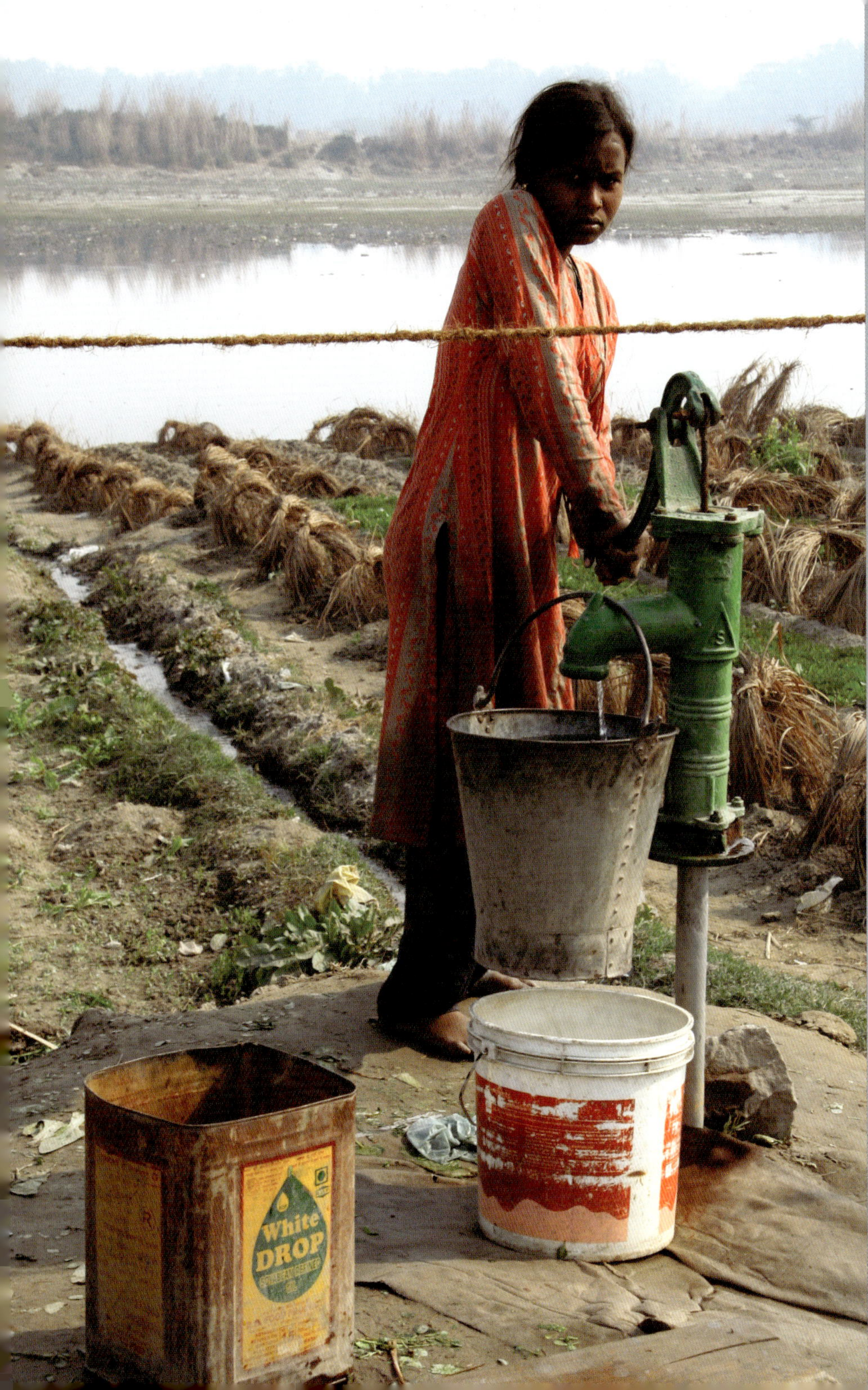

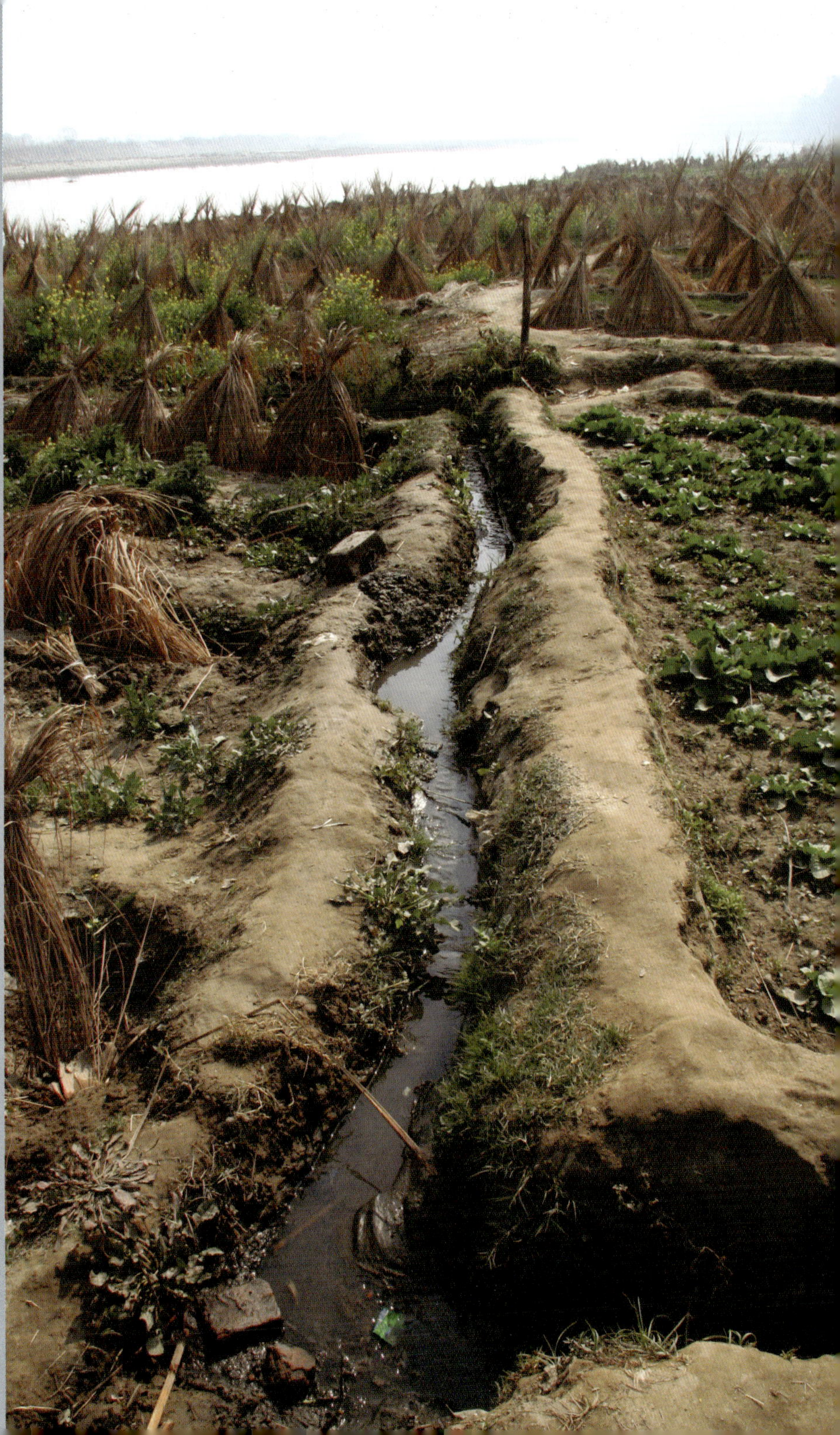

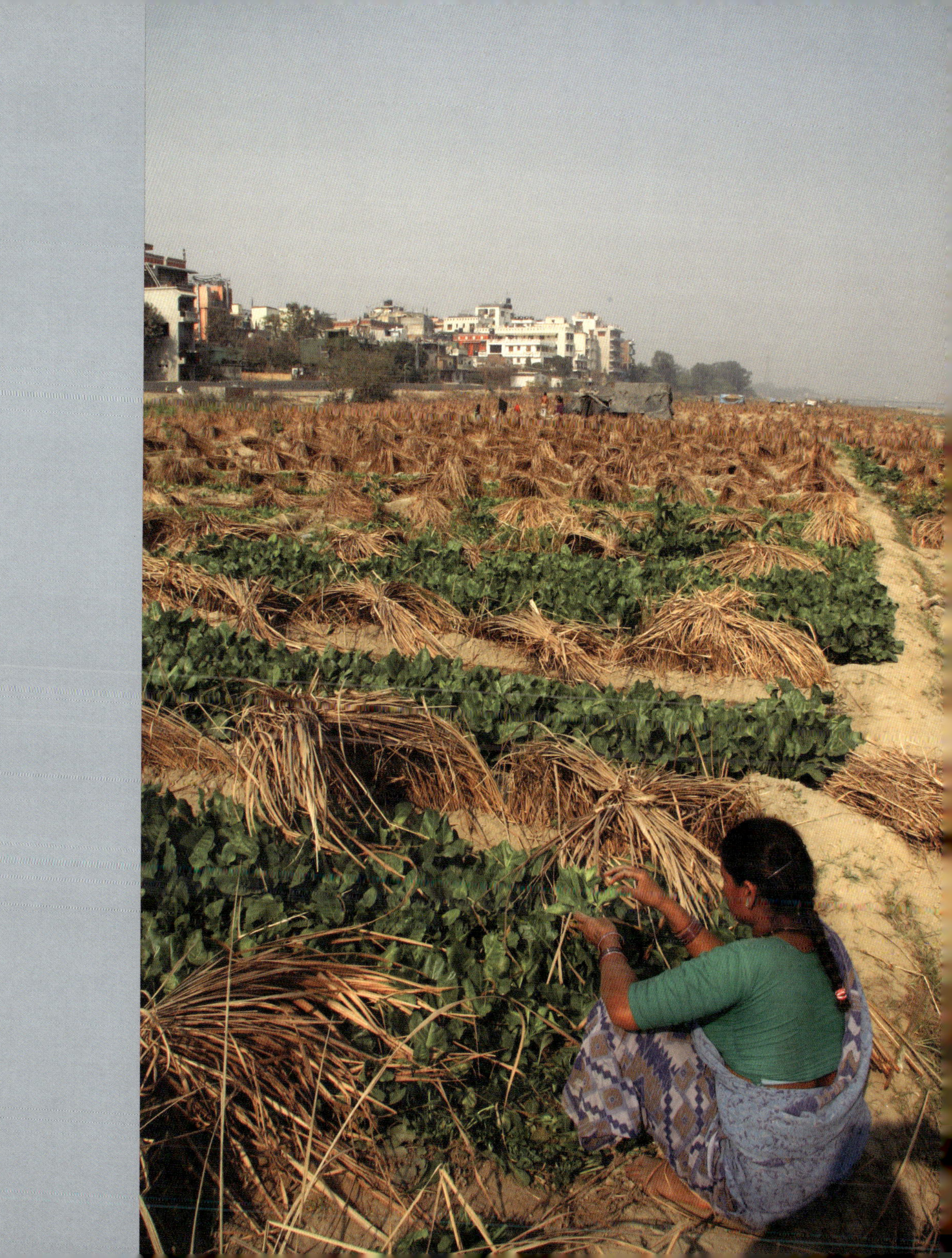

25 JANUARY 2007

10:30AM

tibetan market
houses
their
backs
to the yamuna
find
a house
with its
front
to the yamuna
the farmers
the rag pickers
the forgotten
no further
a boat
slow pace,
thick
water,
black,
still
birds.
death
burning
dumping
wet
old railway bridge
noise
rickshaws
pontoon
shanti van
flyover
construction
gulls
river
stopped
narrowed
access
denied
still,
but birds
still, slow
muck
wash
fields
young wheat
still grows
mustard
flowers
some marigold
dumped
carrion
dogs fight
people sift
remains
distant
non worried
roads
traffic
noise
smoke
I.T.O.
security
identity
explanations
given
call it a day.

4:30PM

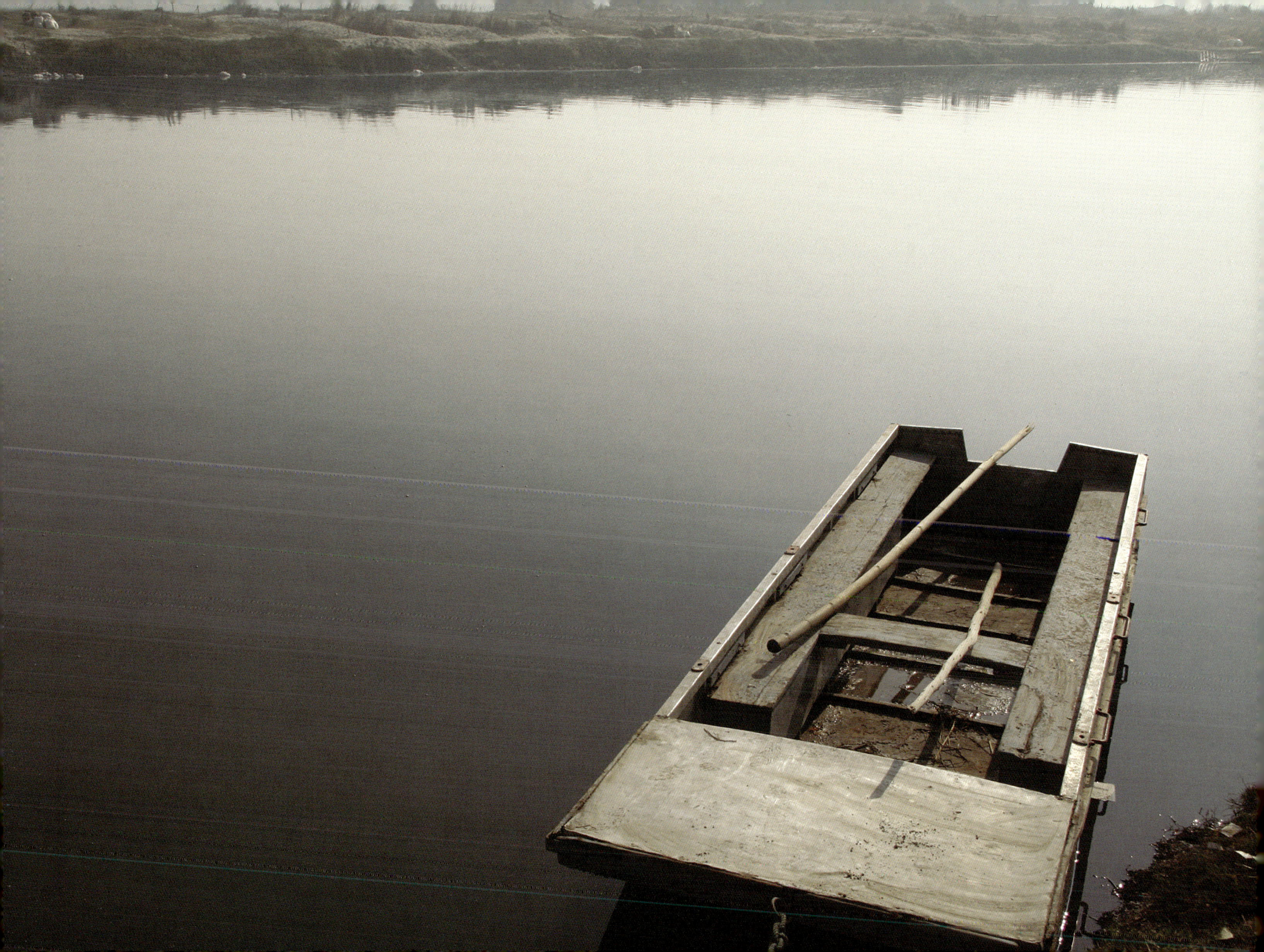

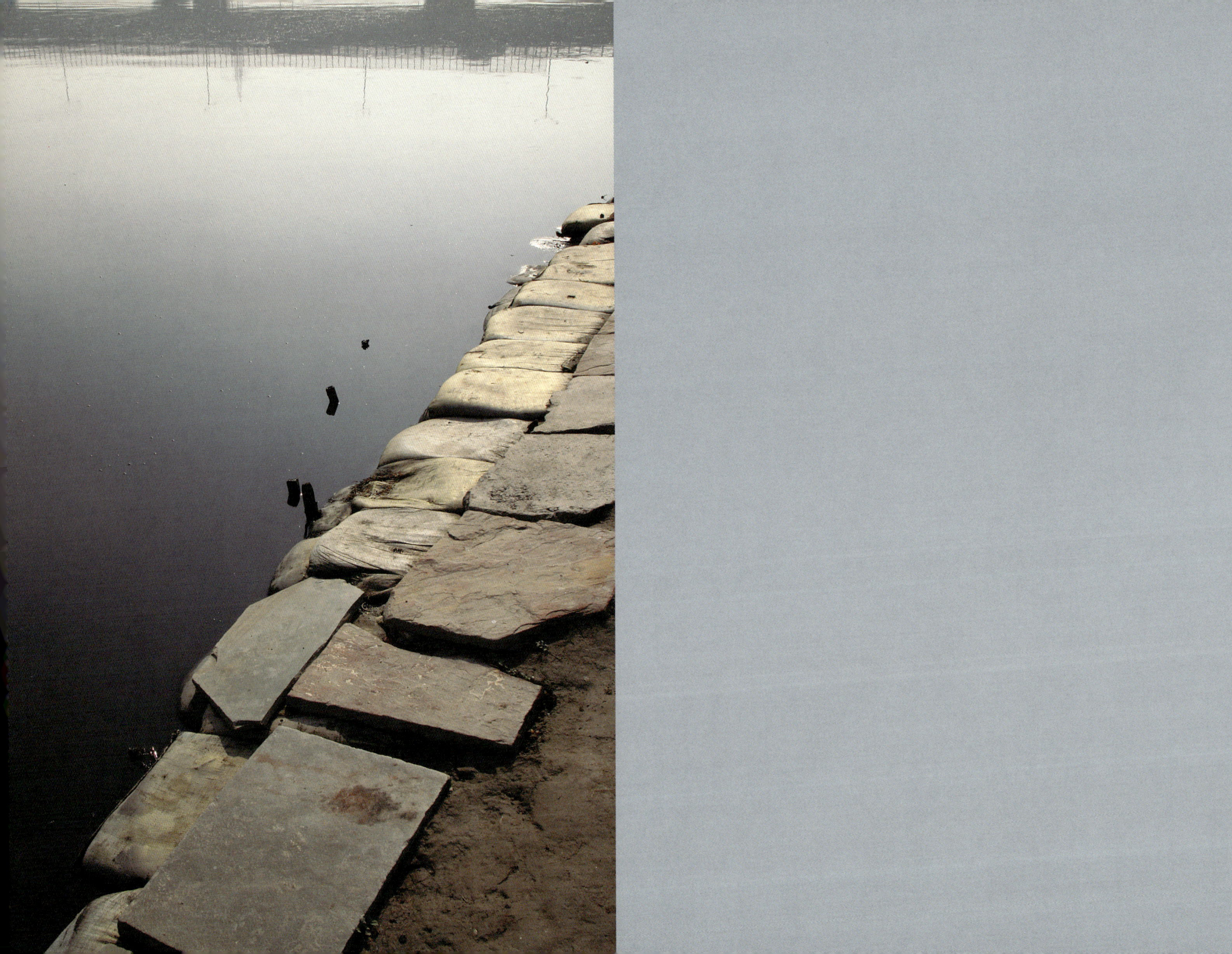

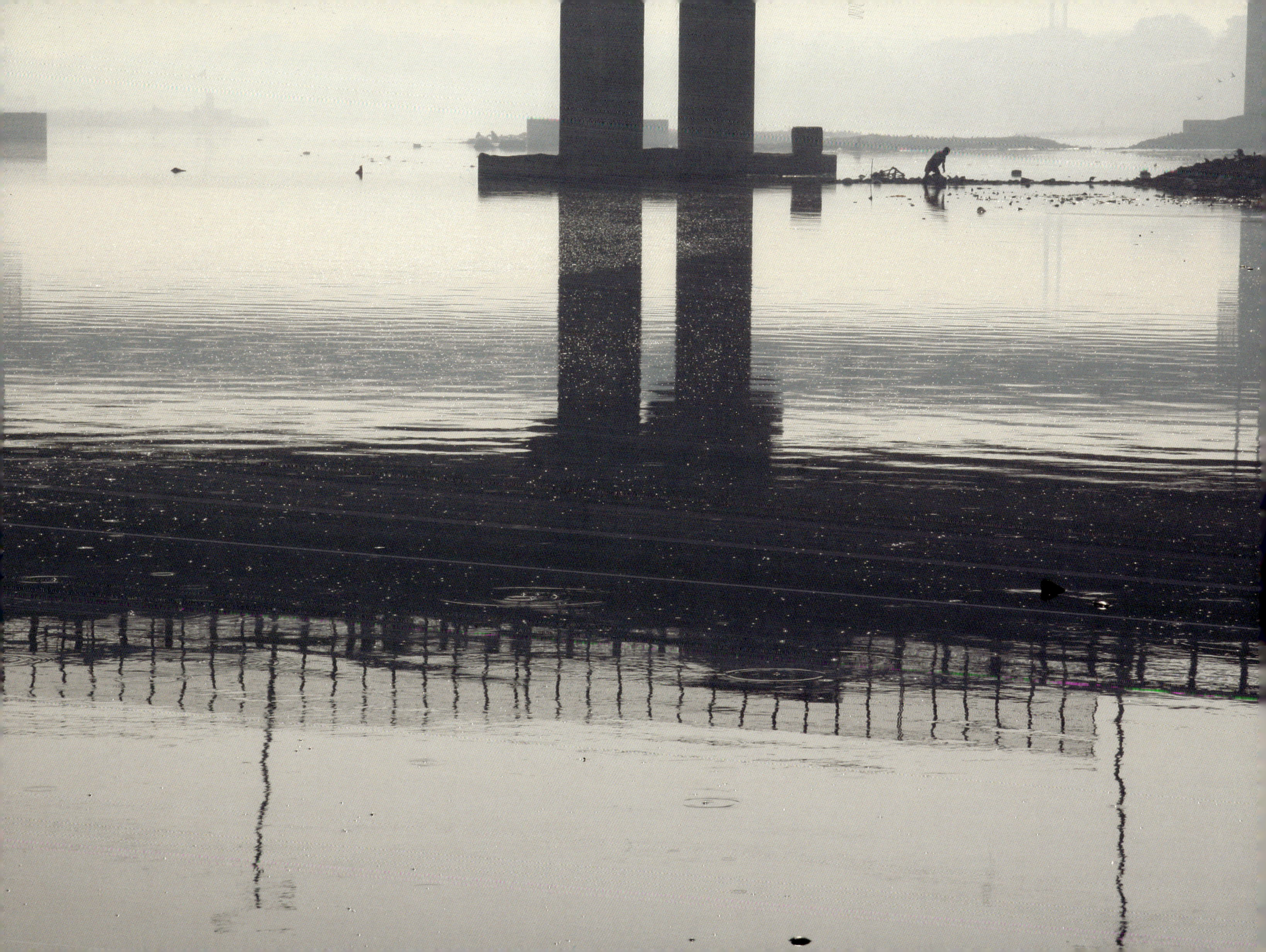

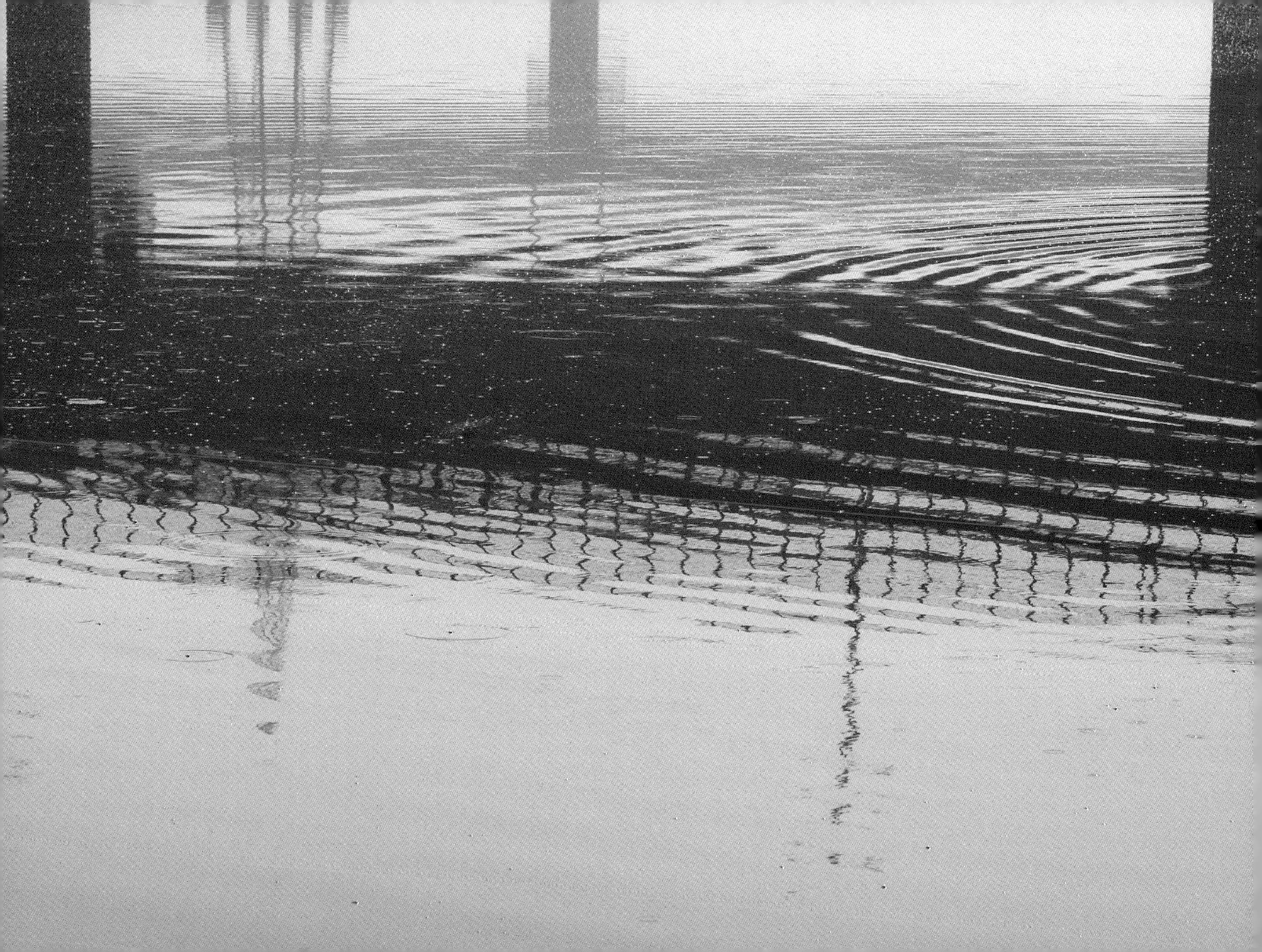

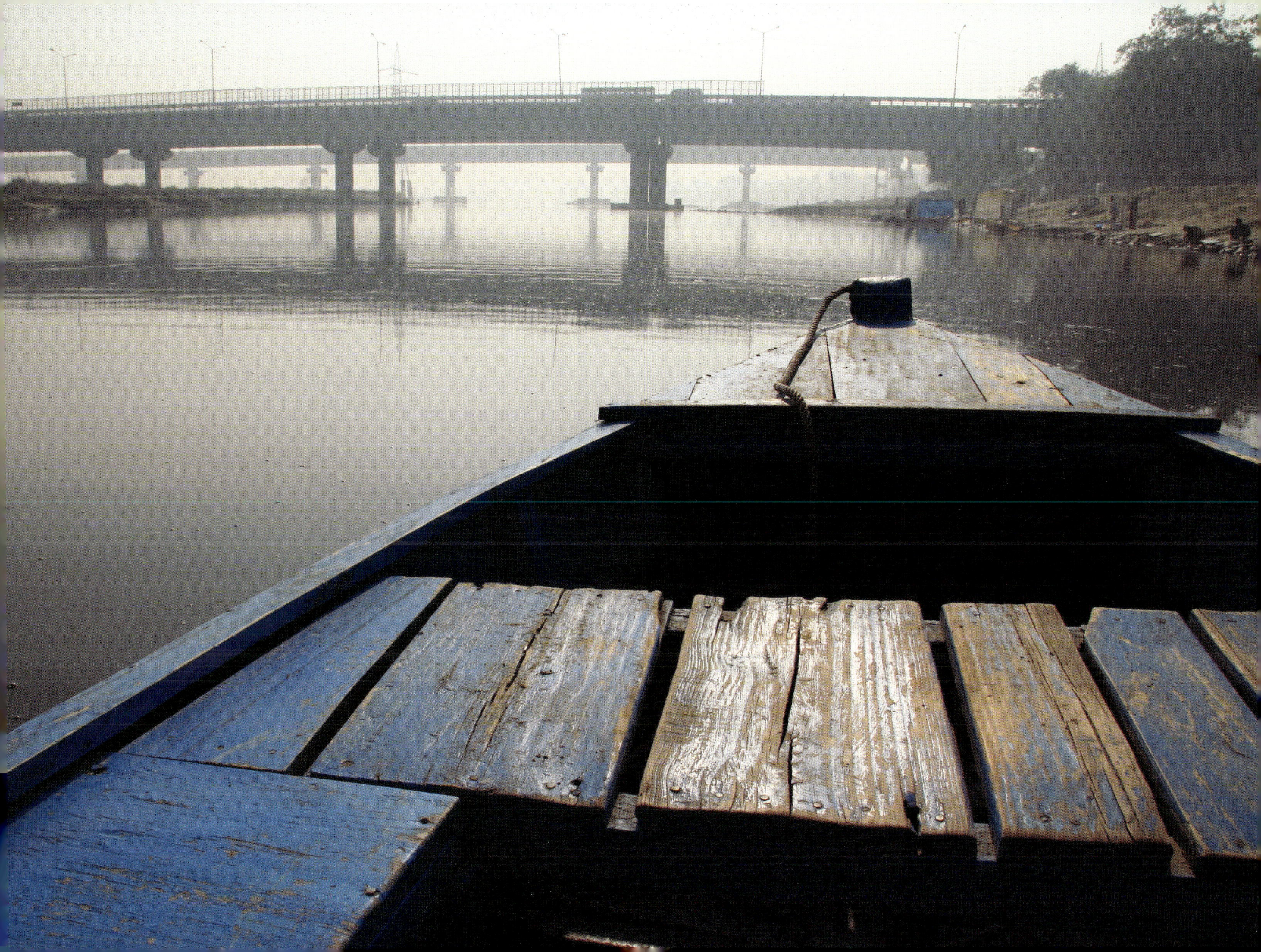

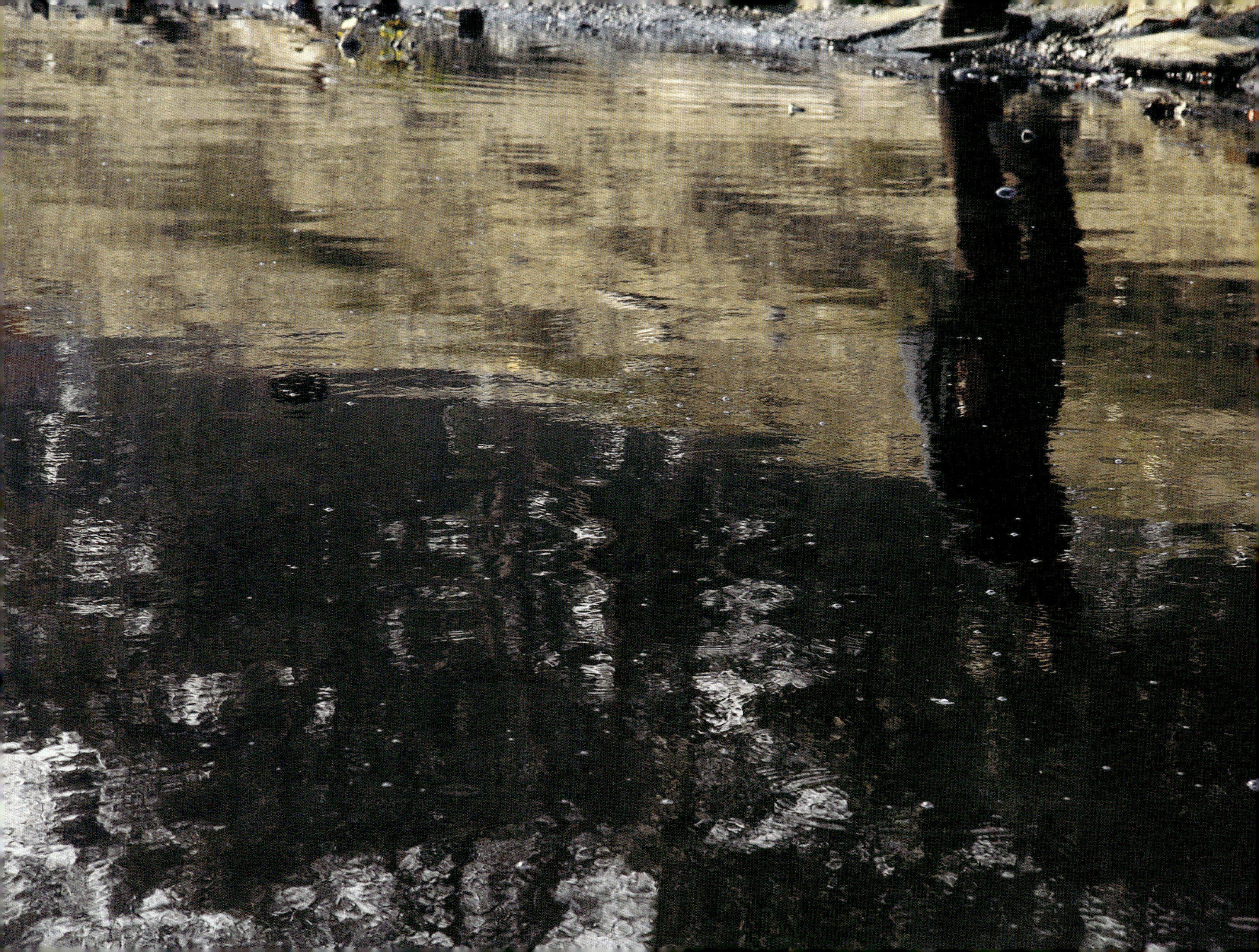

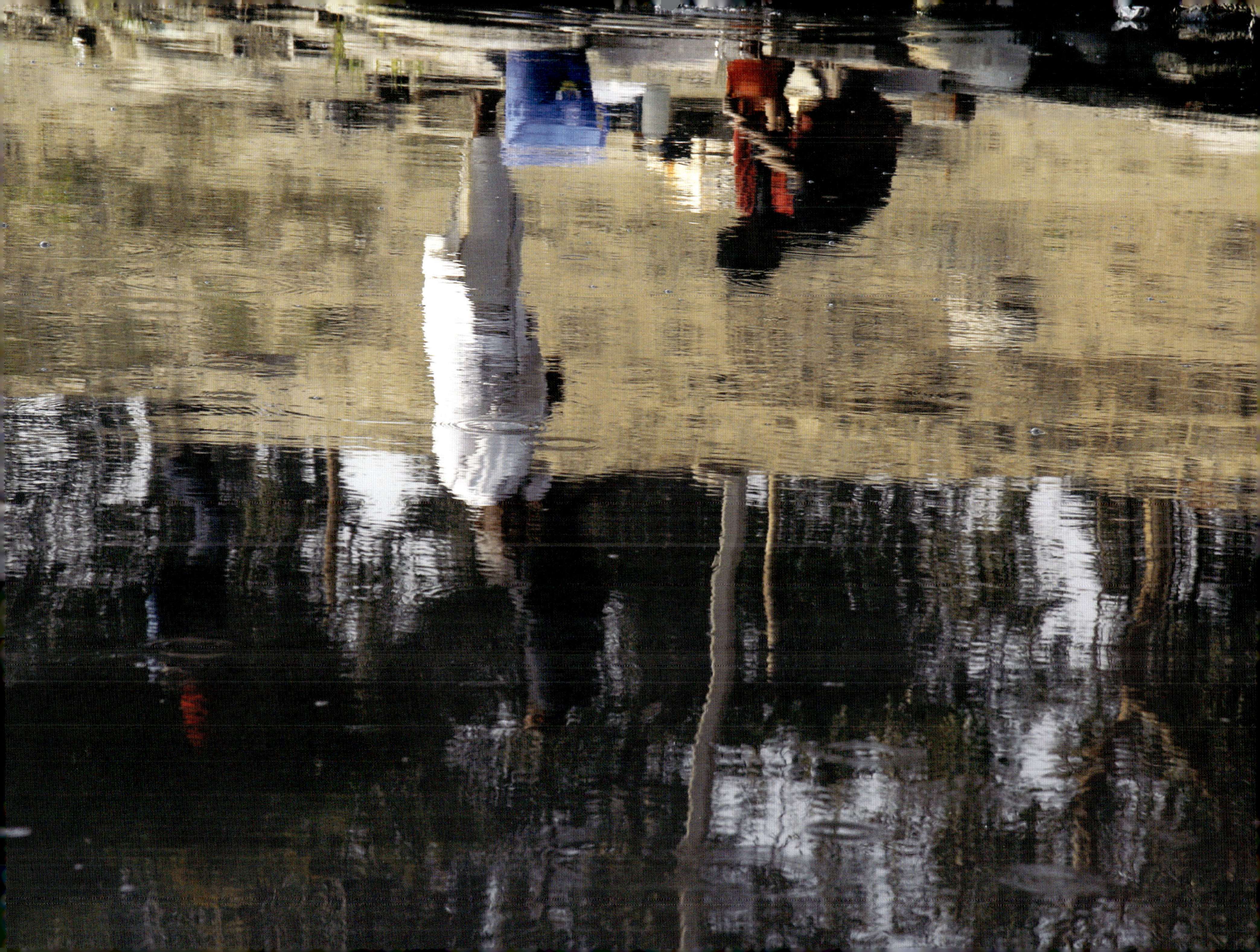

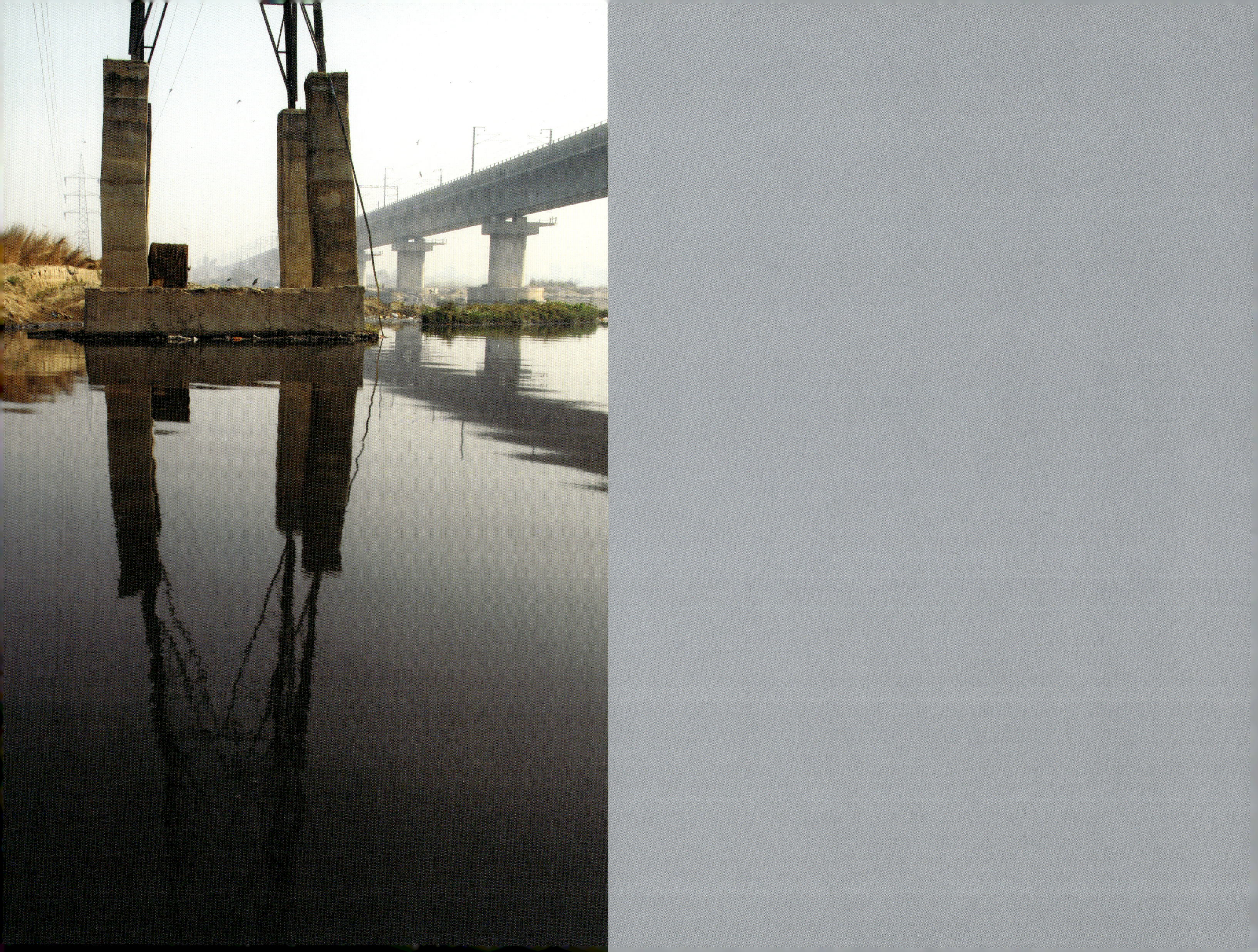

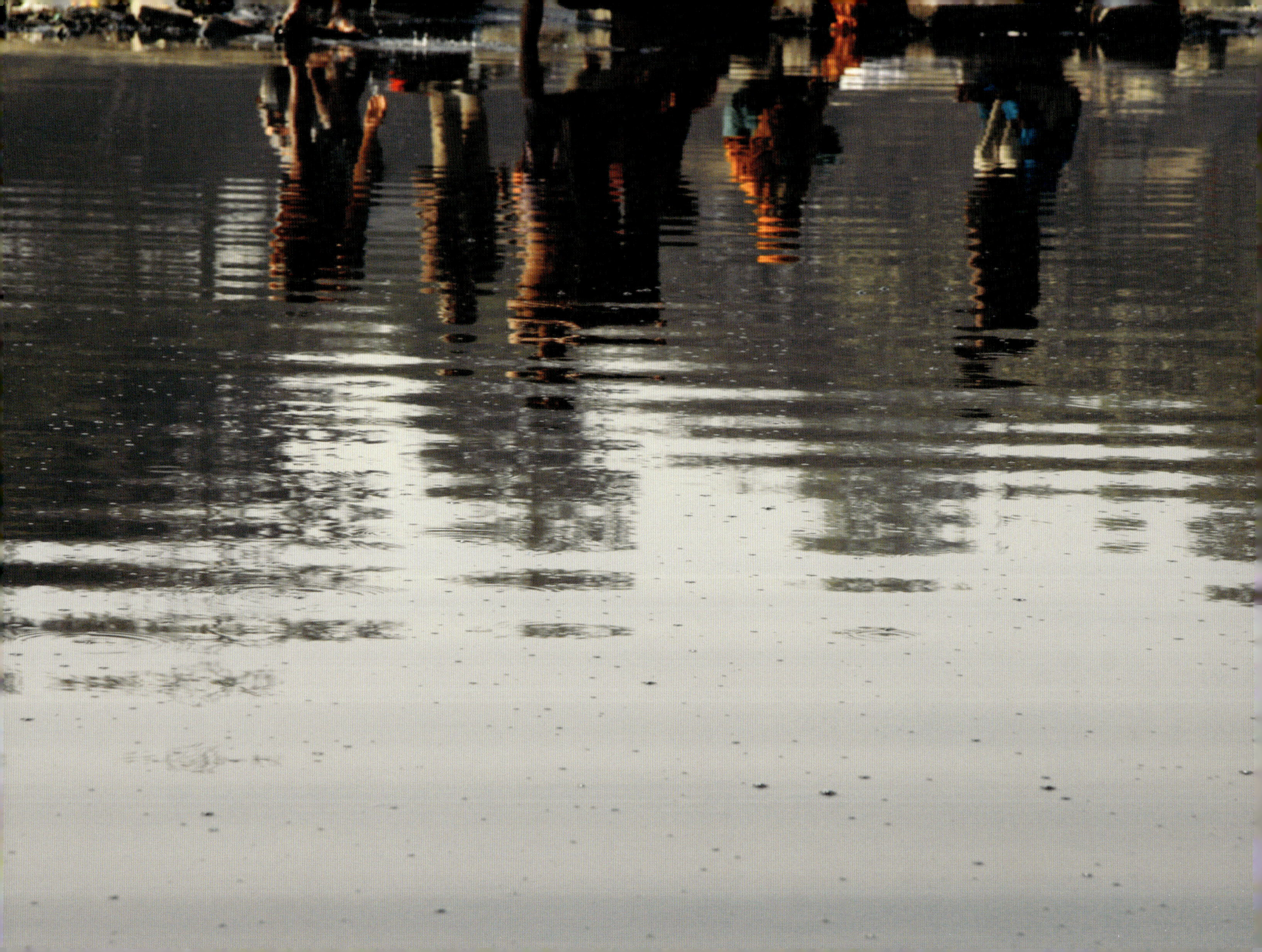

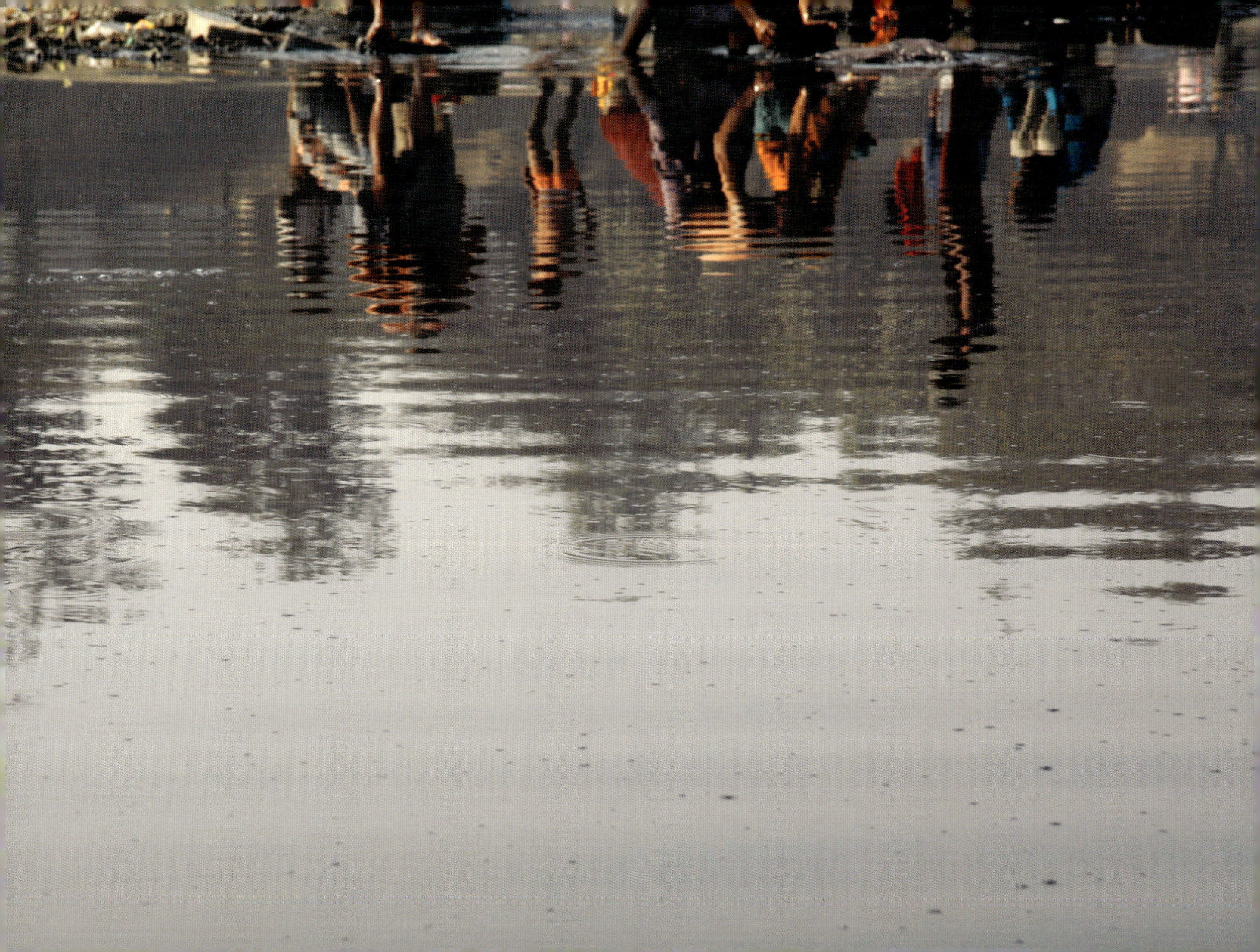

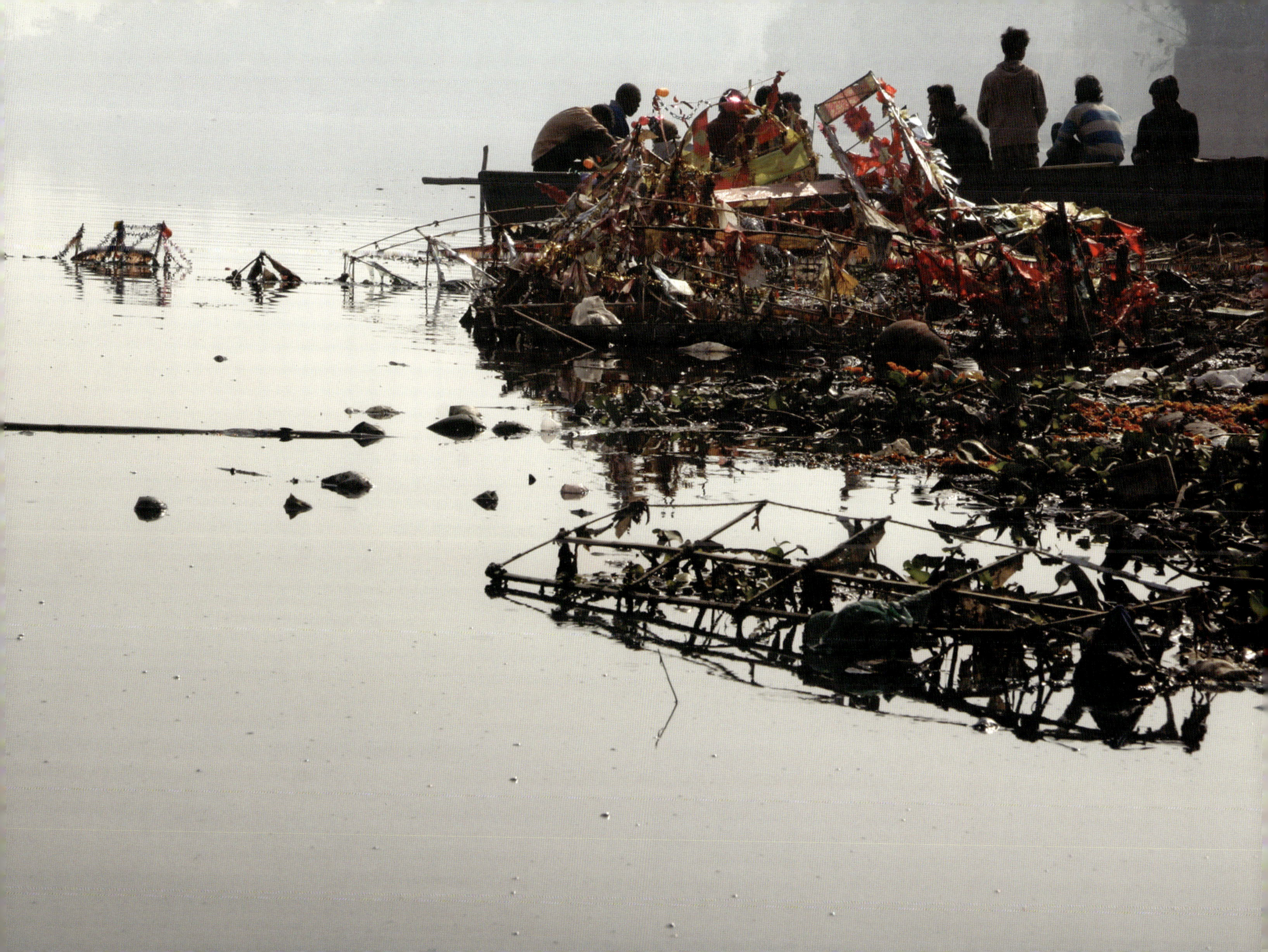

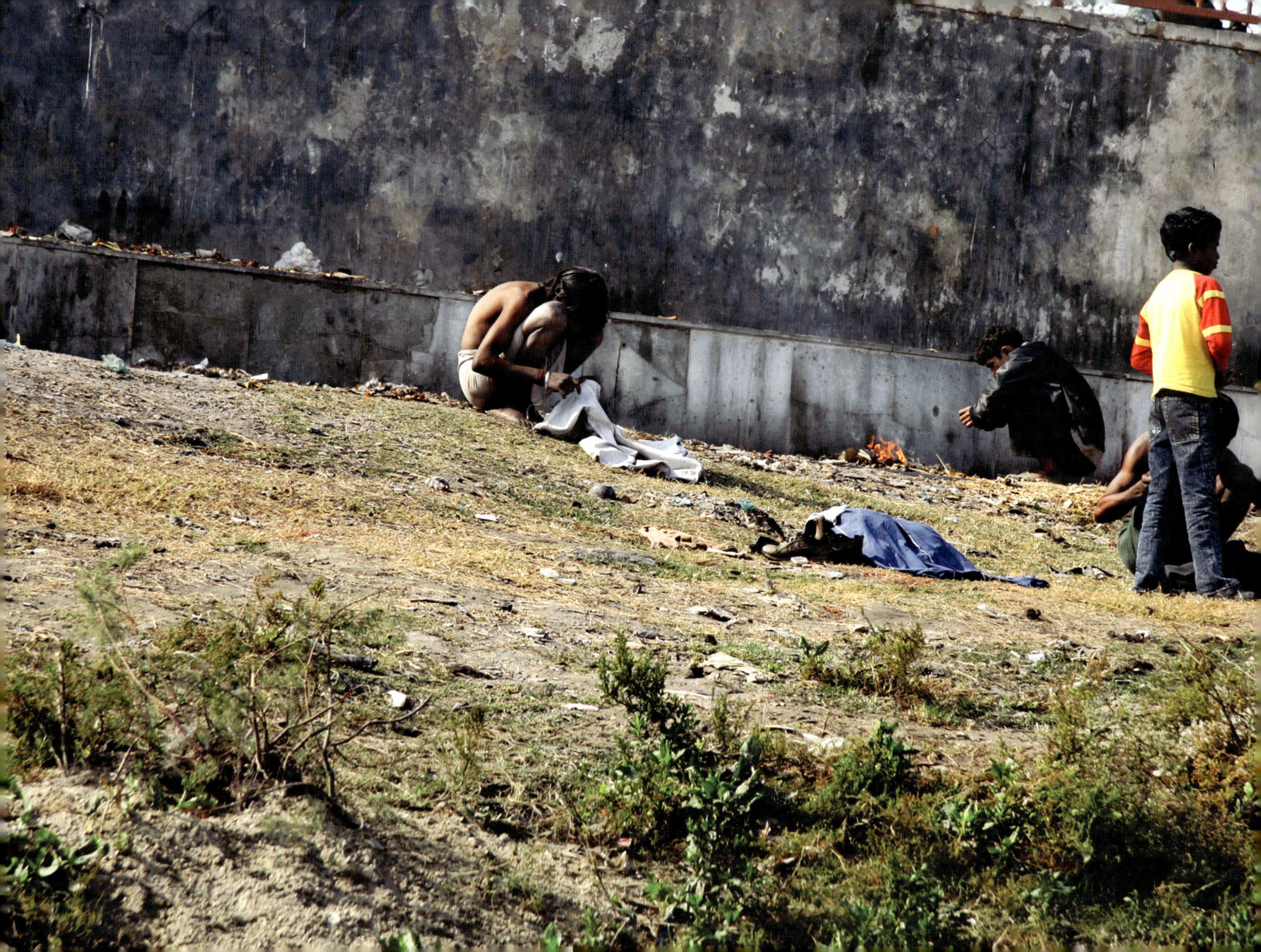

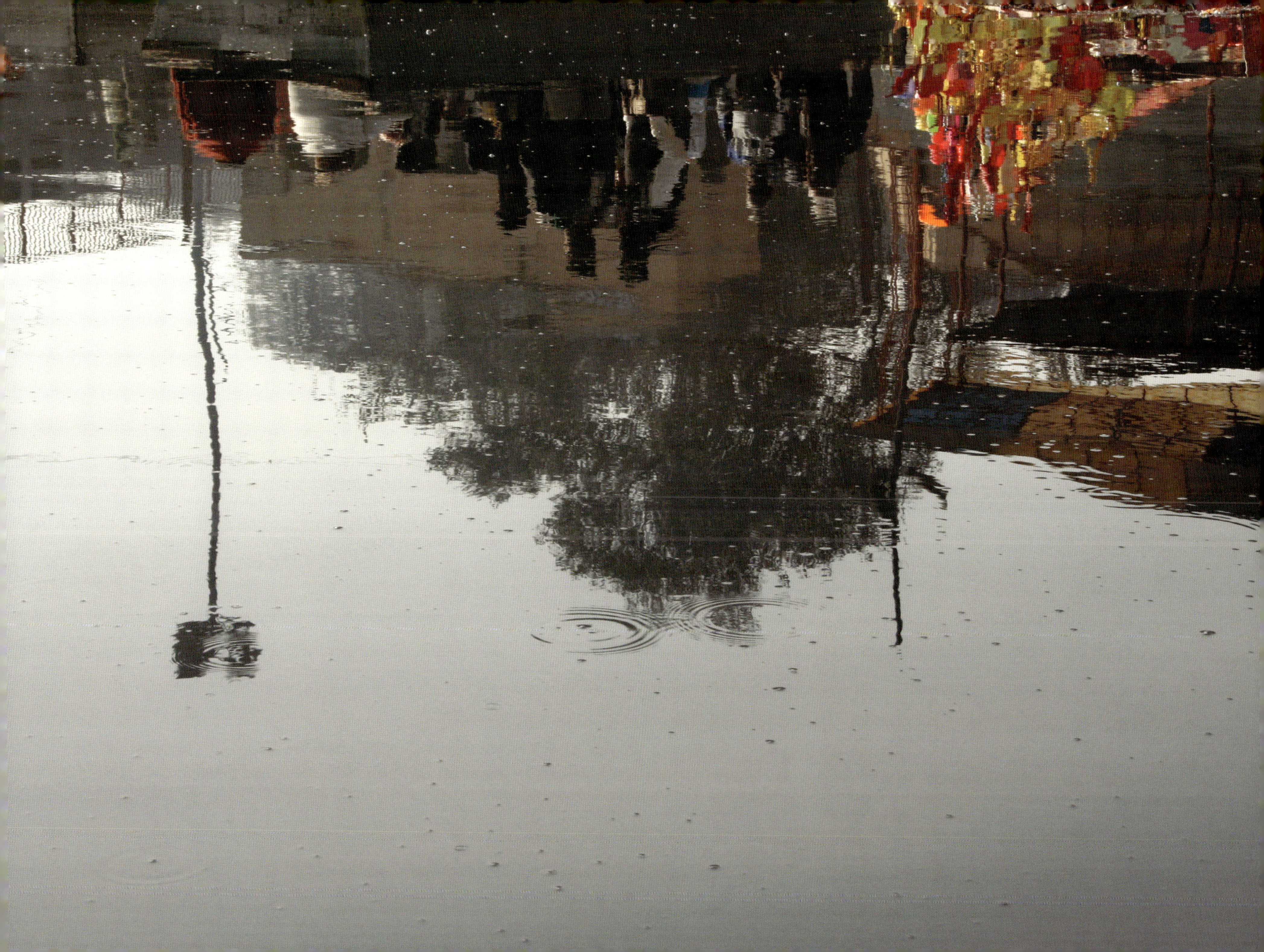

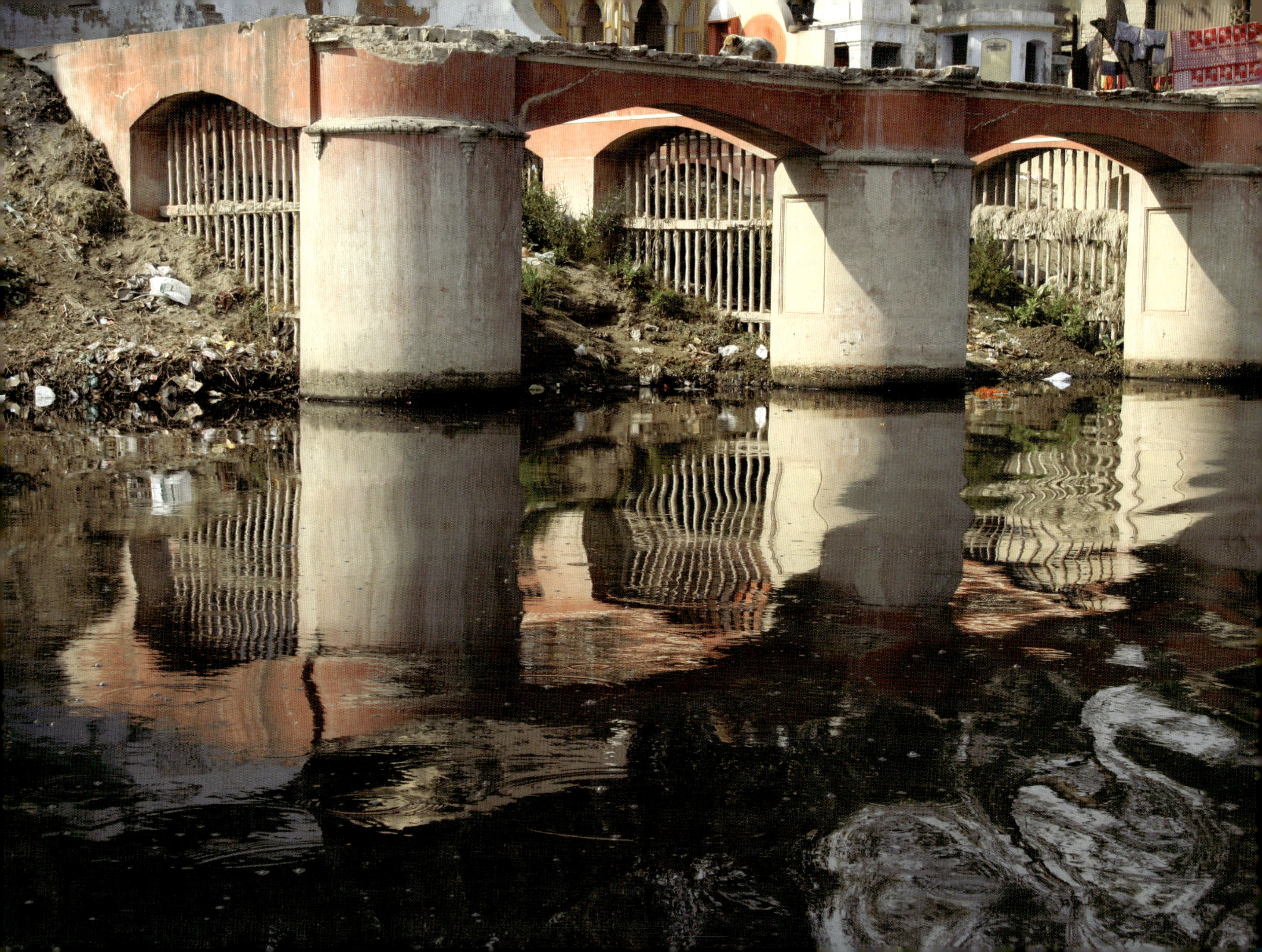

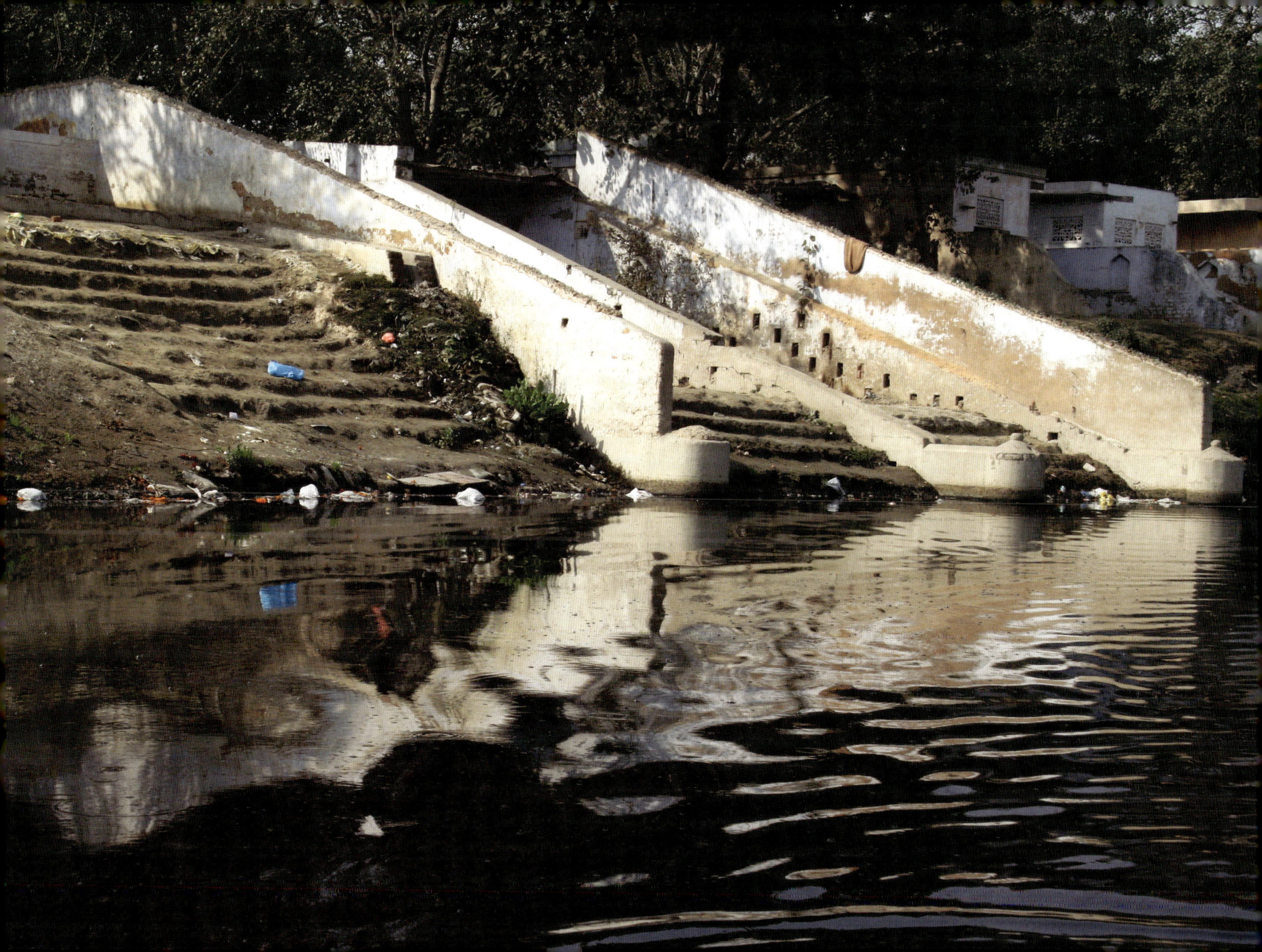

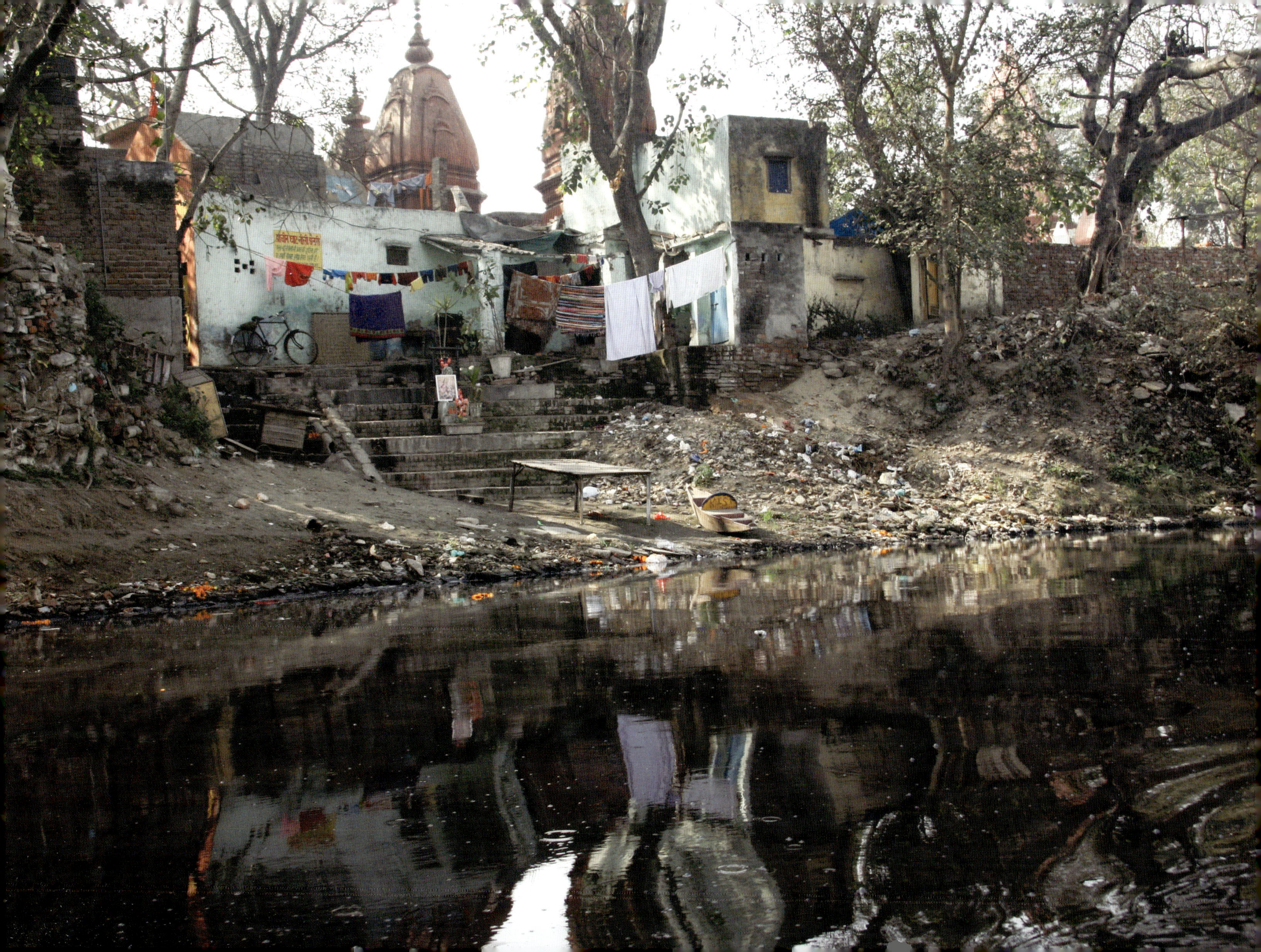

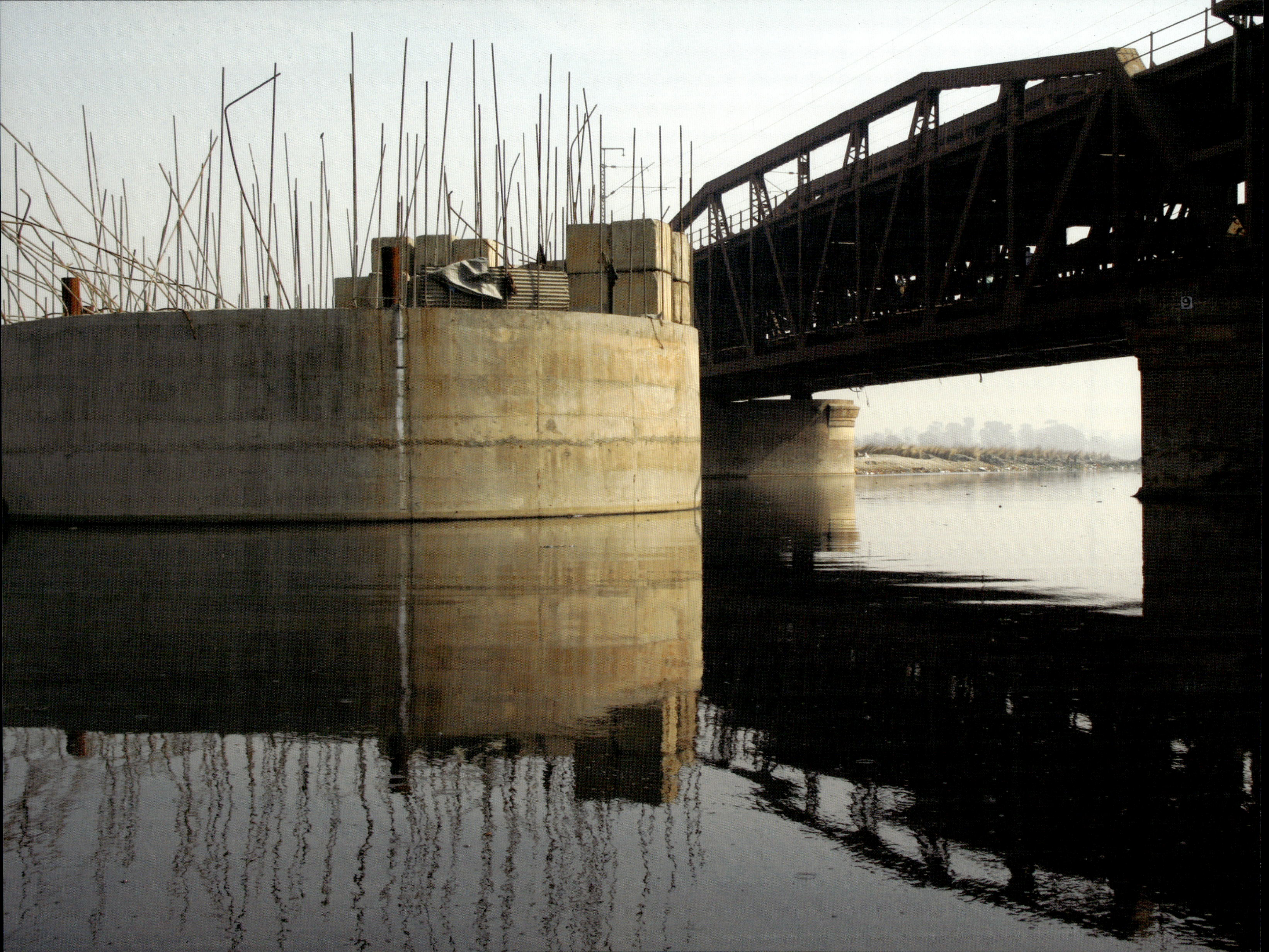
9

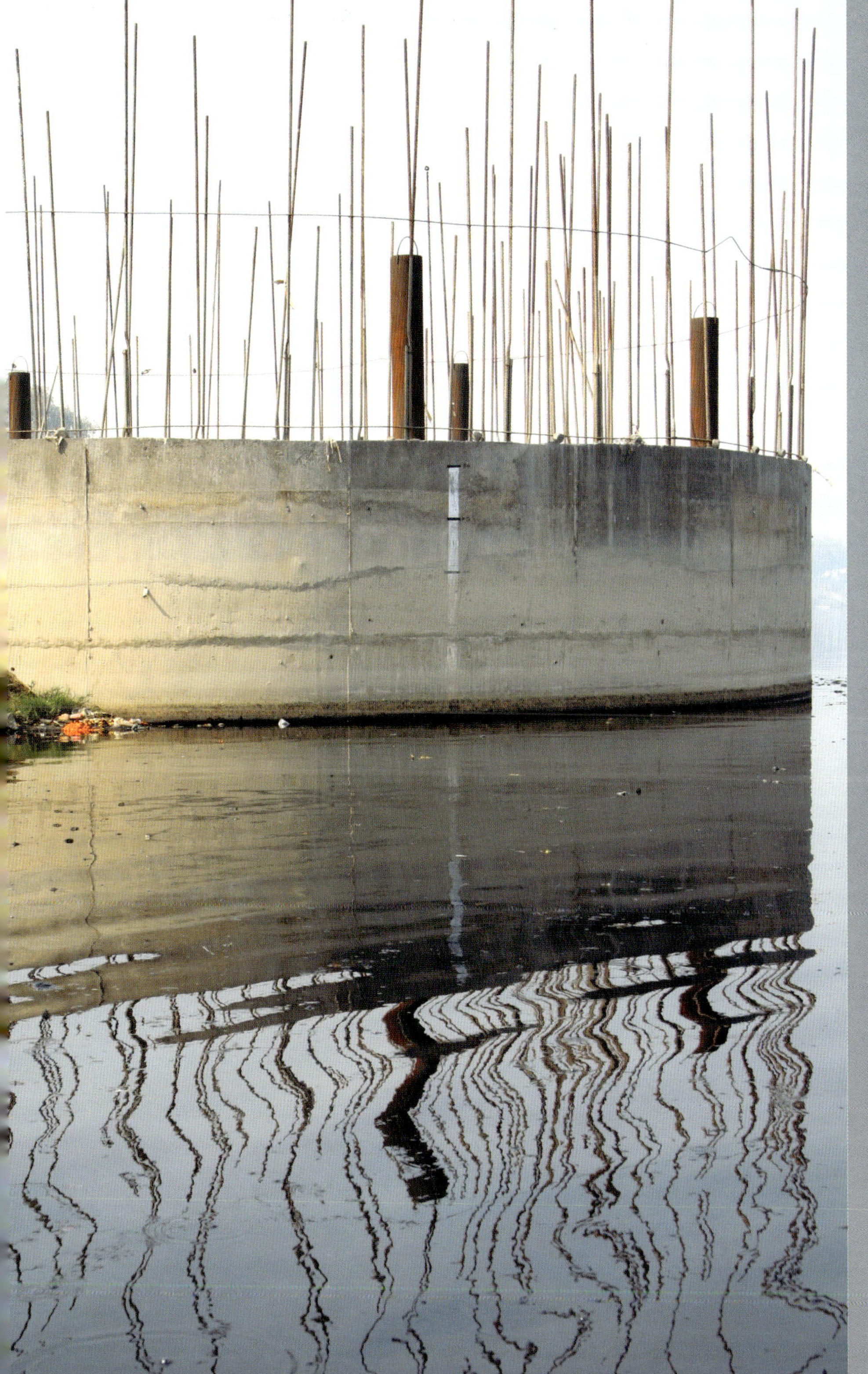

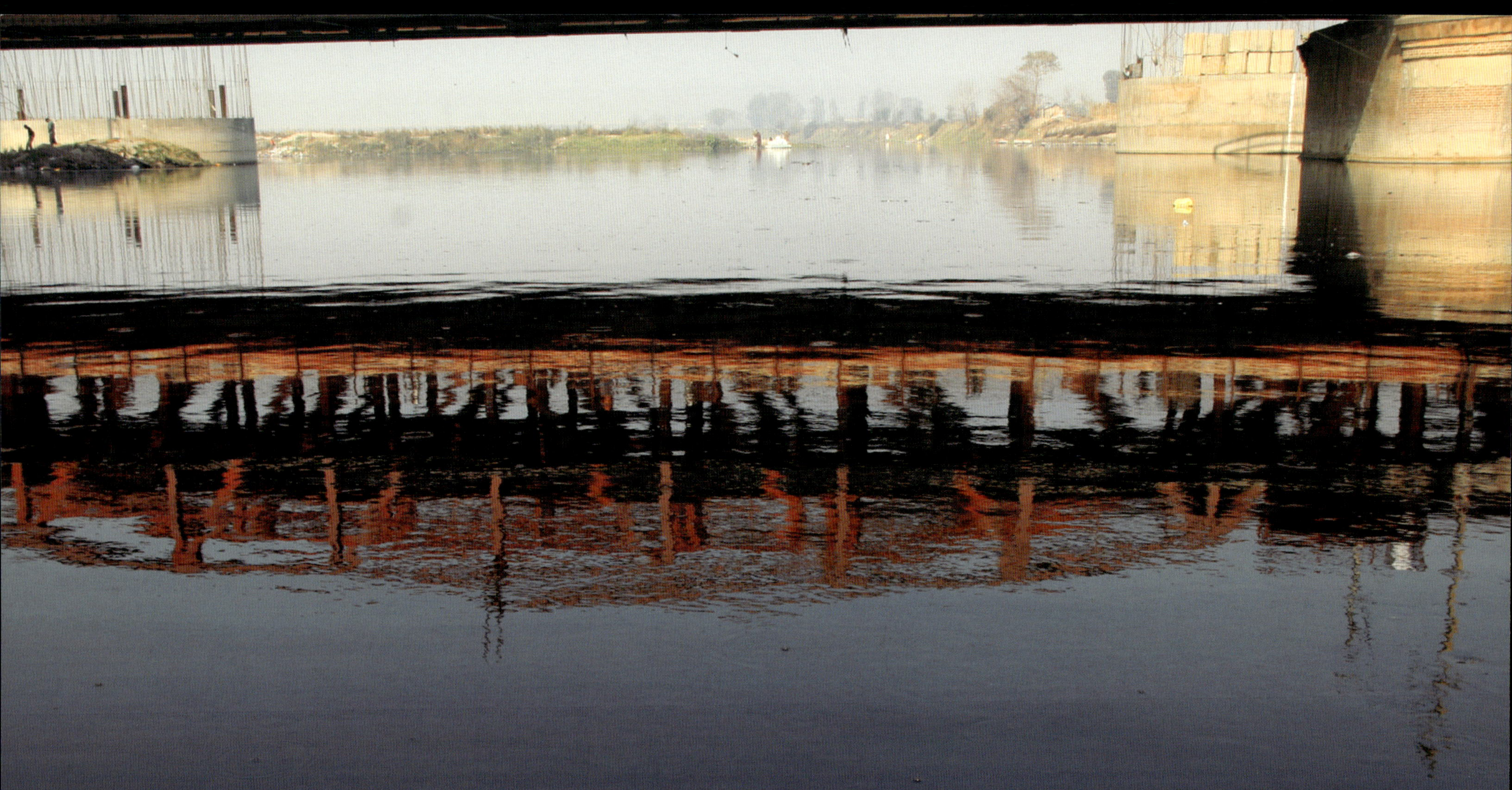

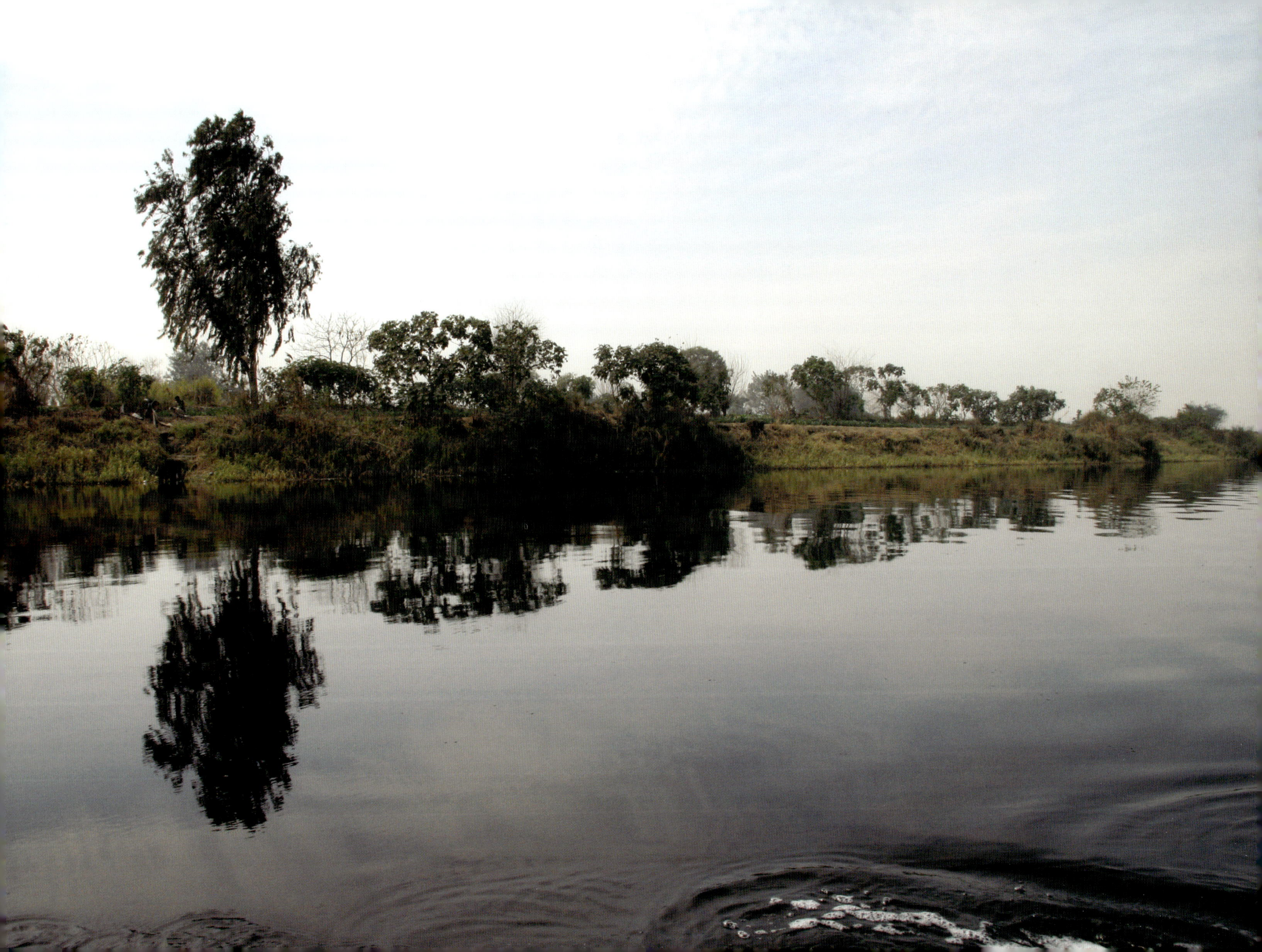

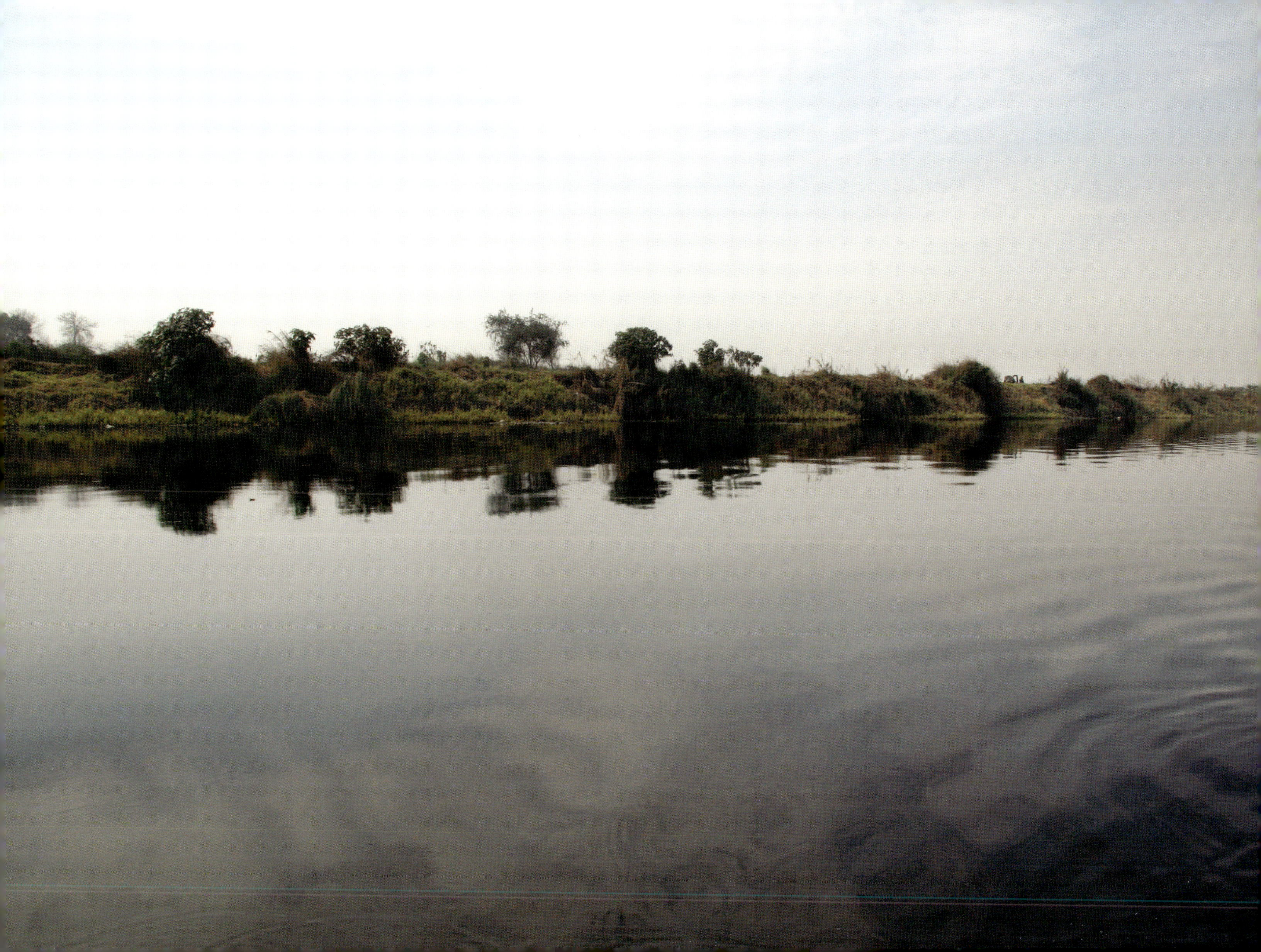

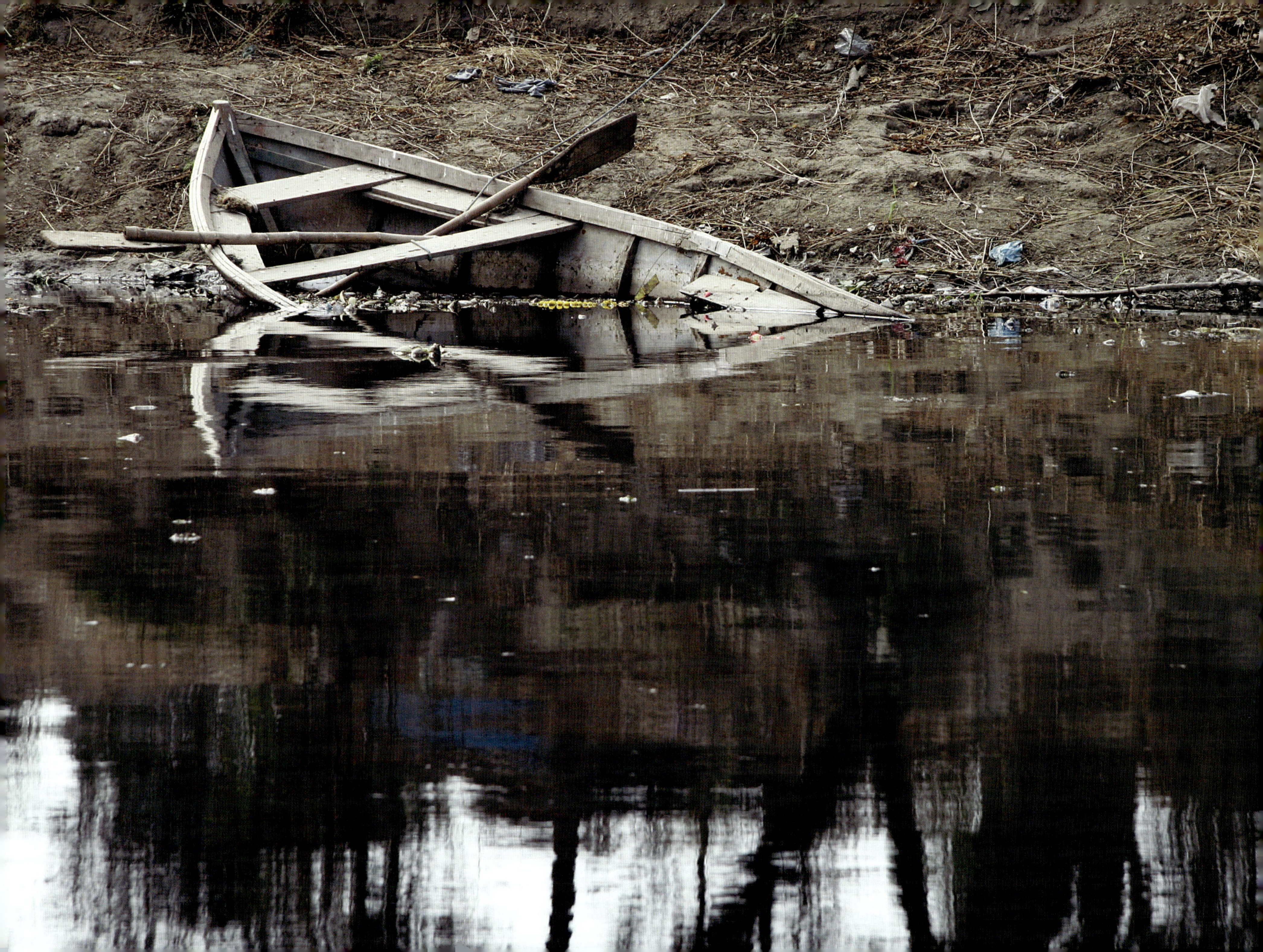

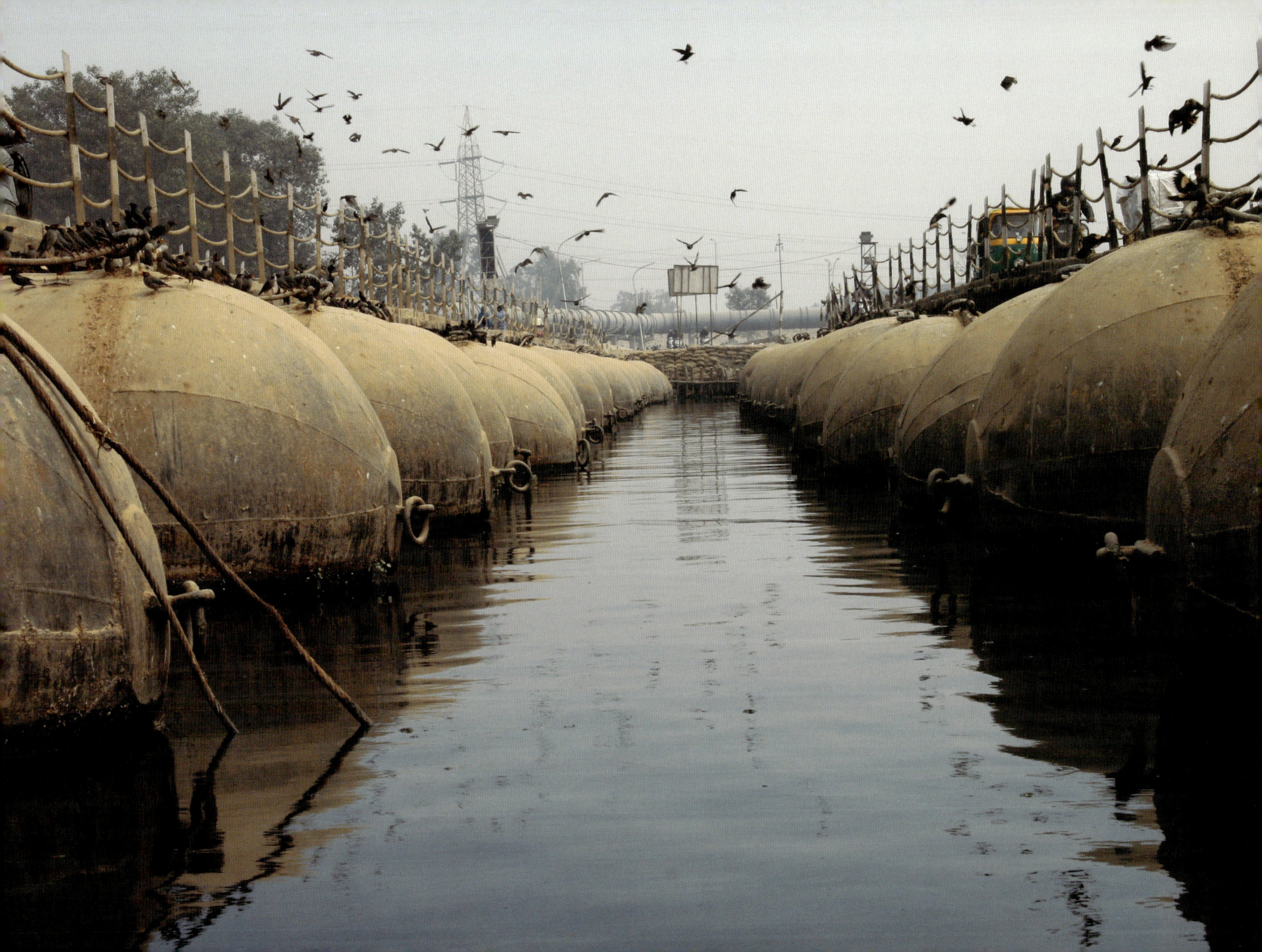

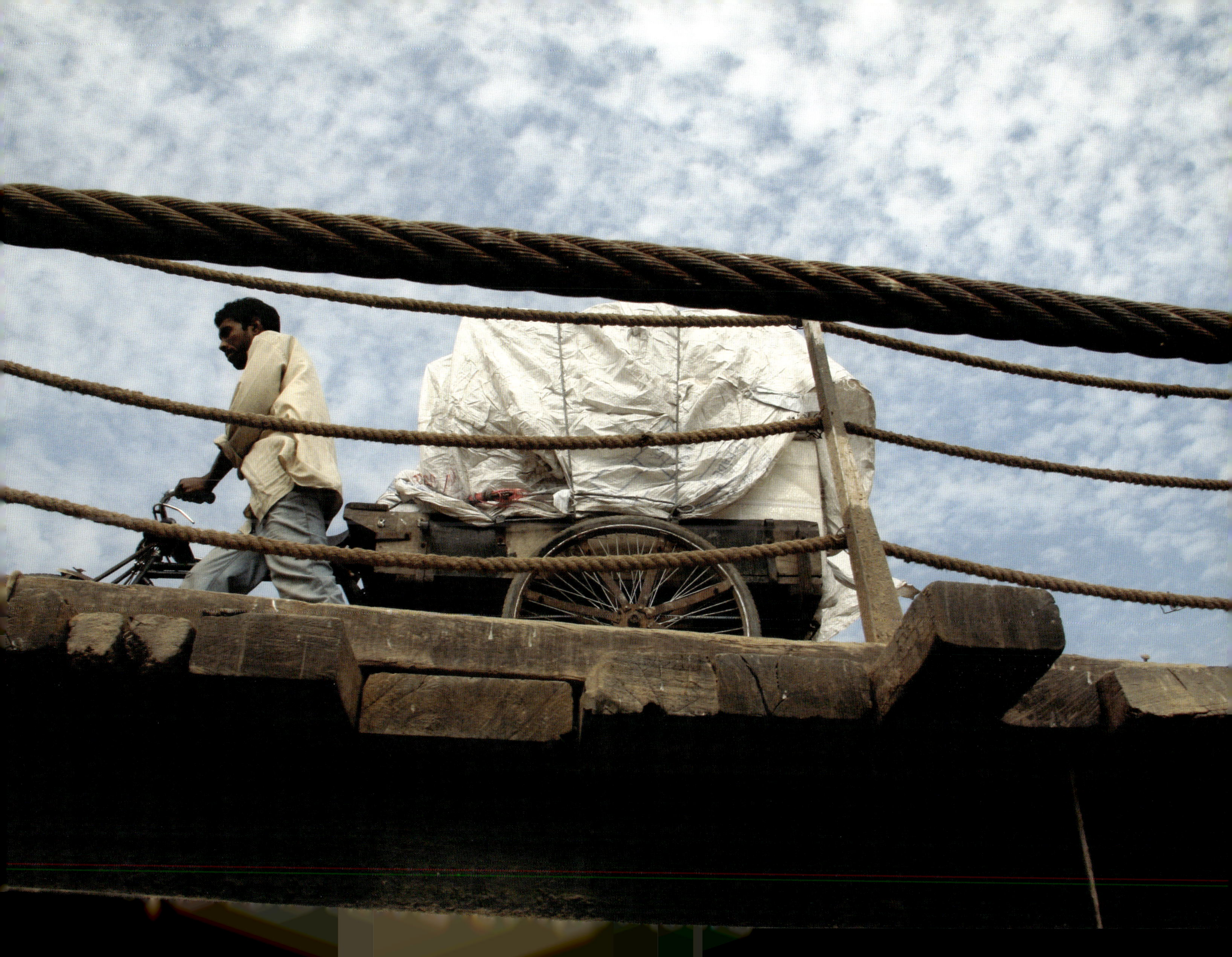

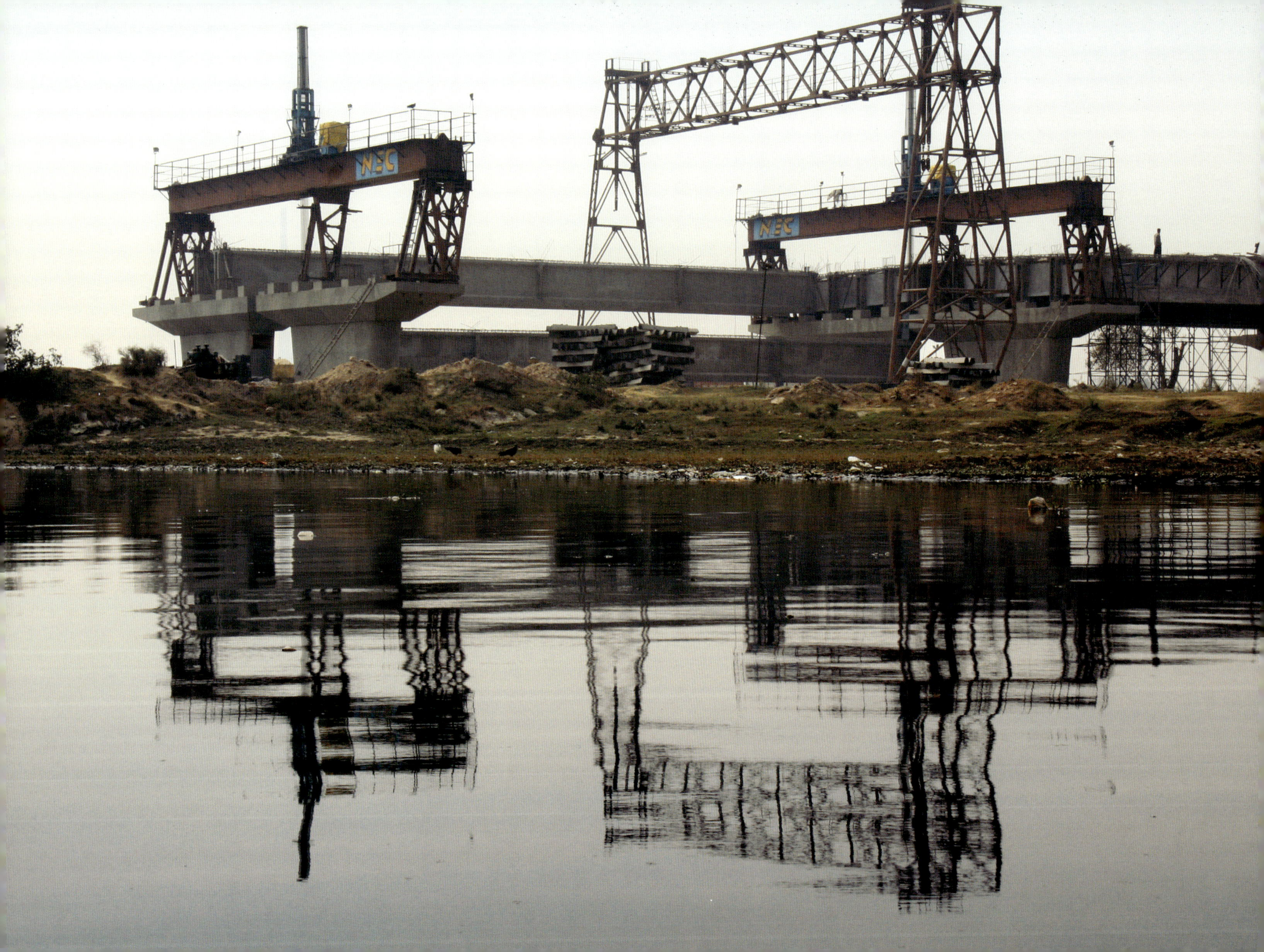
NEC
NEC

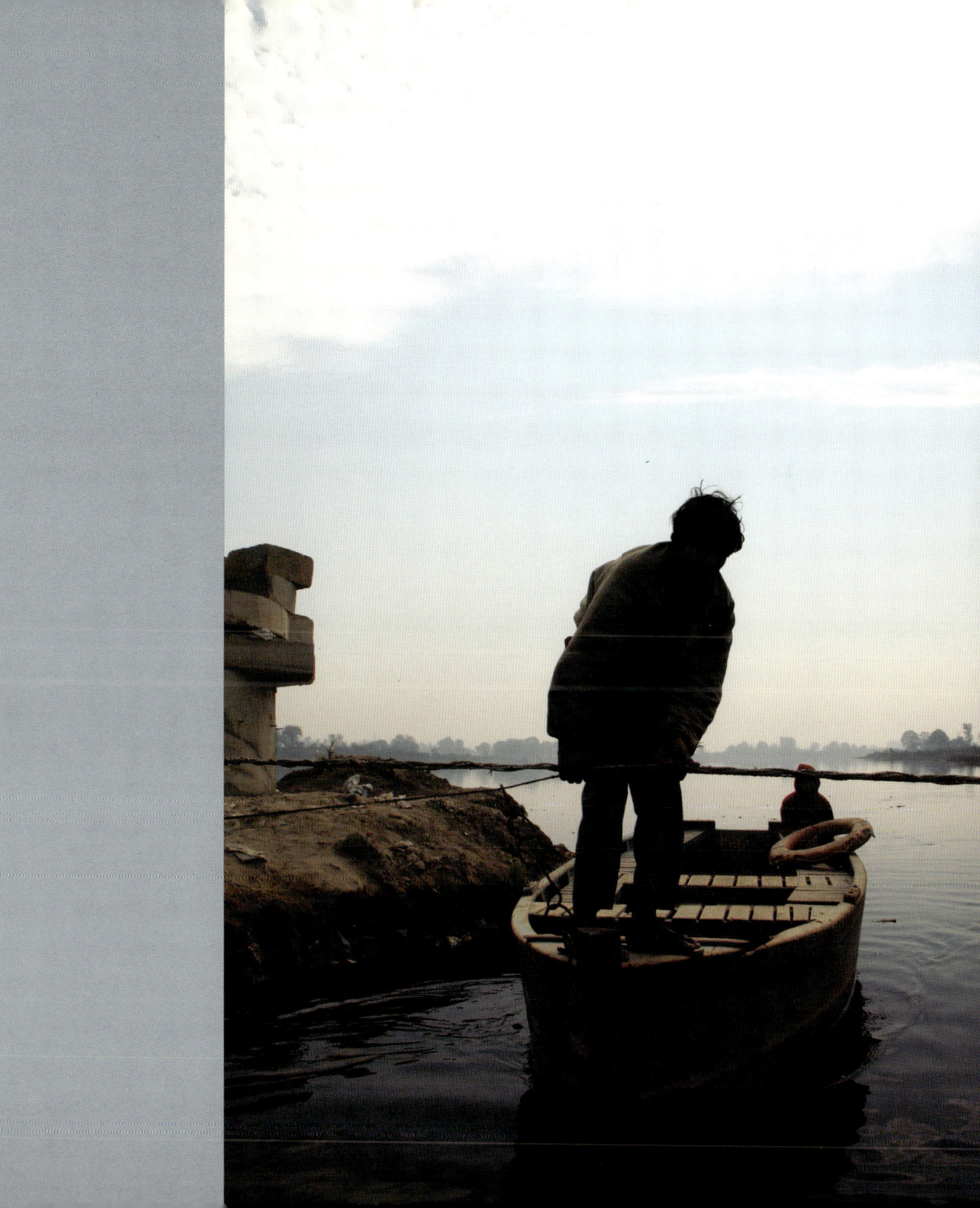

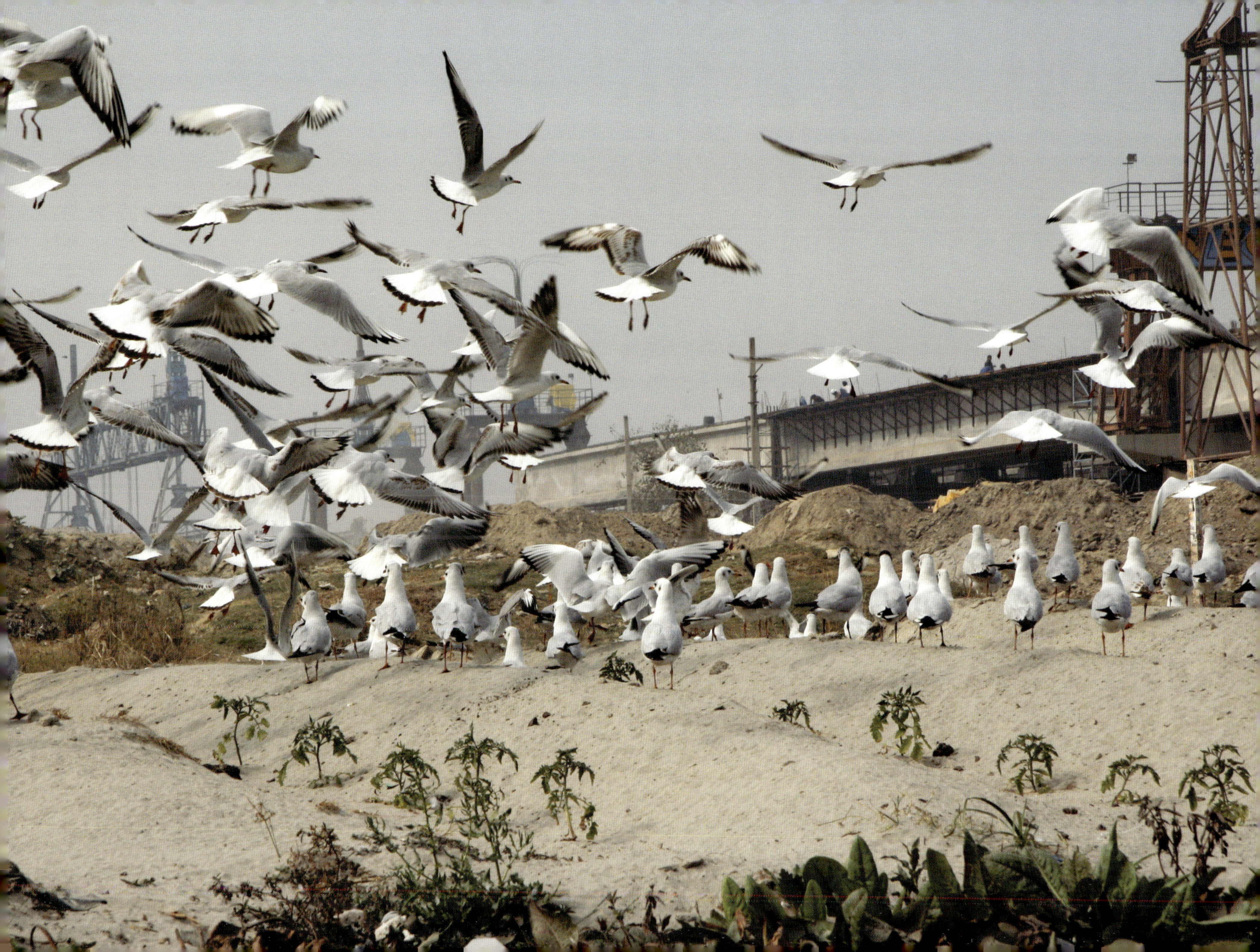

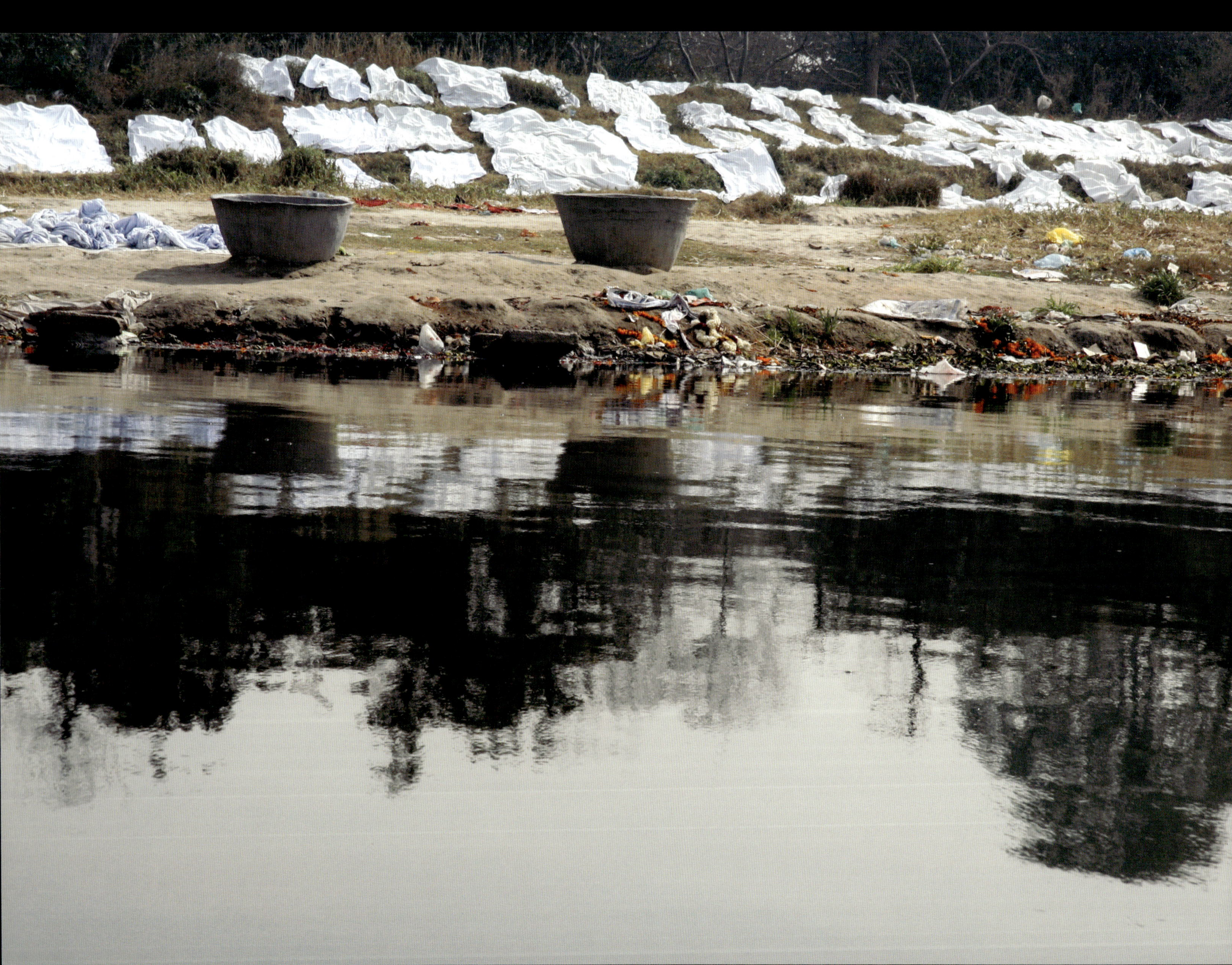

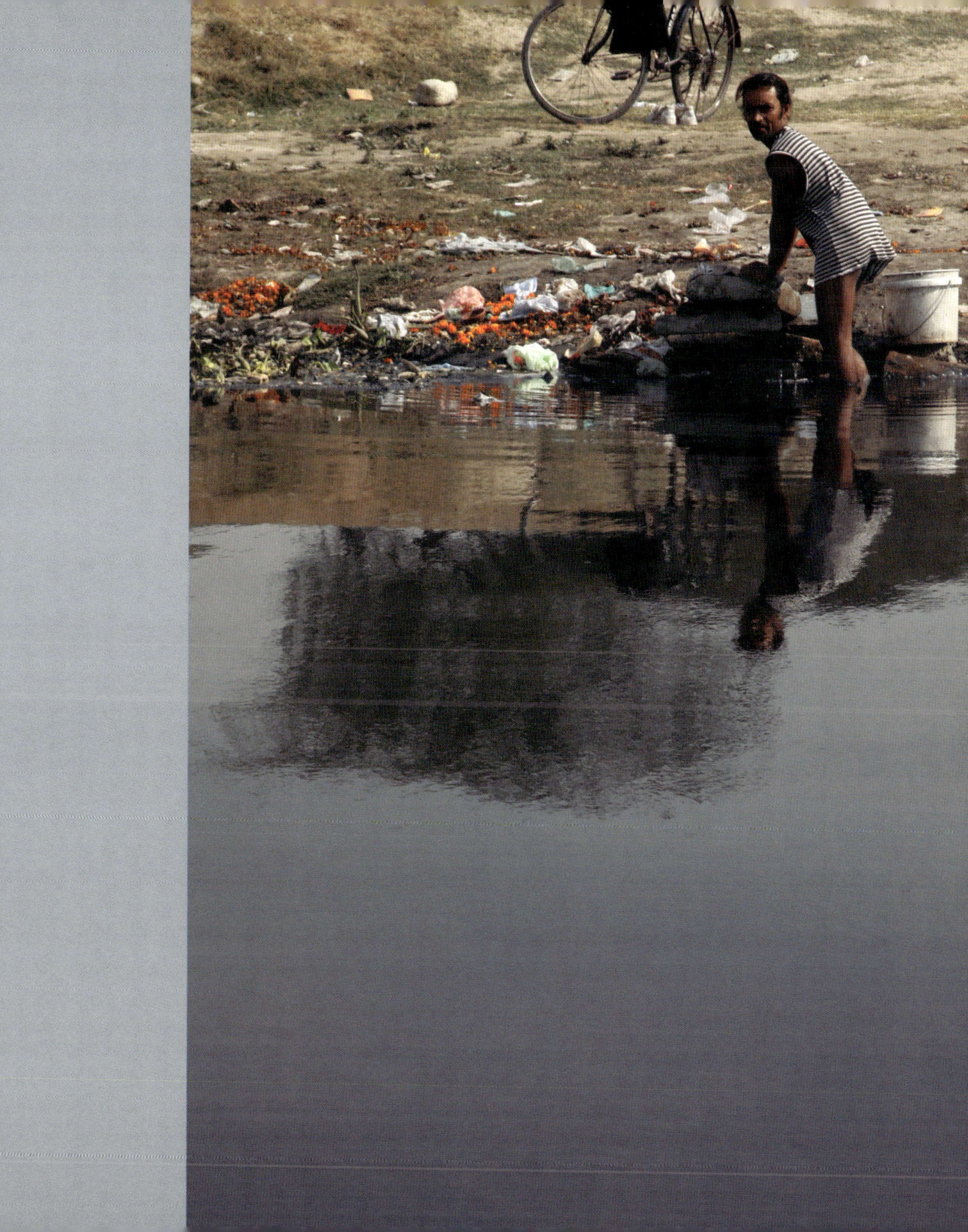

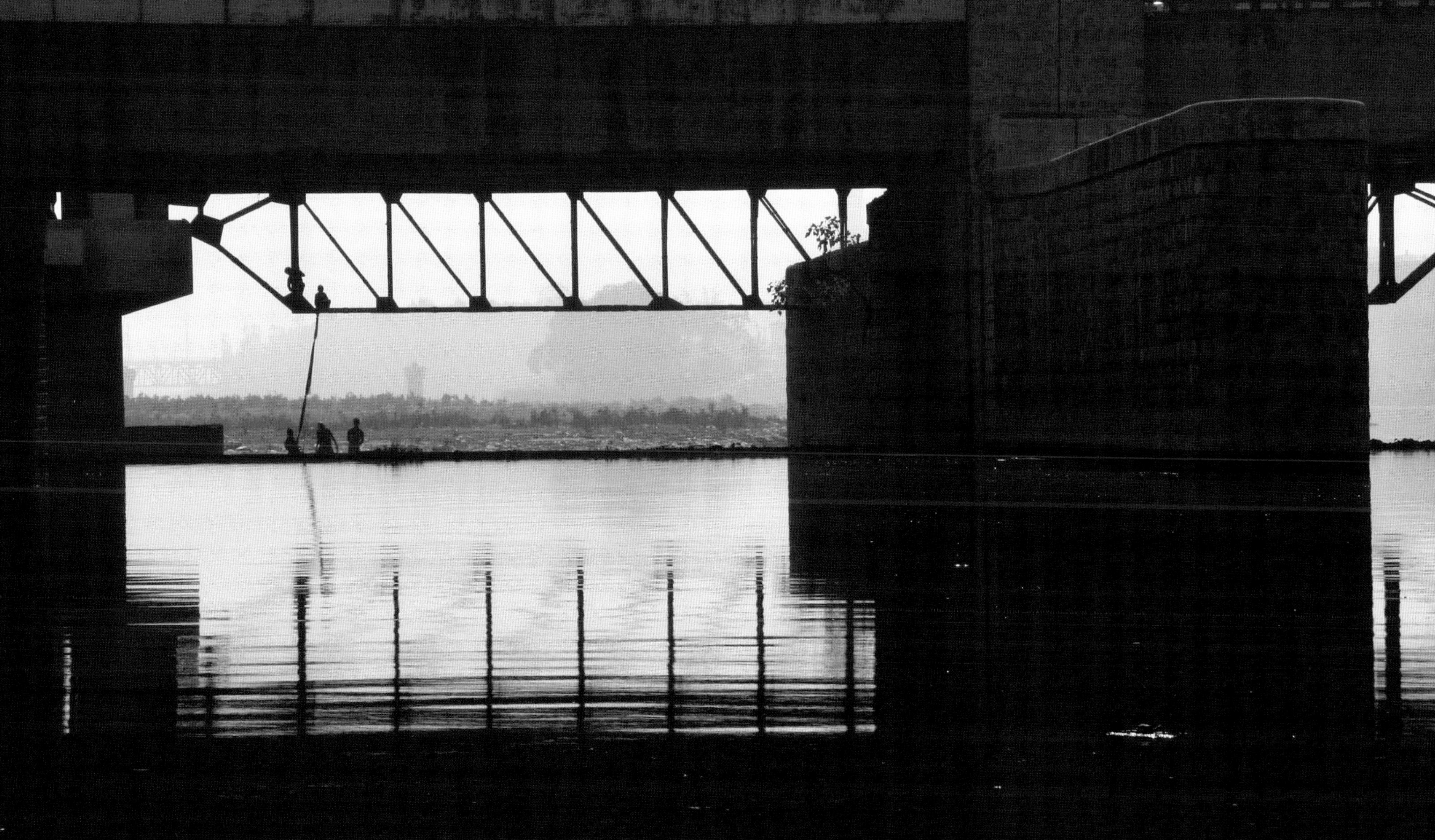

27 JANUARY 2007

8:30AM

no access
to the
yamuna
walk
past
noise
power
station
on the road
demolished
basti
at the river
bank
jumping over
barbed wires

fog,
surreal
paths,
fly
ash
sinking
ground
inlets
sewage
two birds
black
water
the day
very foggy
the river
through rubble
homes
abandoned
walk
the day

low
visibility
no river
drain
mist
path
along
the river.
fly
— ash
fields
desolate
walk
abandoned

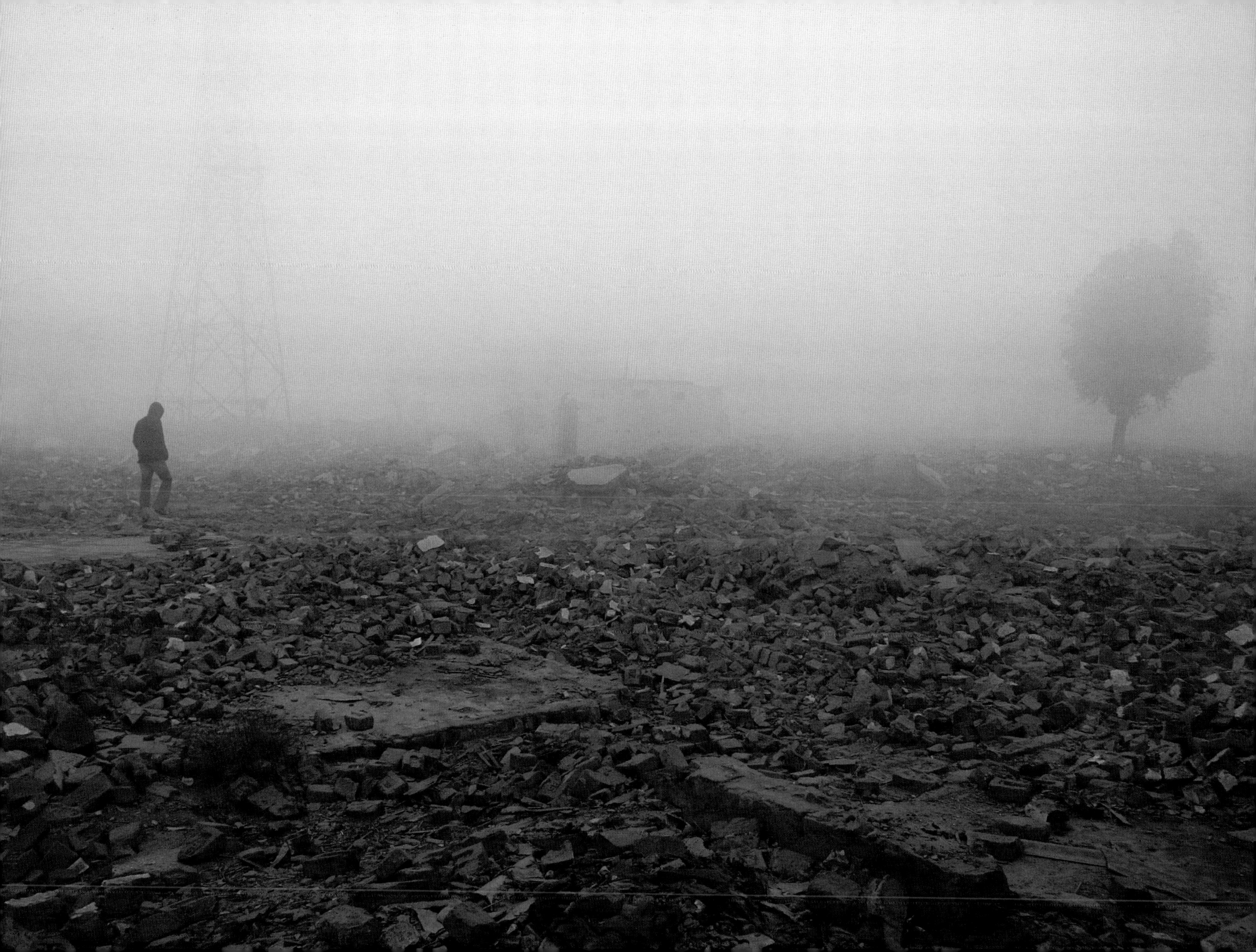

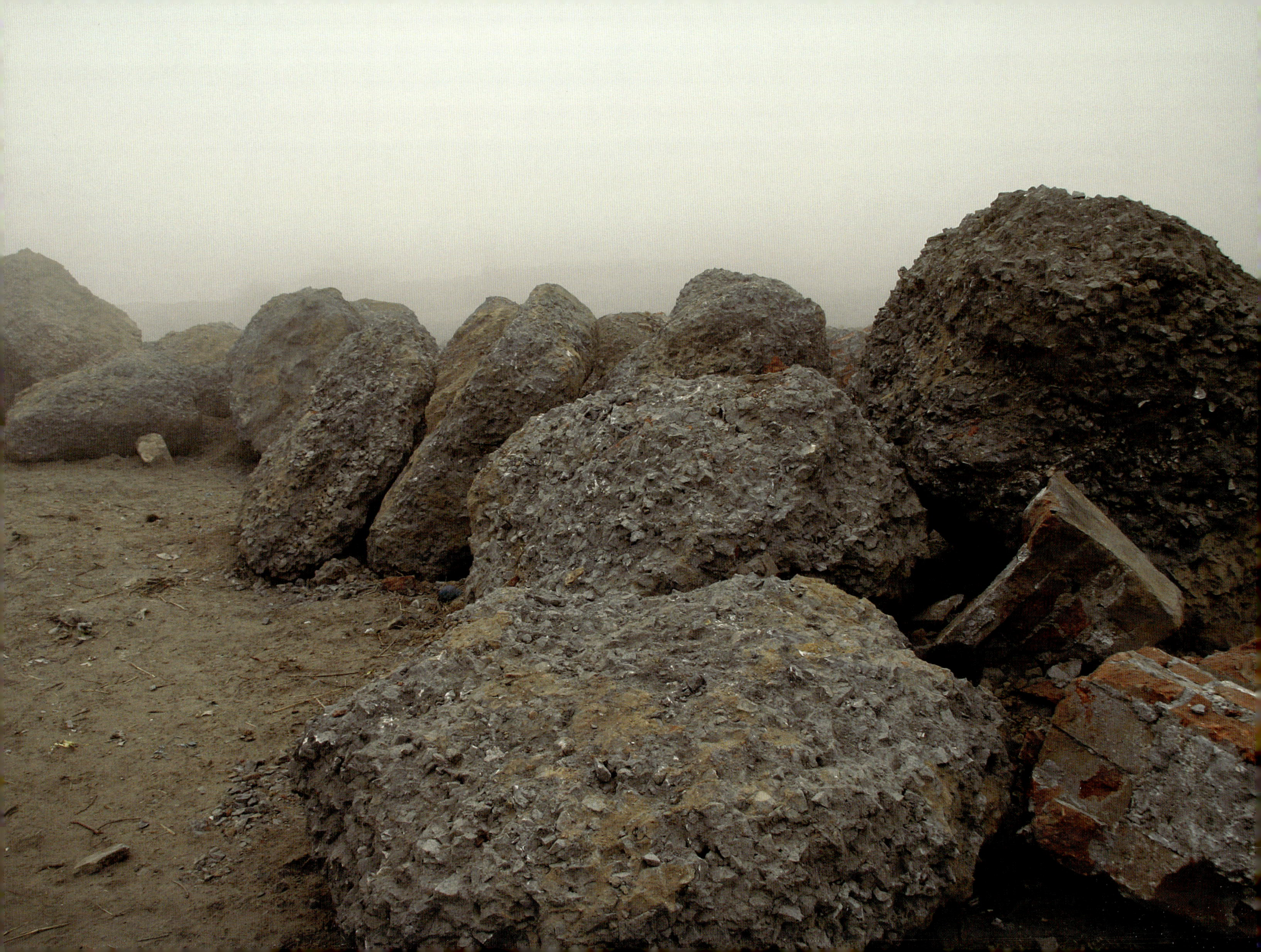

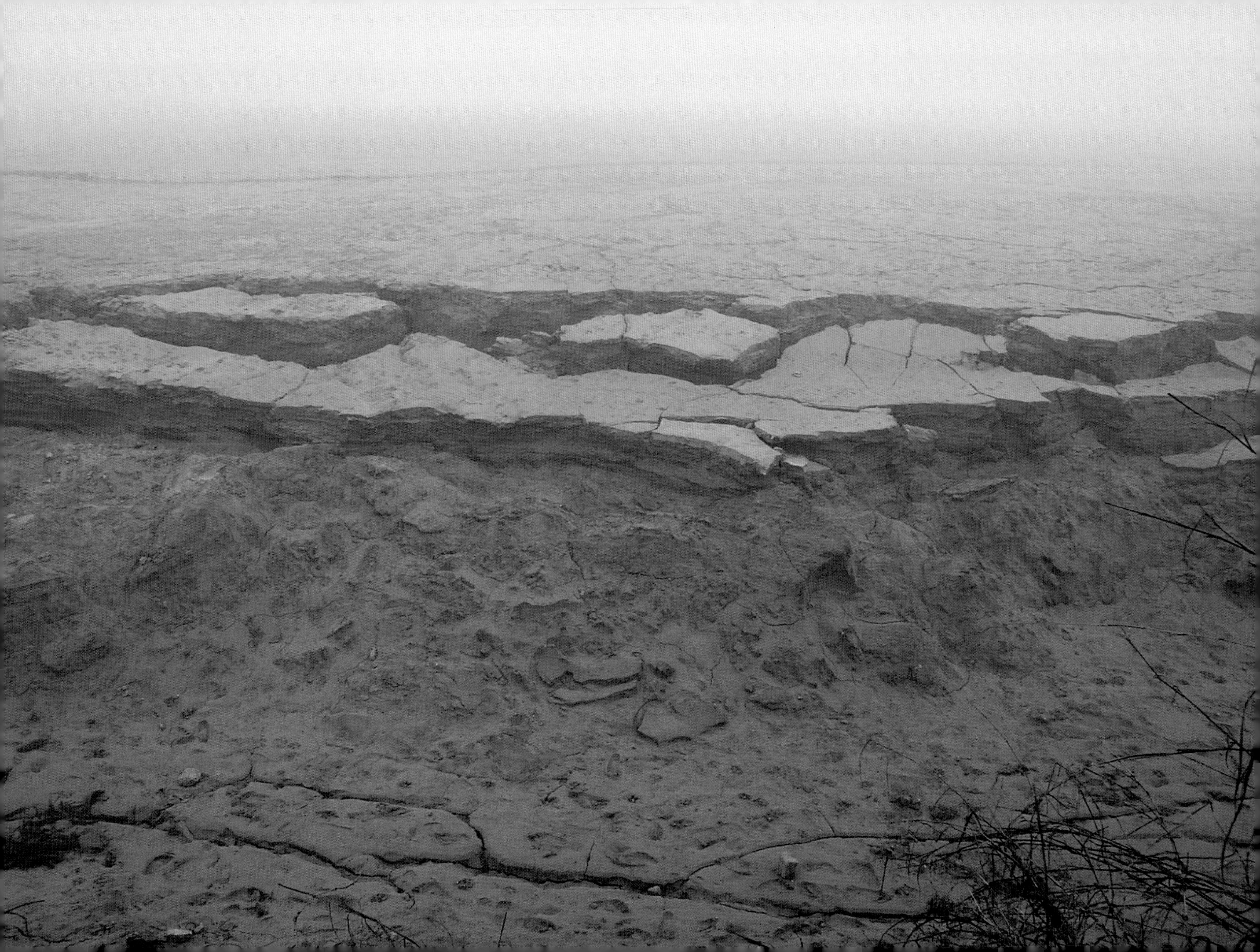

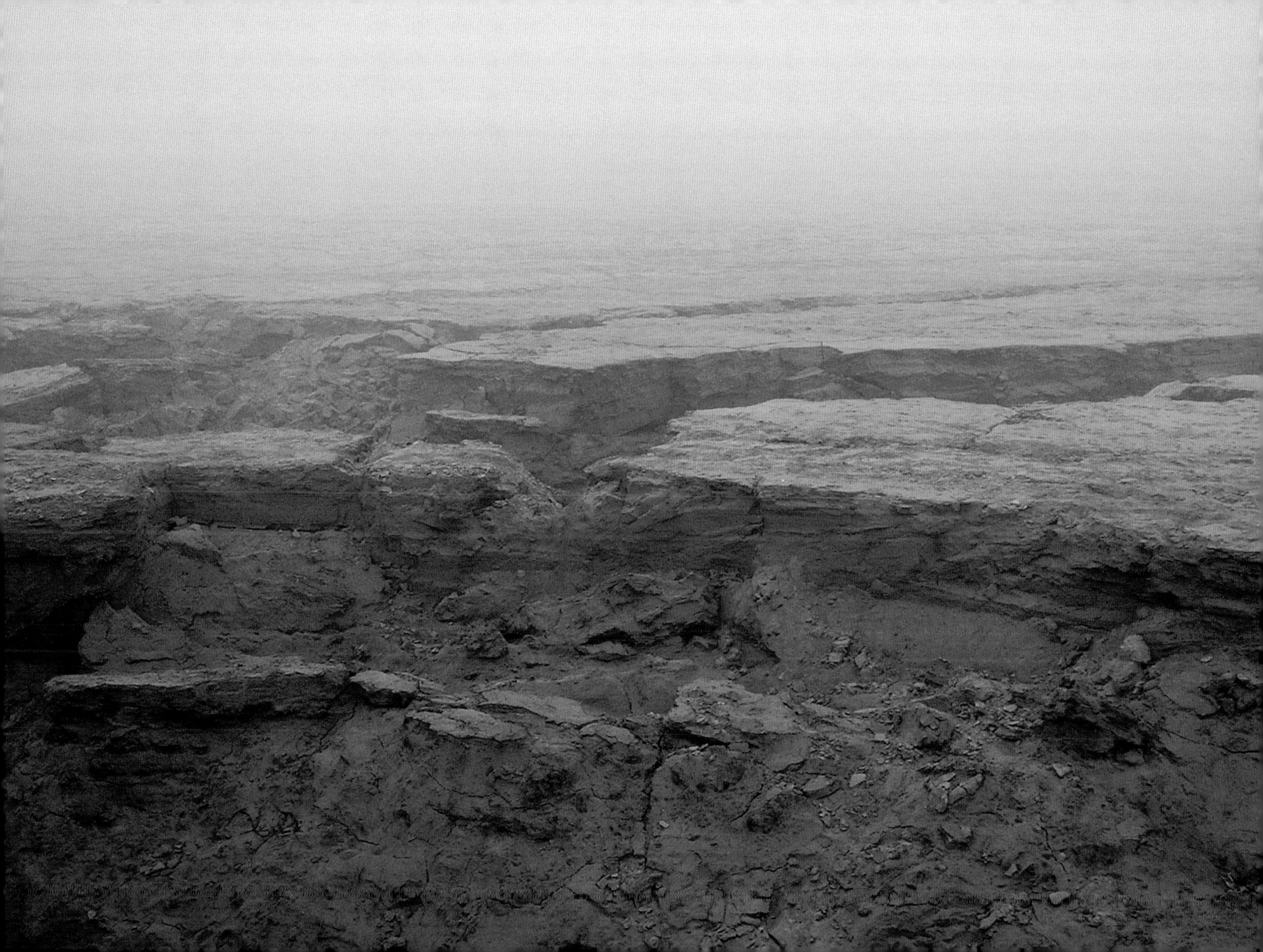

28 JANUARY 2007

start again
the same place,
making
our way
through fields
sewage
irrigated
under
Nizamuddin
Bridge
two beggars
sun
home,
no way,
to the
road again
to walk
to cross
the drain
up to
the road.

DND
tollway?
Ashram?
slip
down again
plastic
wages
scrap shops
river
not in sight
down again
winding path
flat
global village (?)
under the DND
jamia
sewage
washing
cricket
death
river

no access
navy
training
the road again
agra canal.
and the
bird sanctuary
you
are not
allowed
inside (?)
outside
jump over
canal works
fencing
birds
pigs
okhla barrage
call it a day

3:30PM

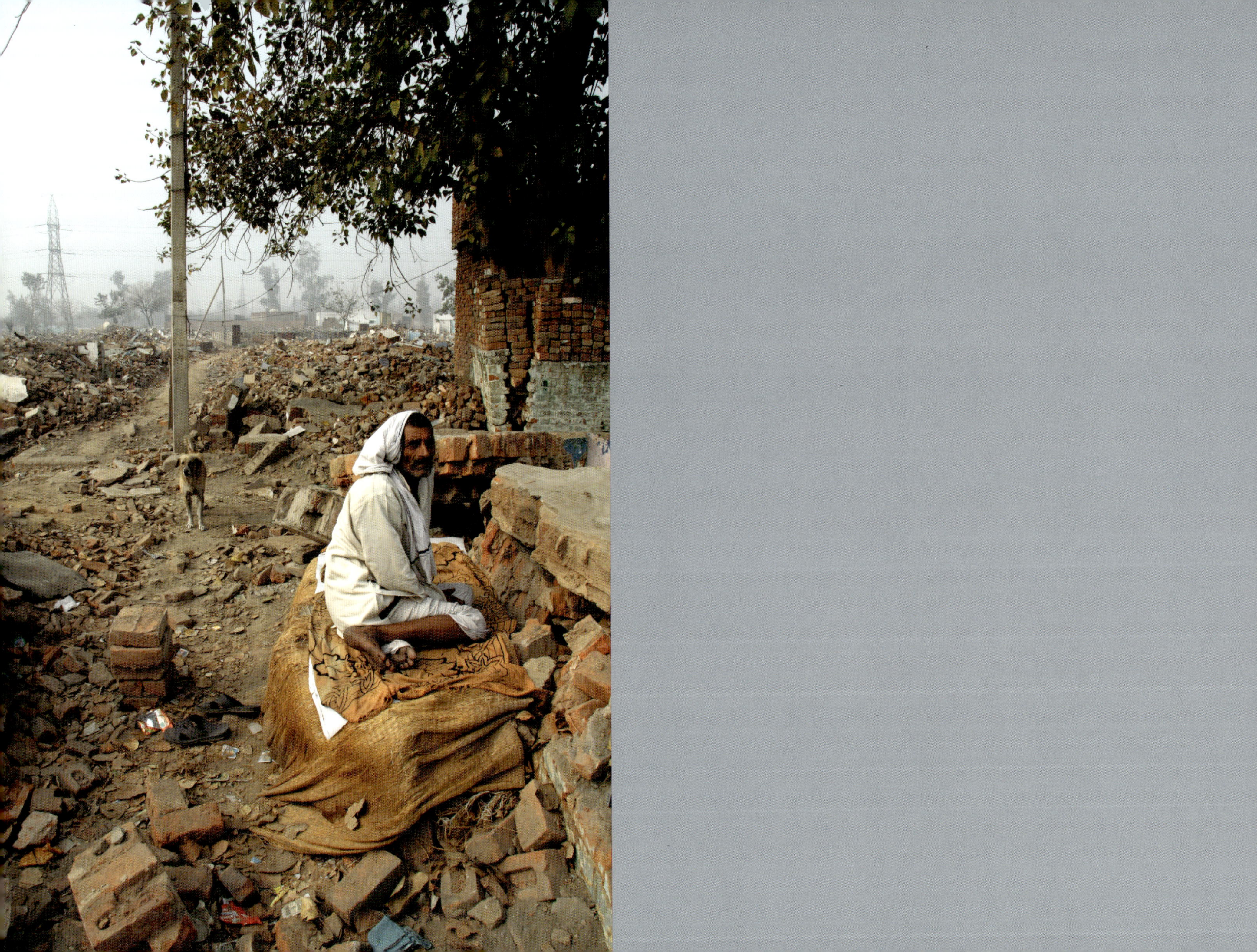

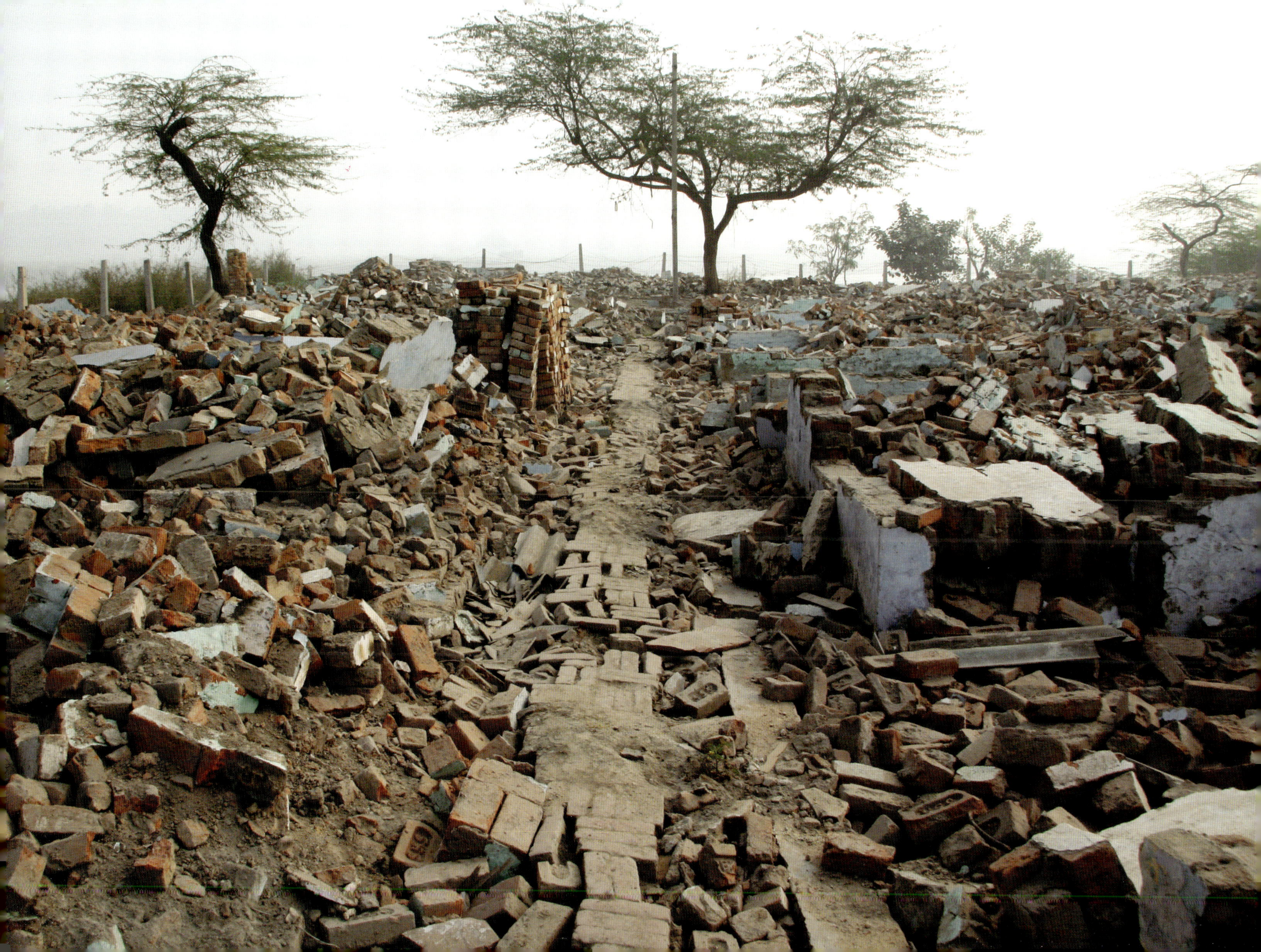

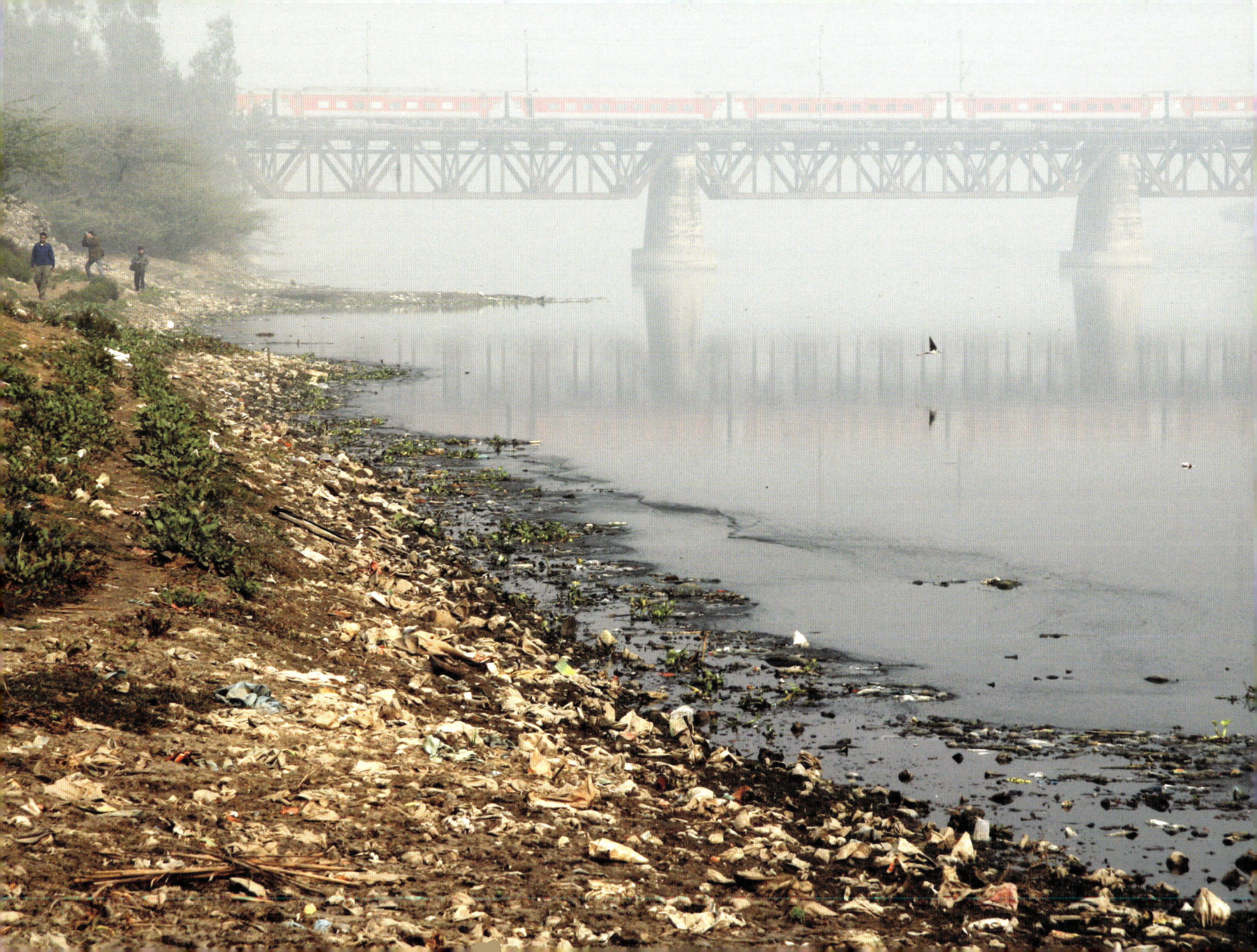

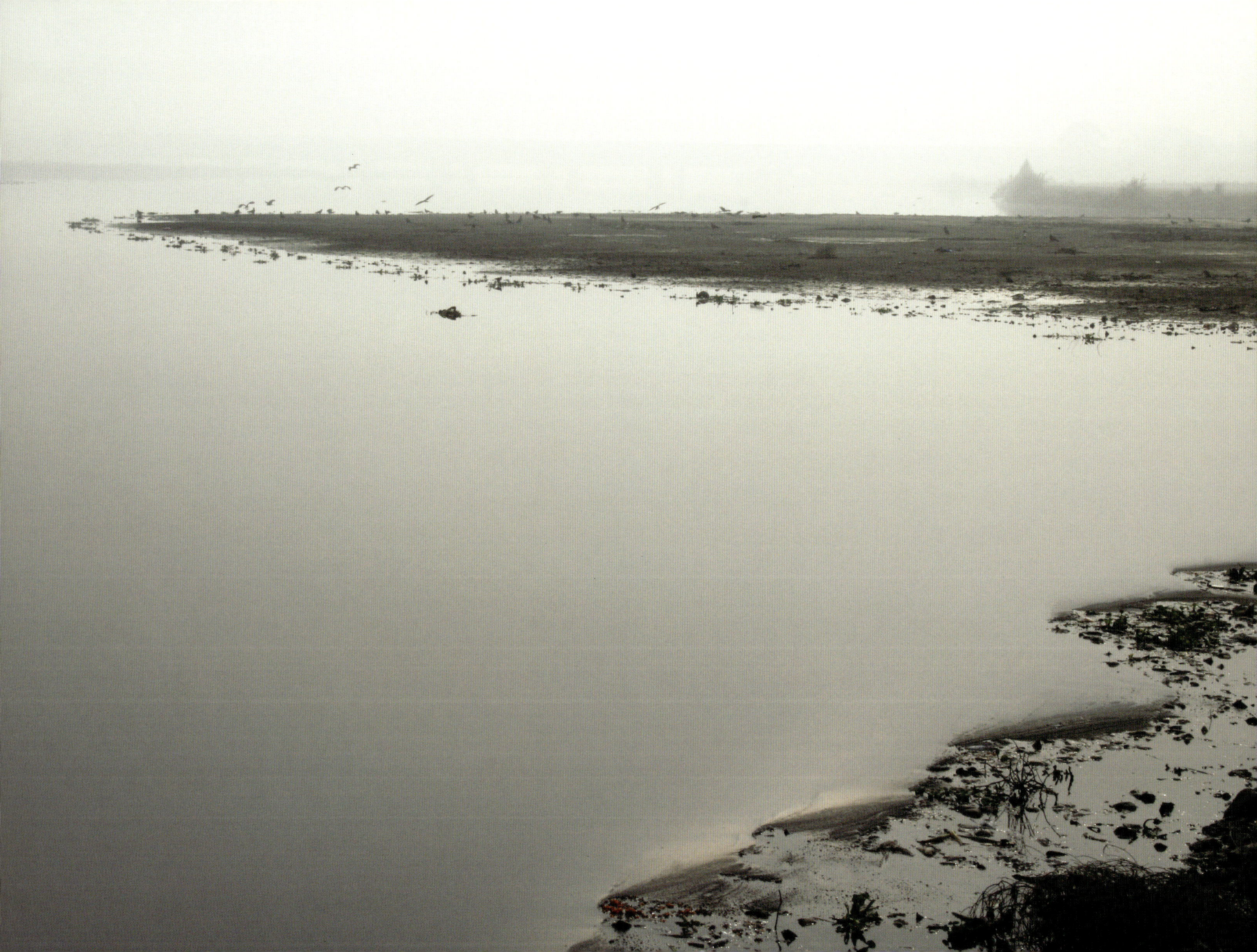

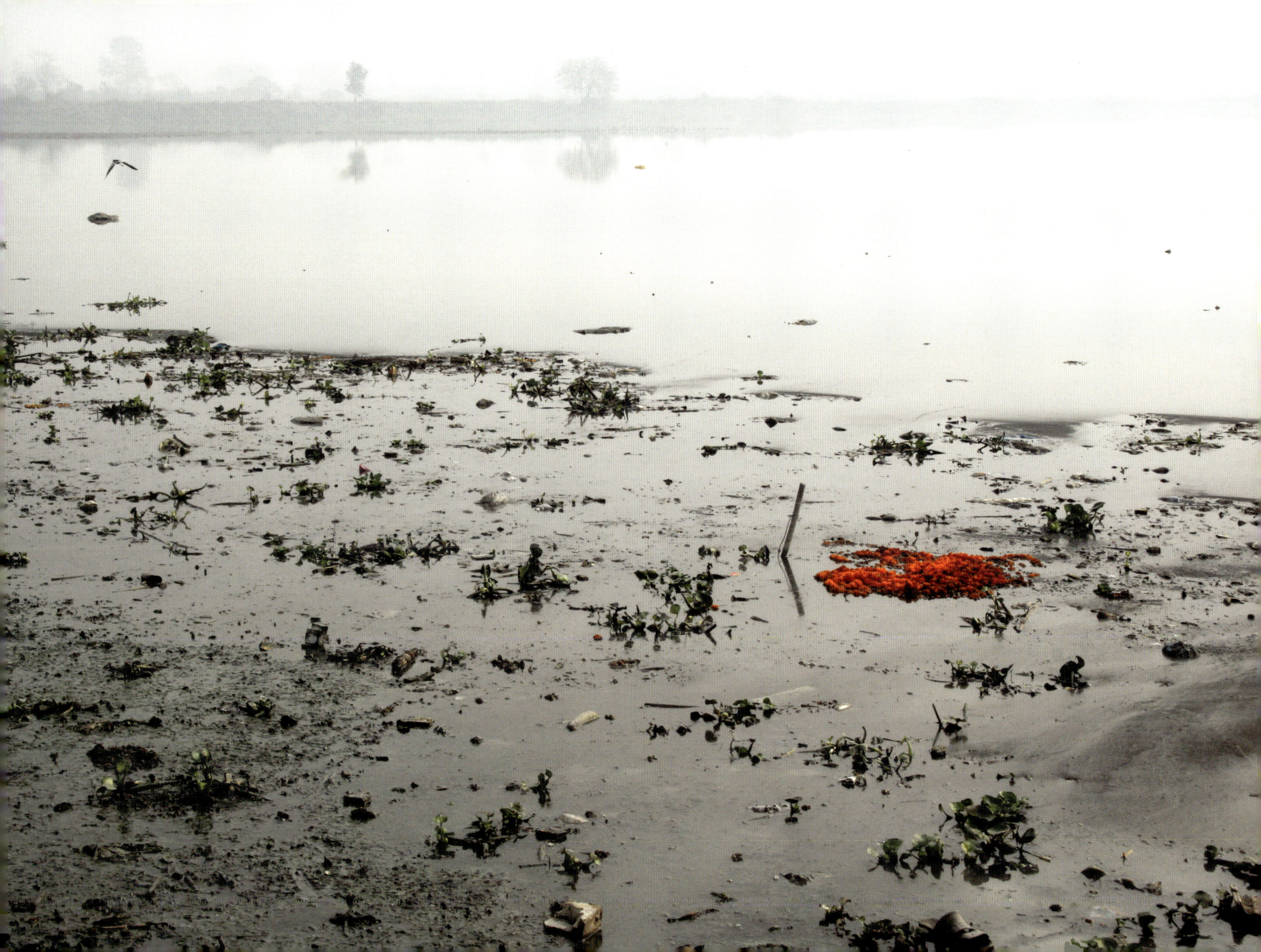

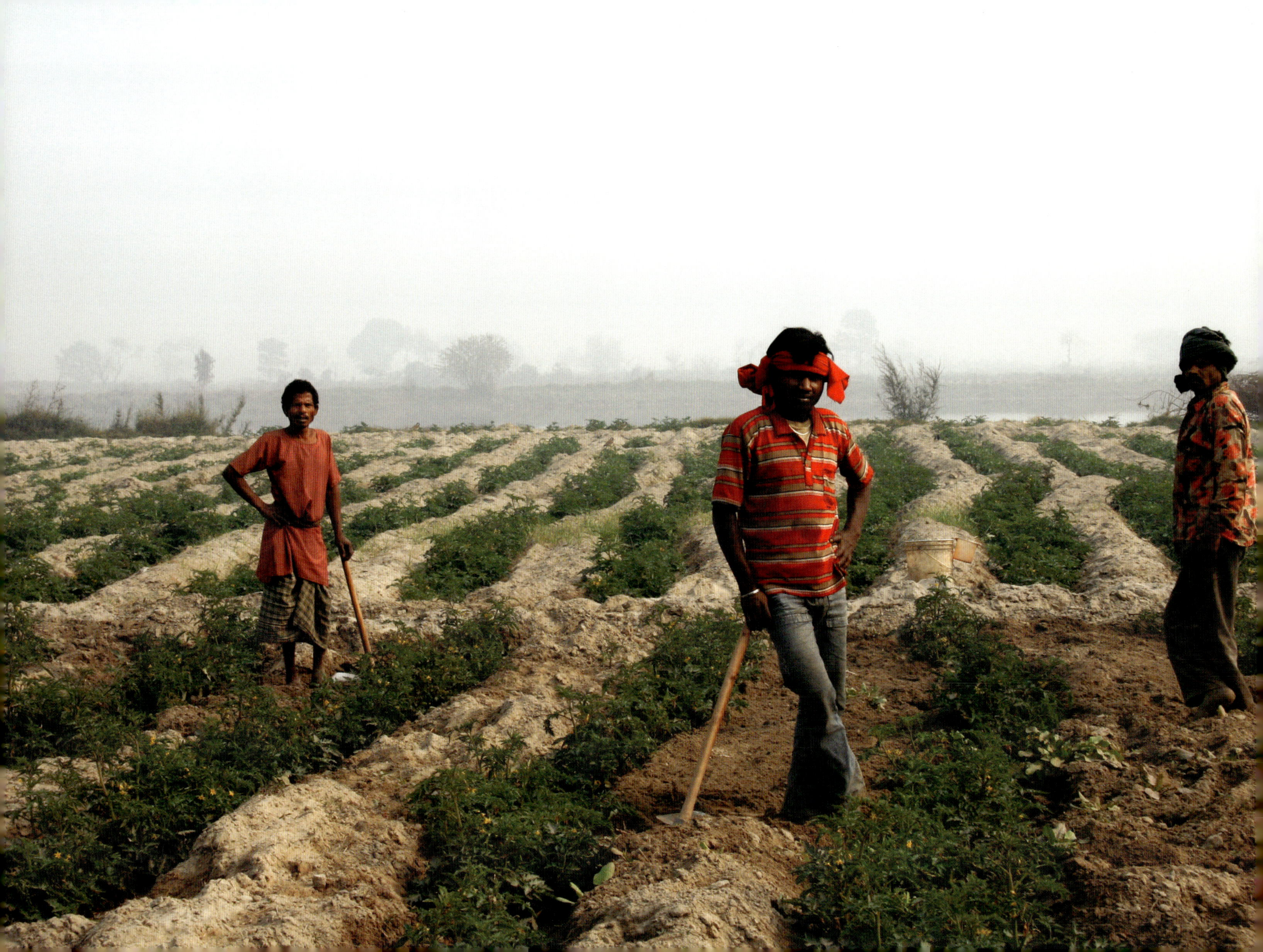

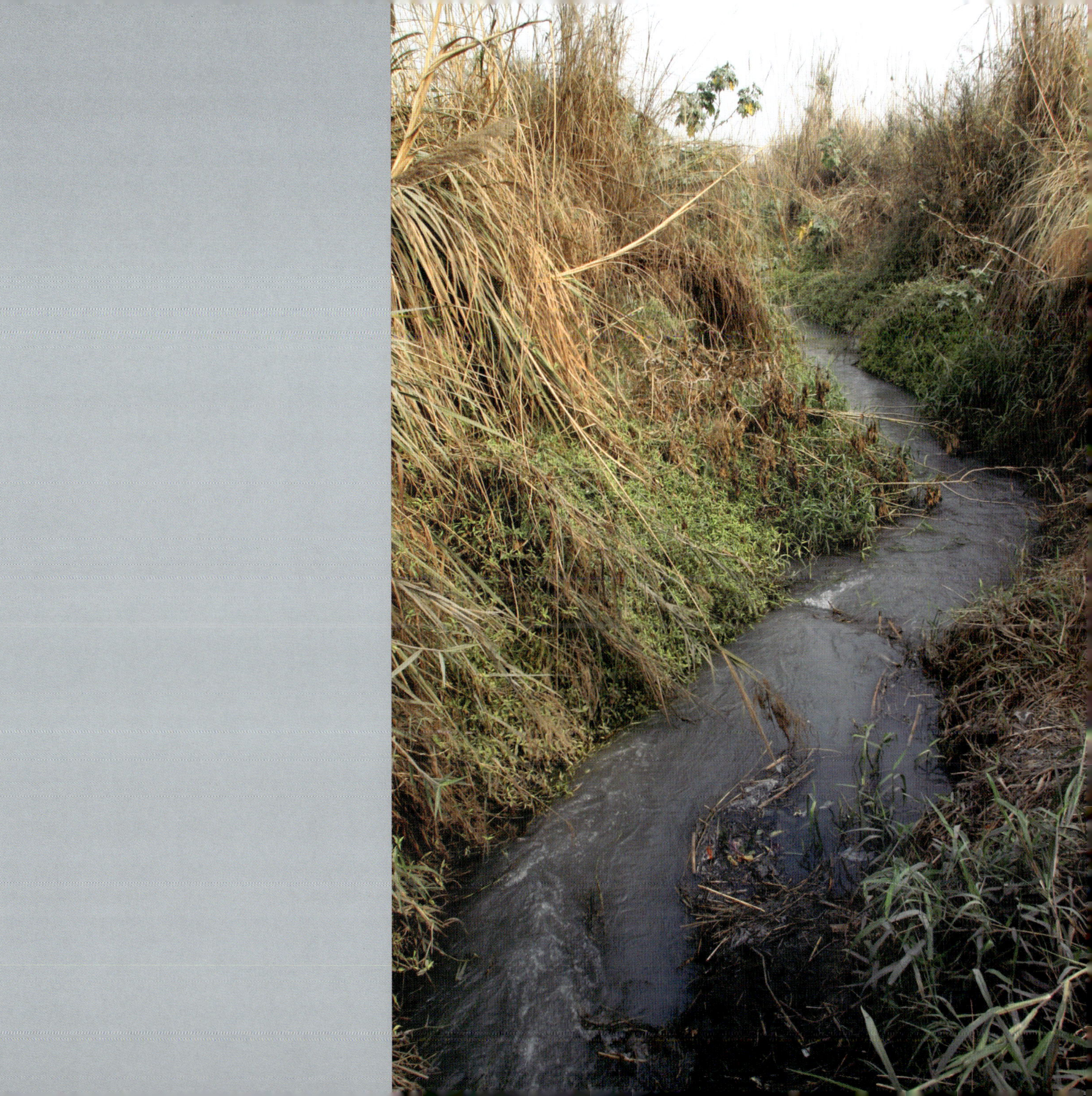

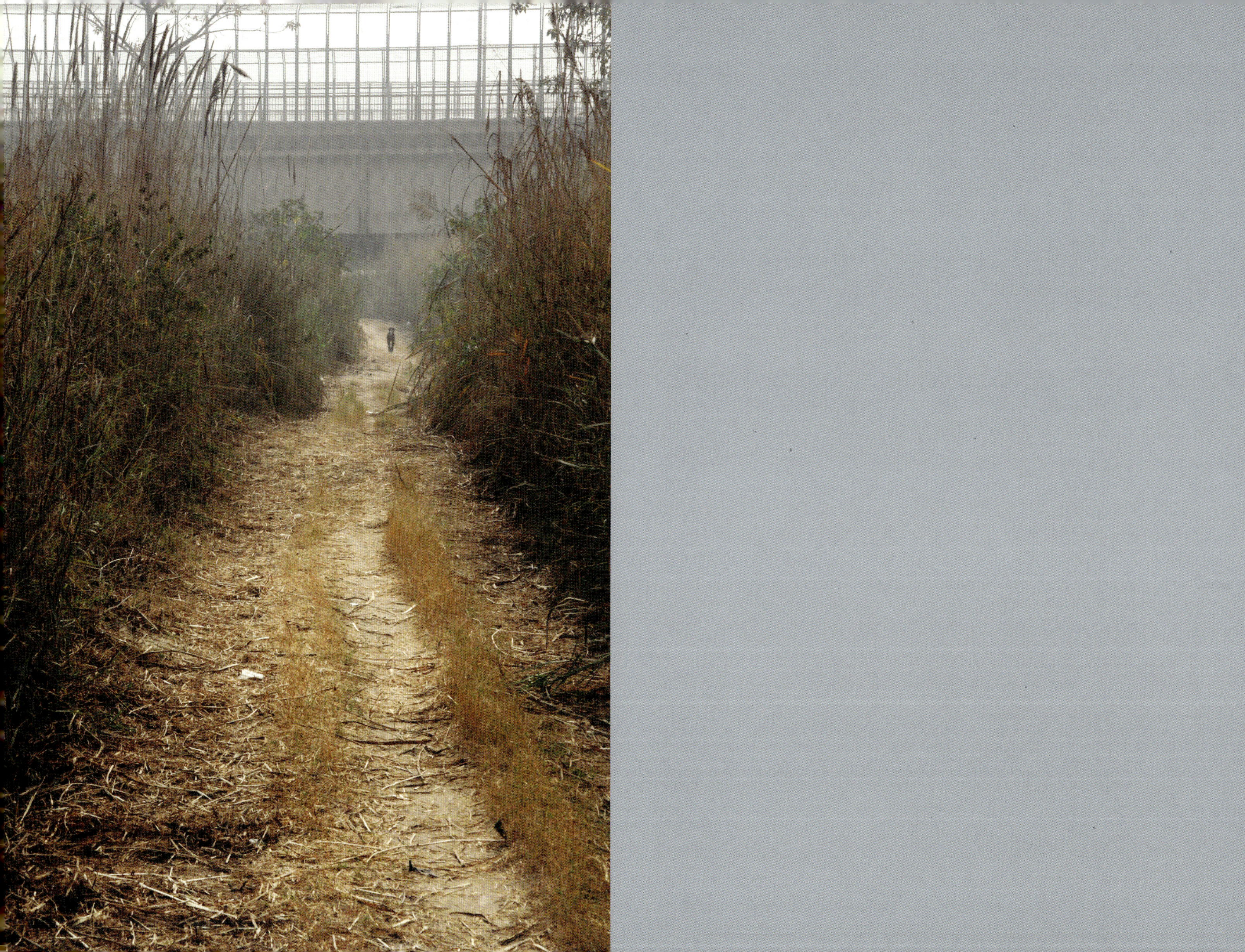

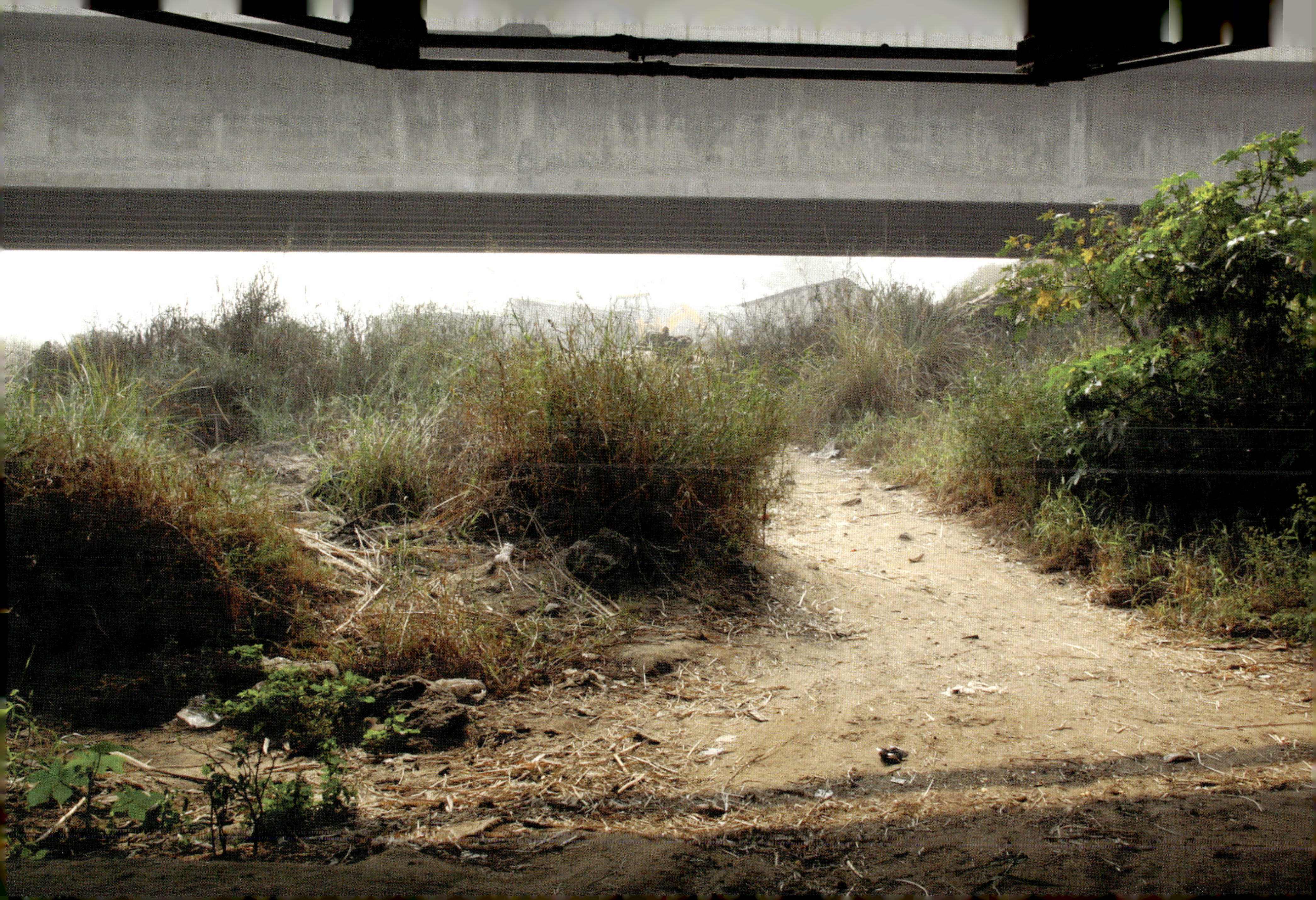

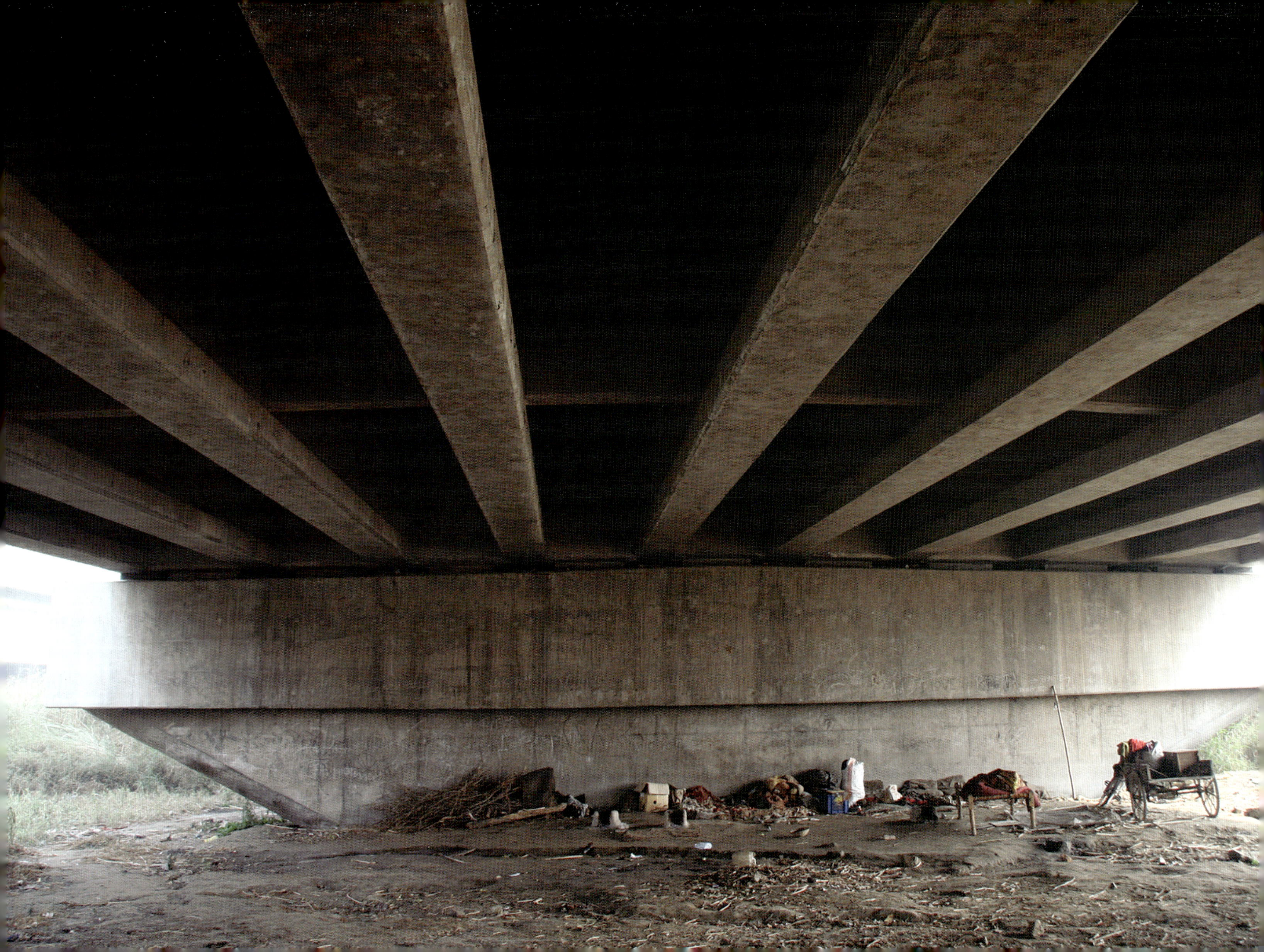

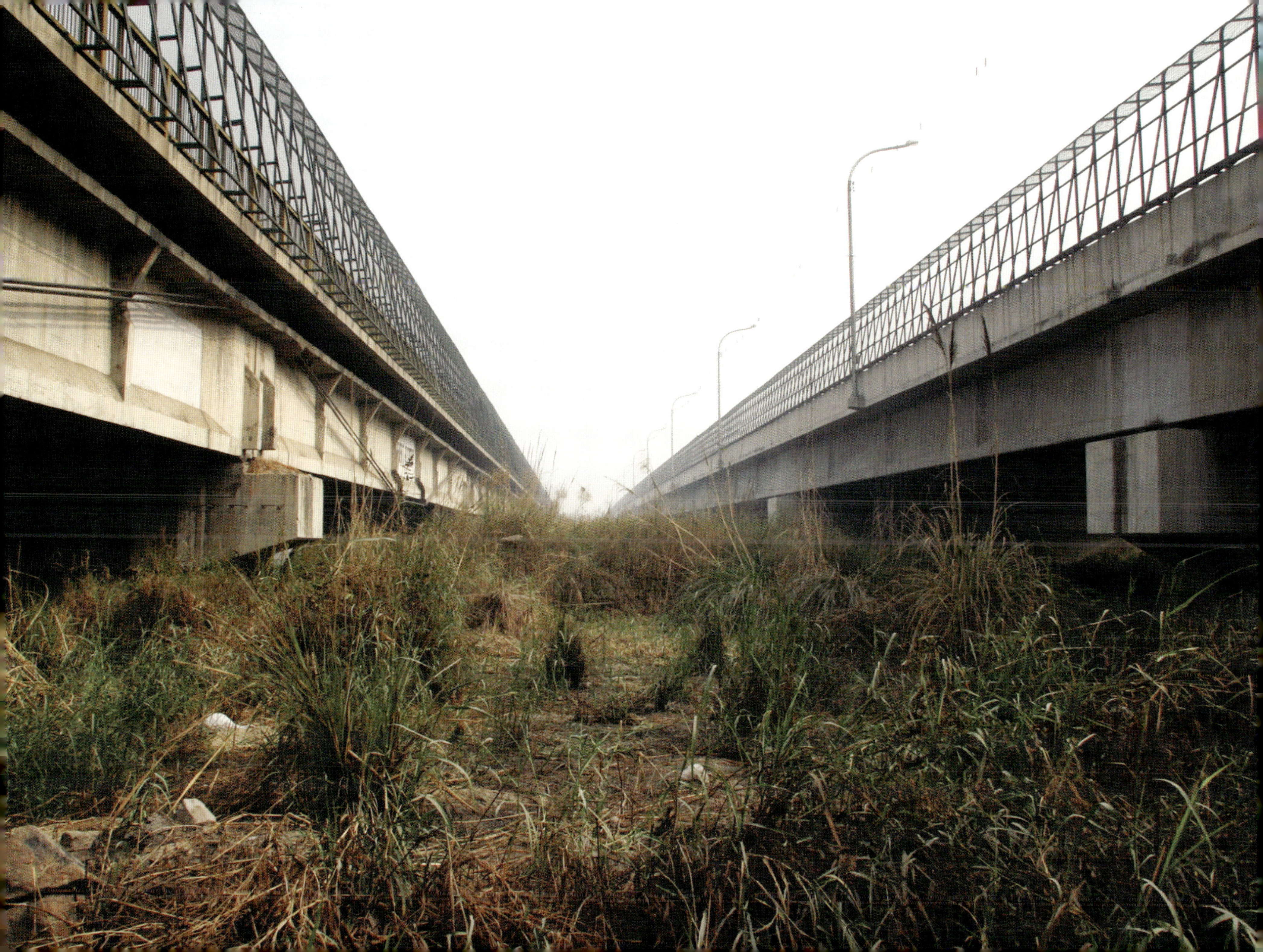

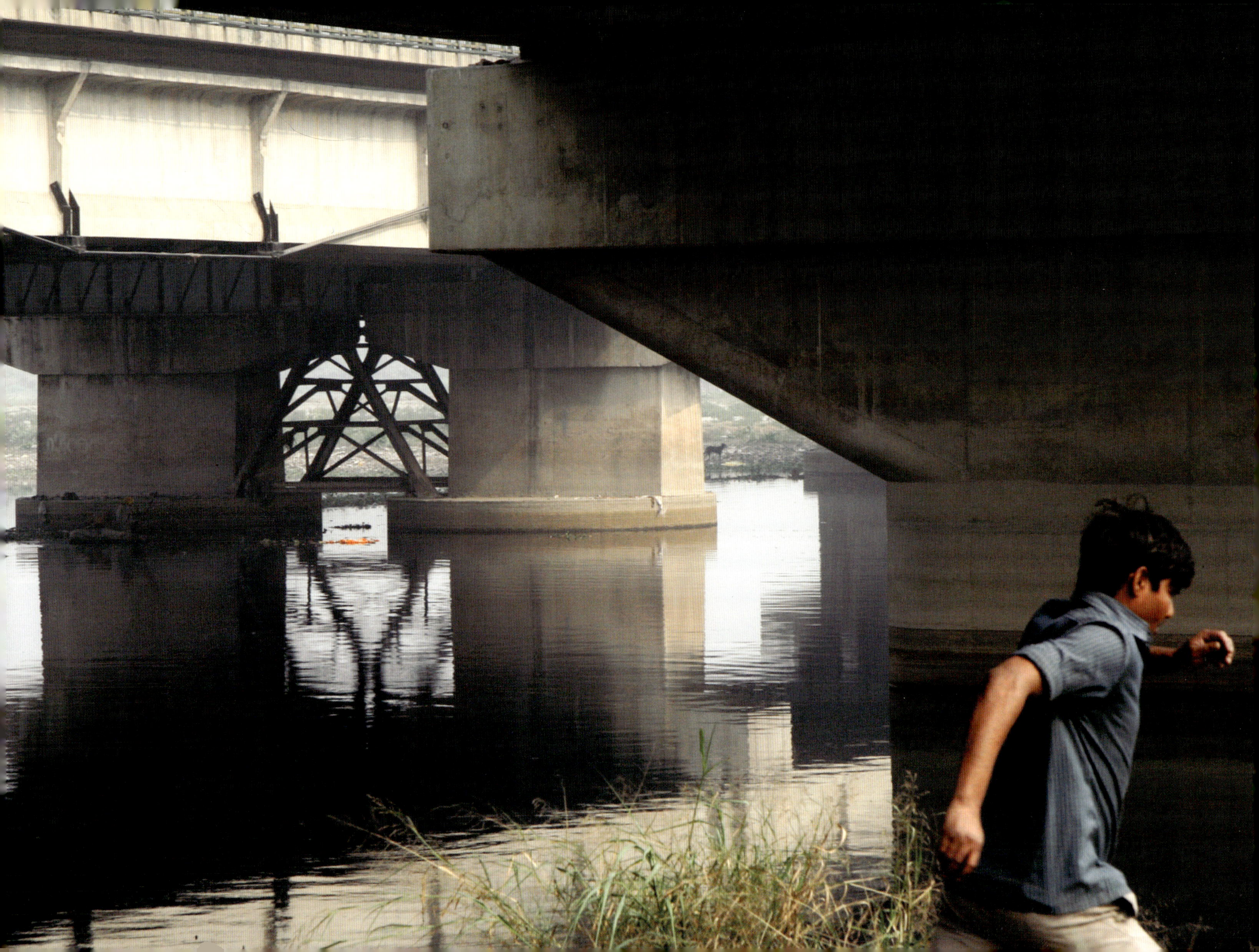

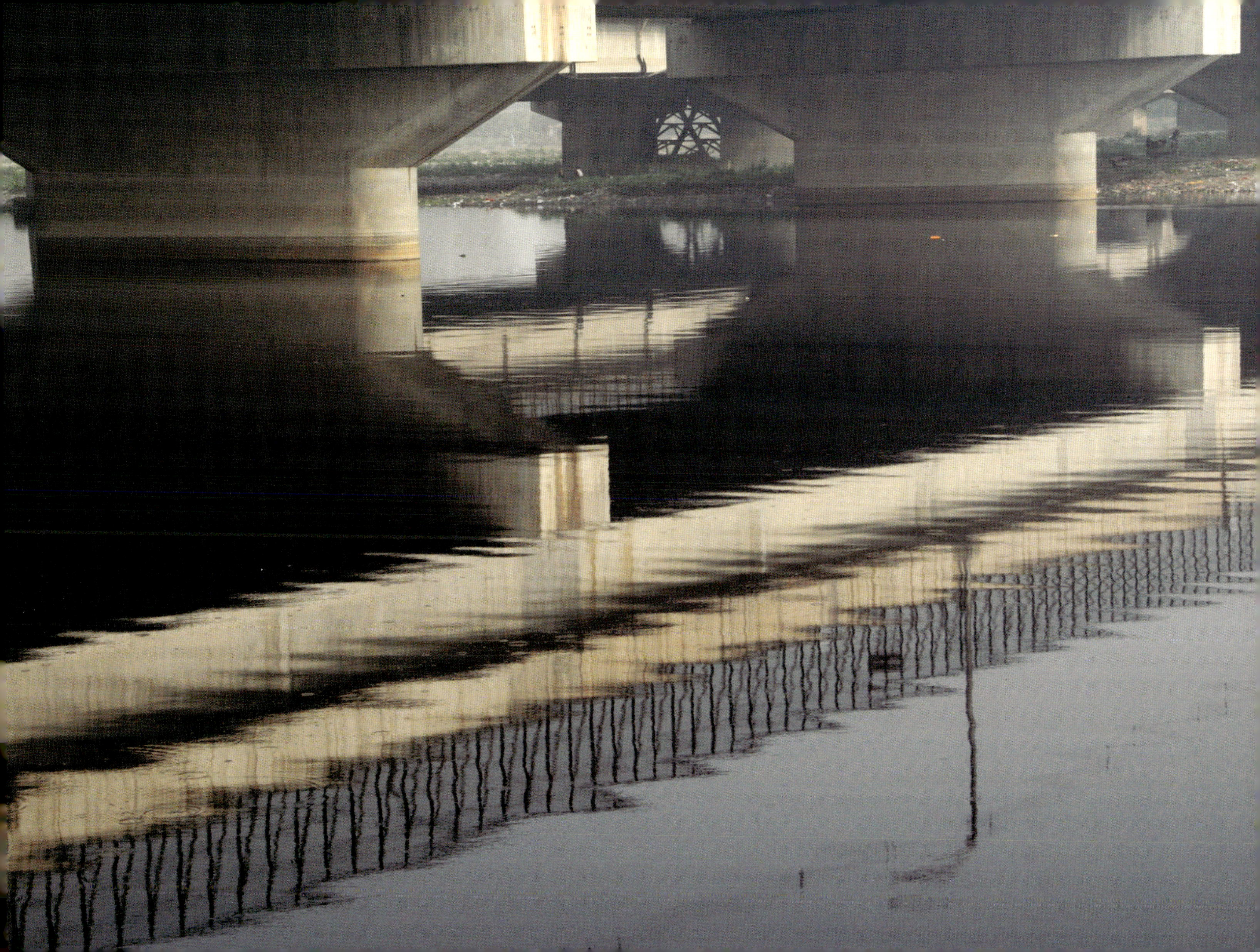

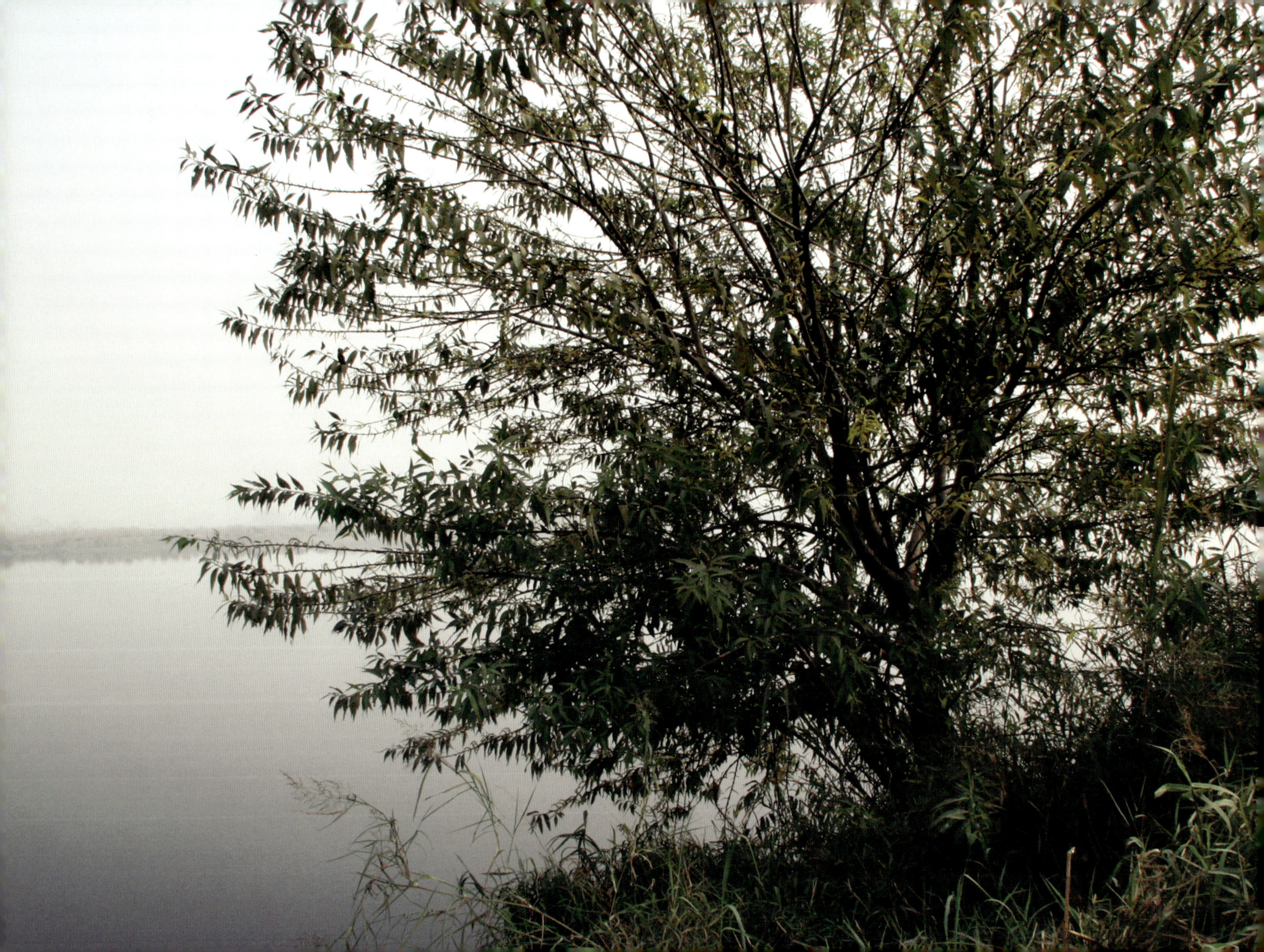

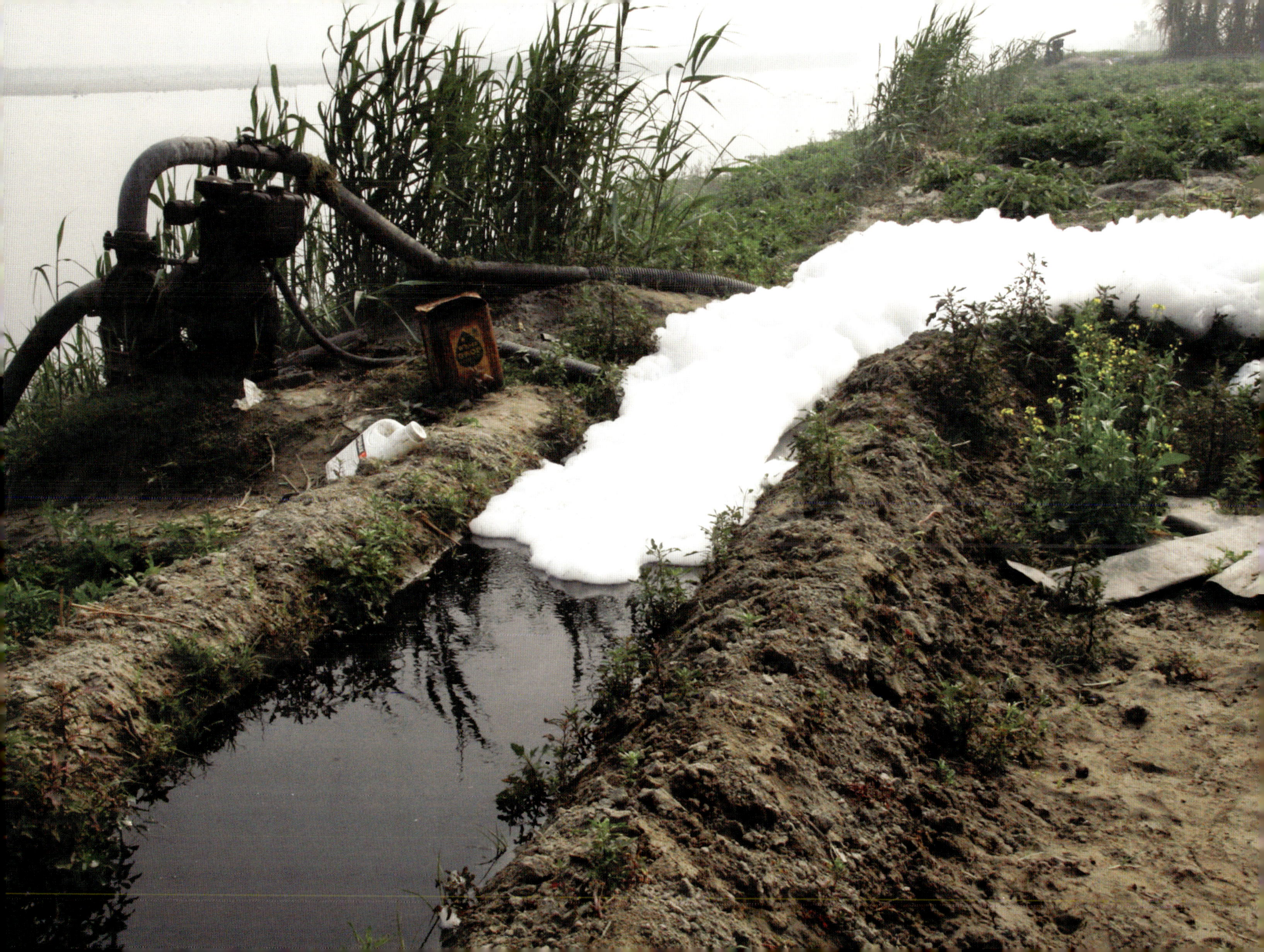

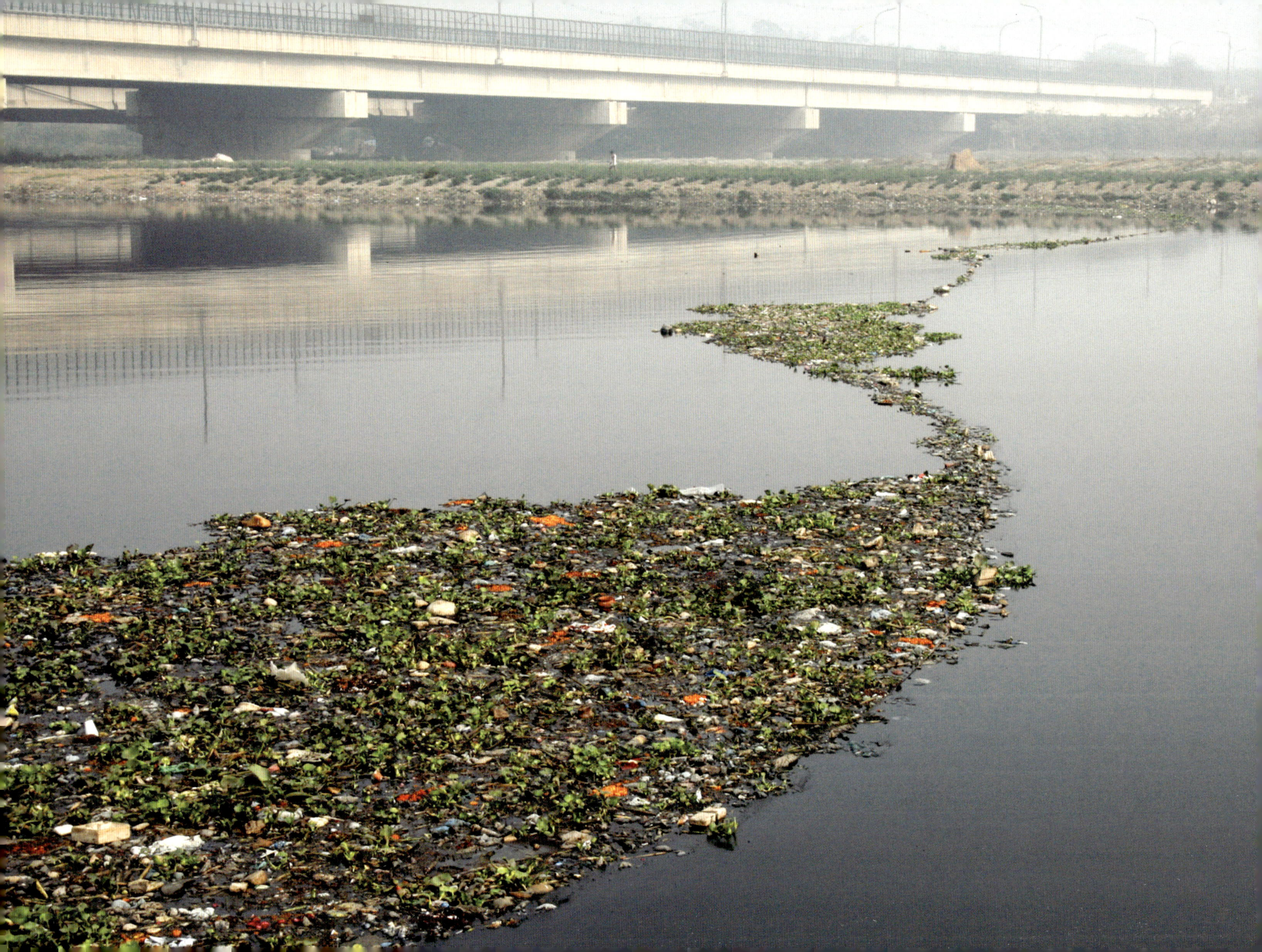

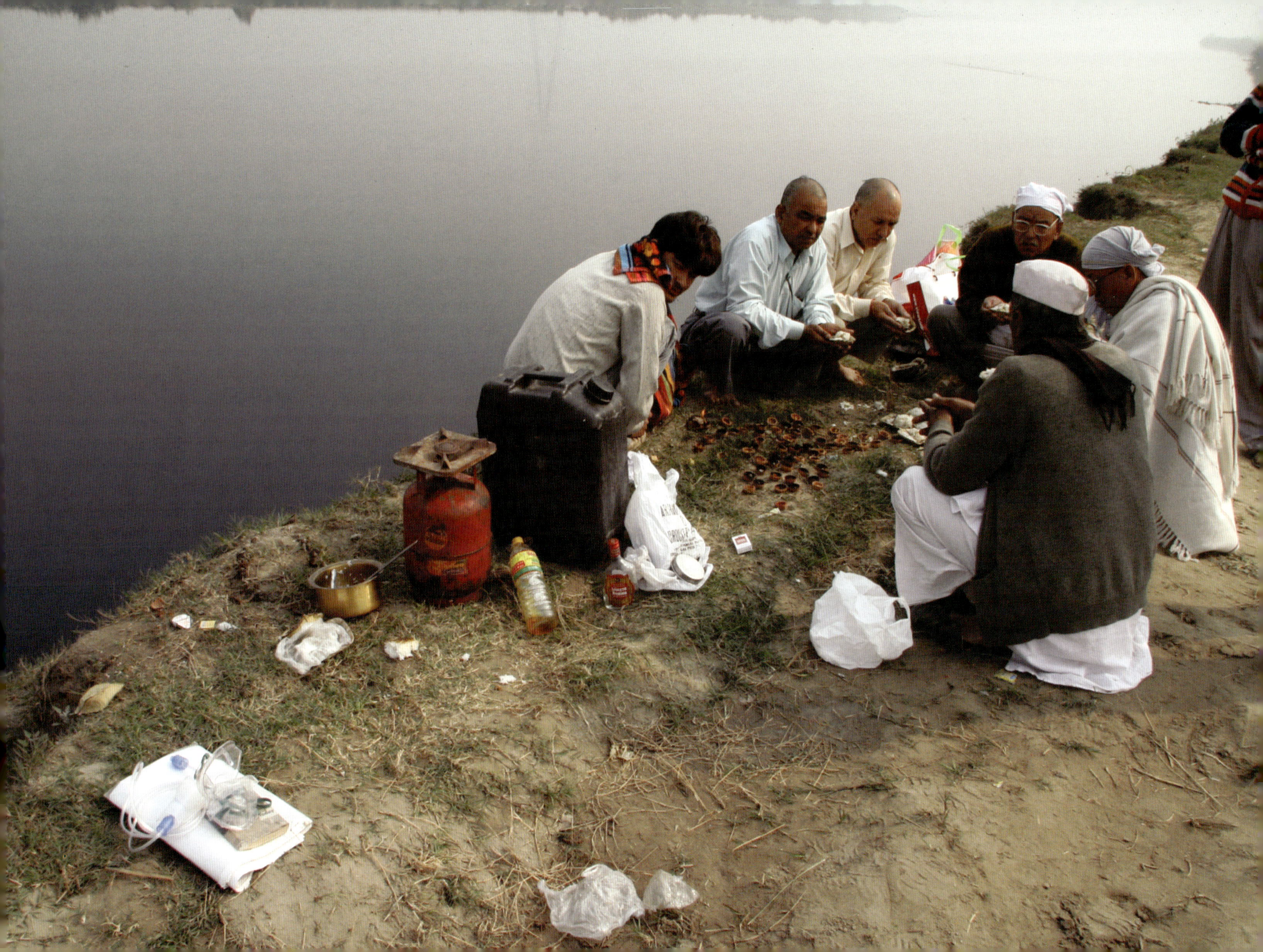

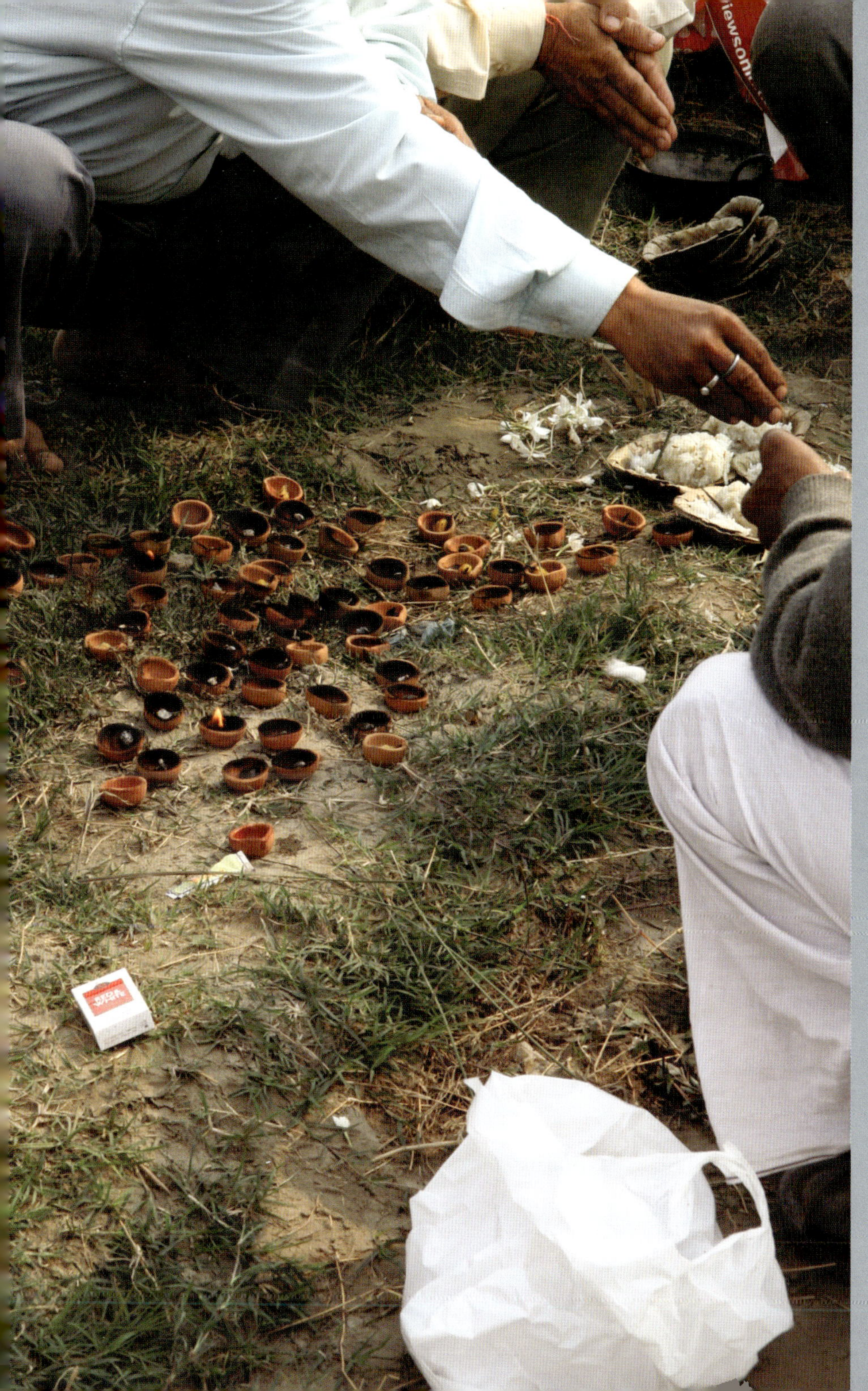

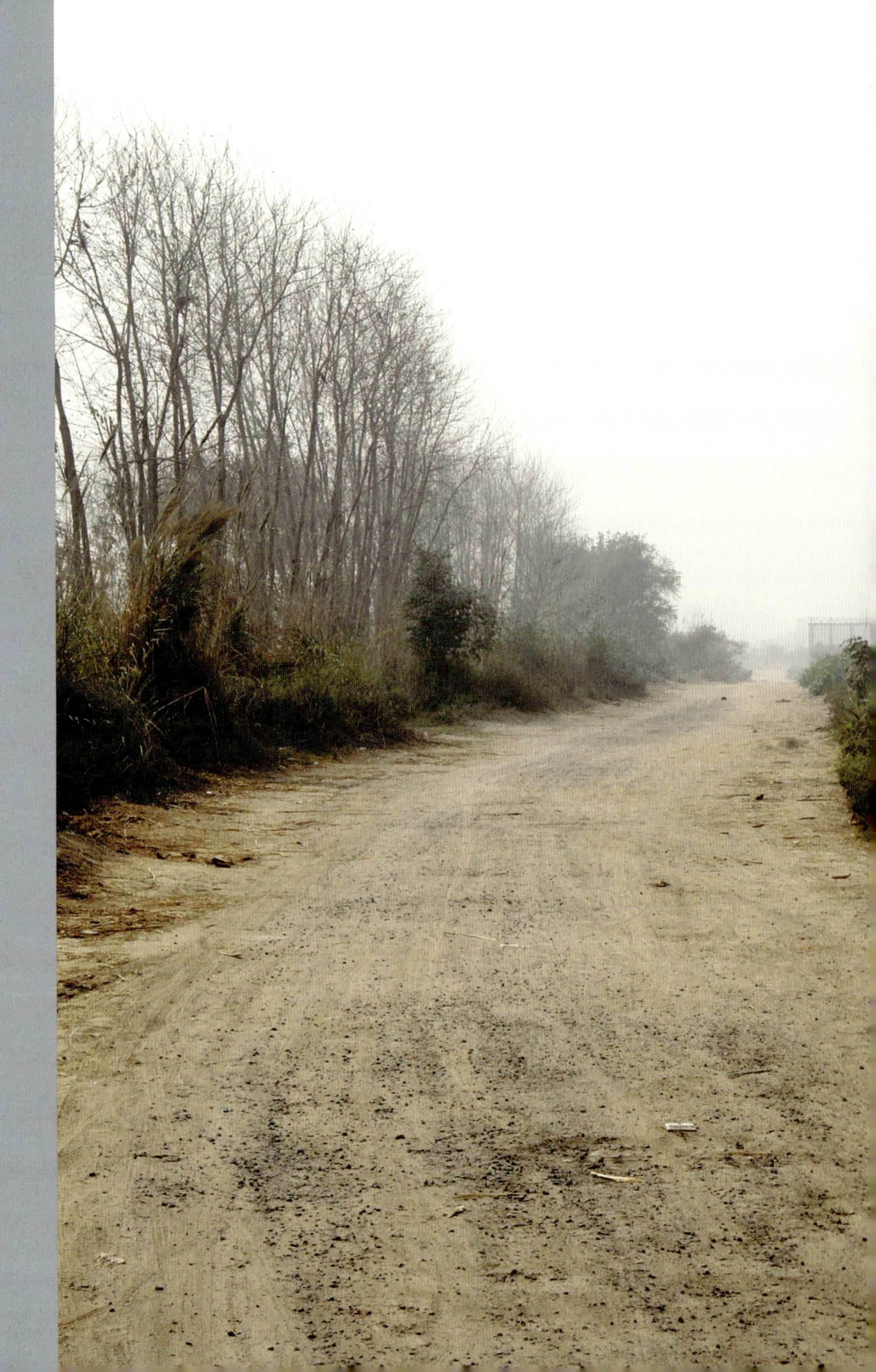

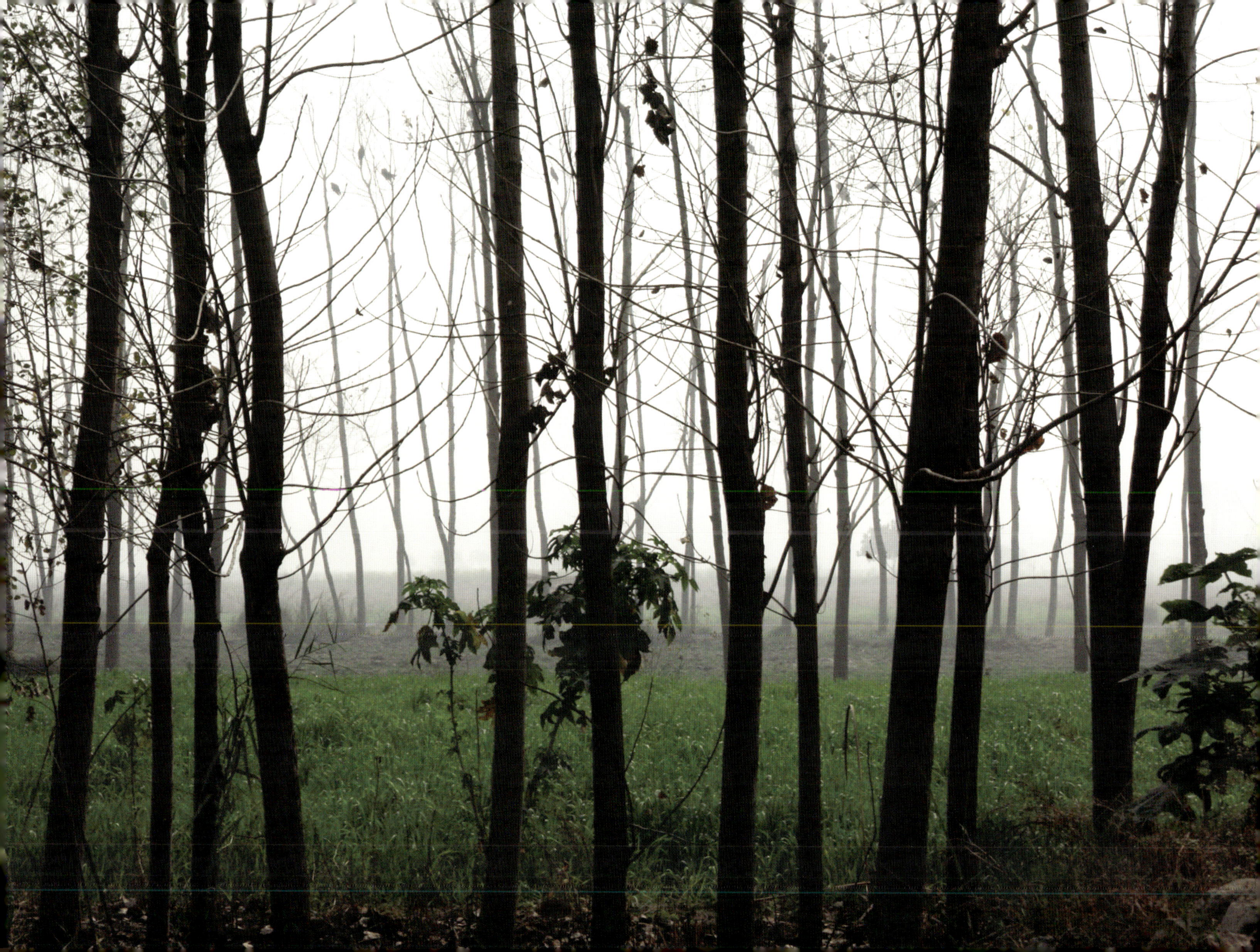

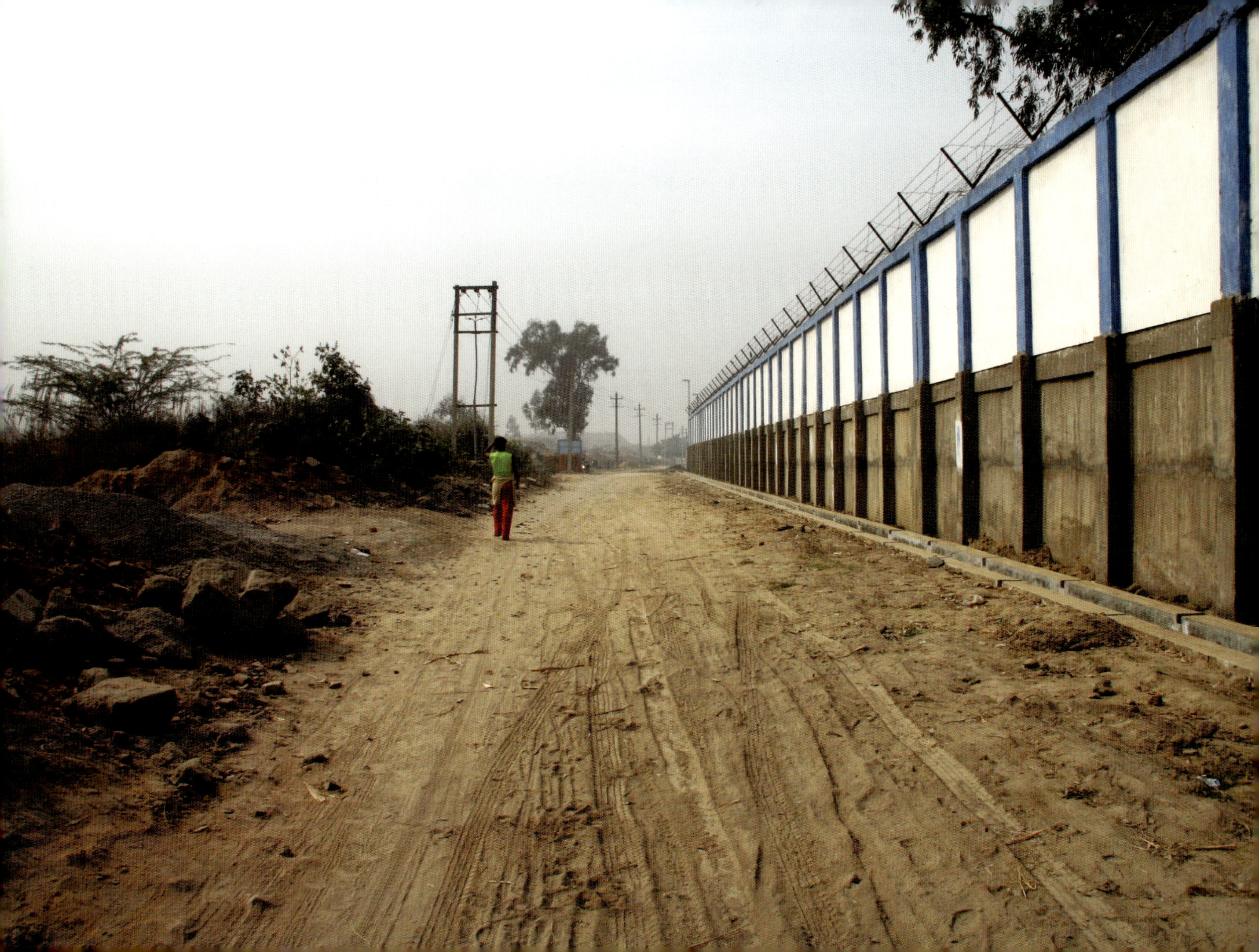

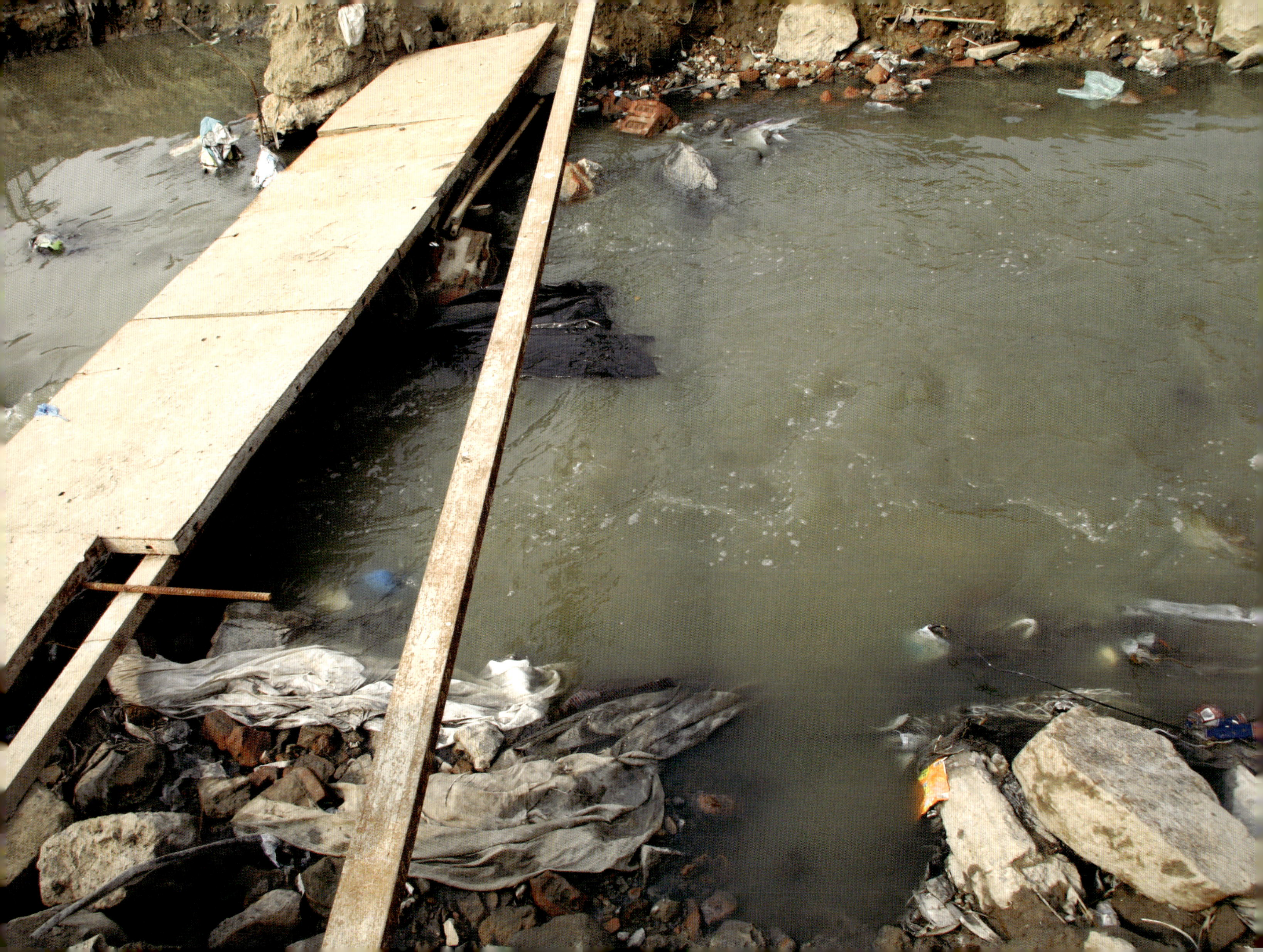

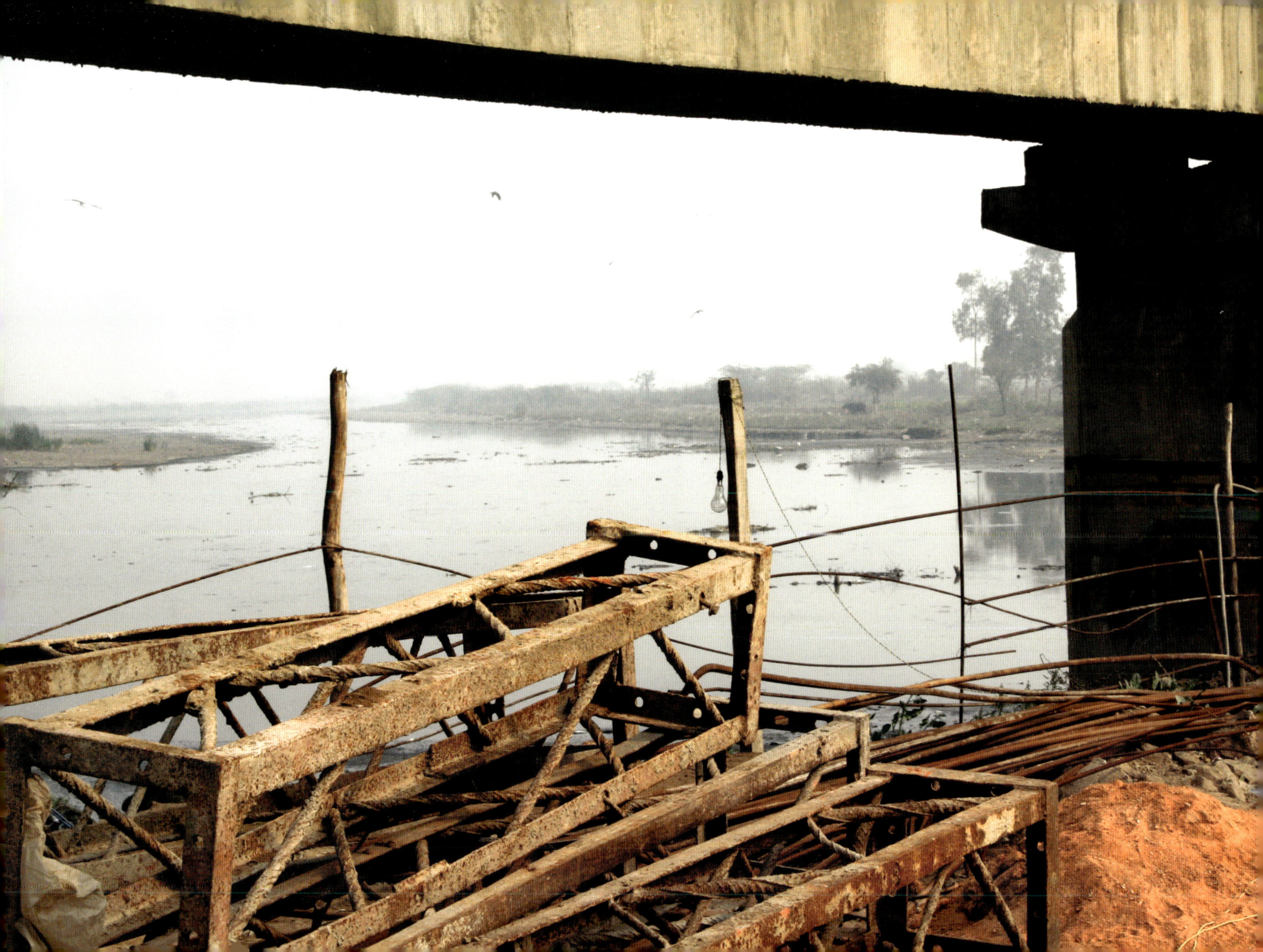

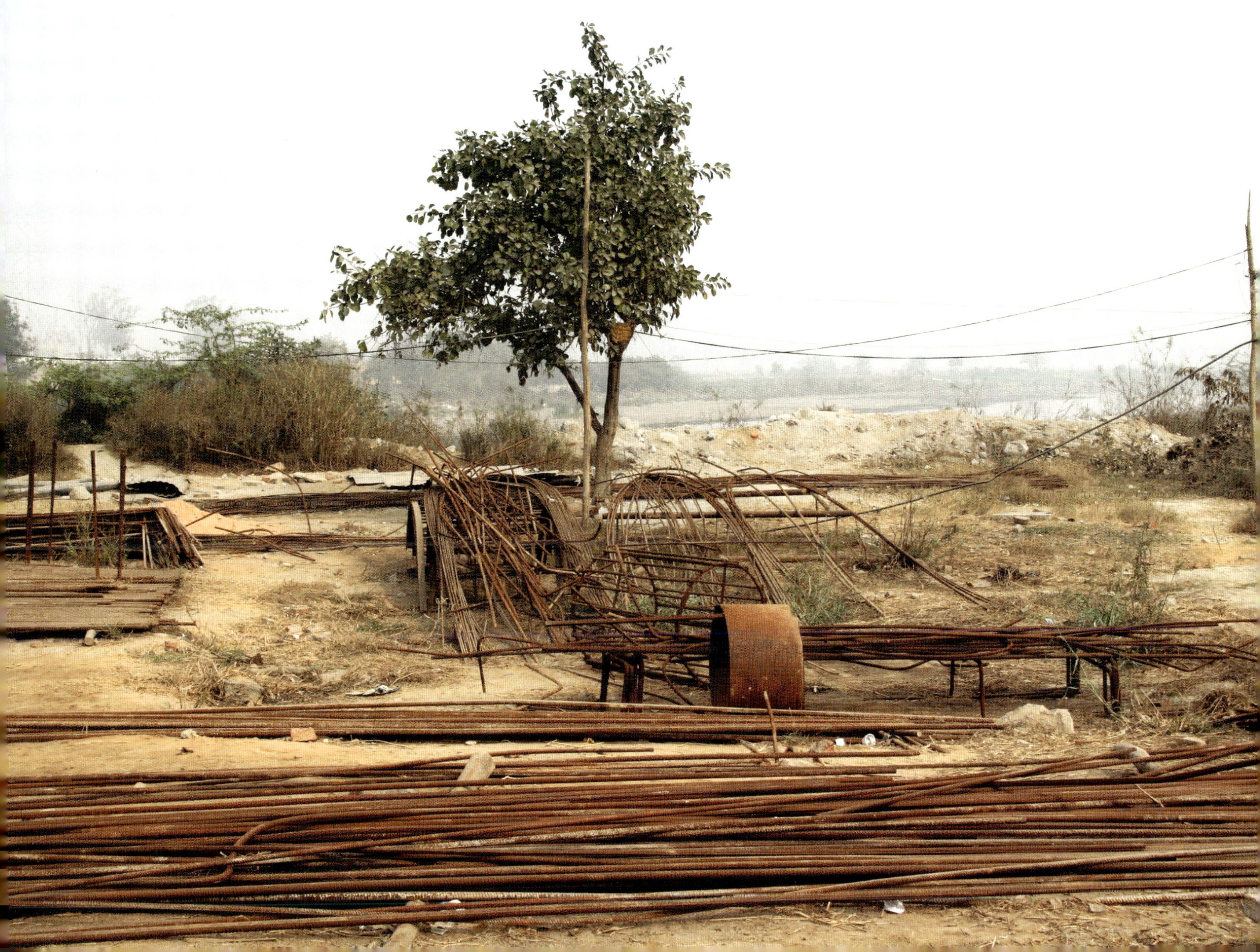

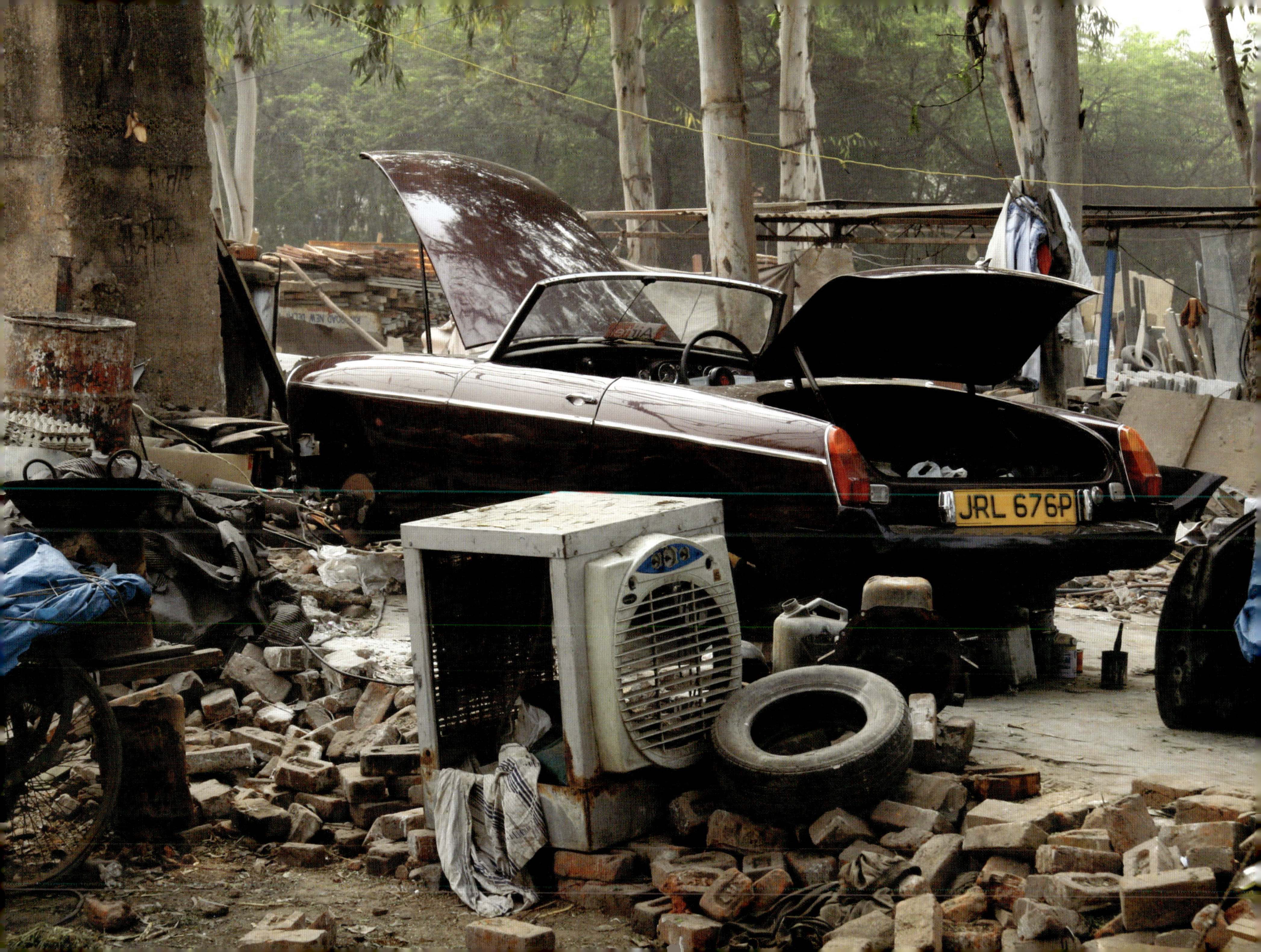
JRL 676P

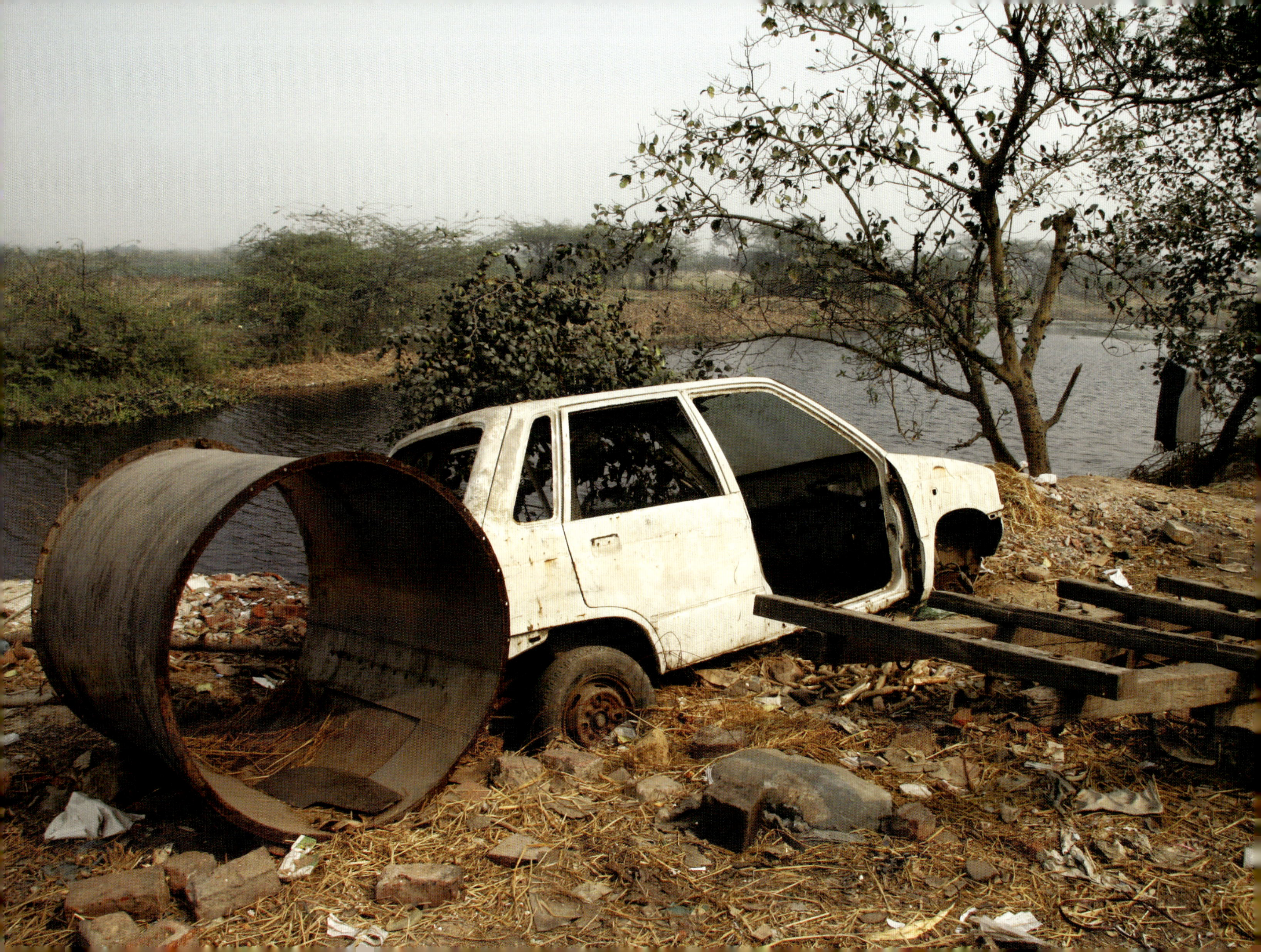

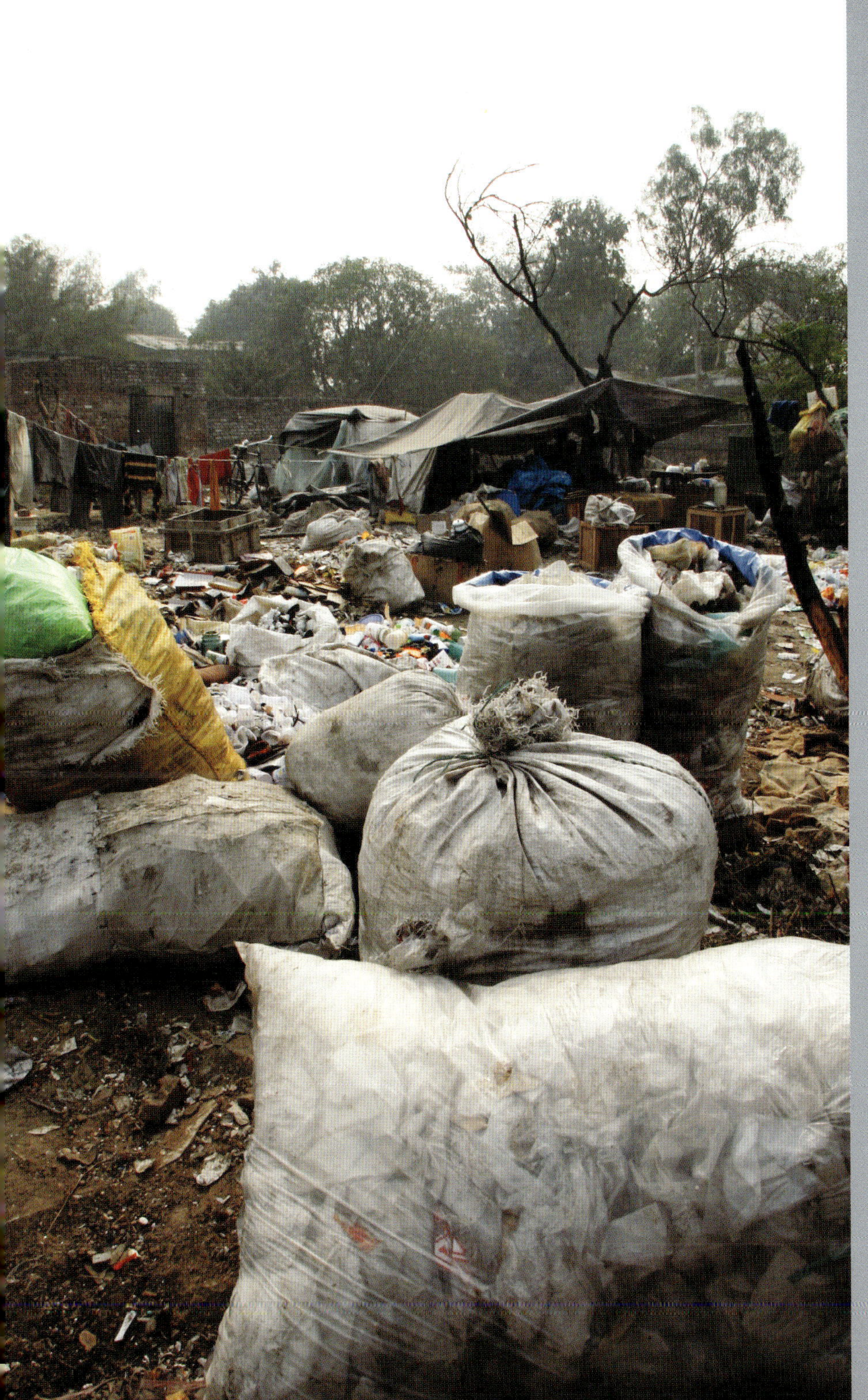

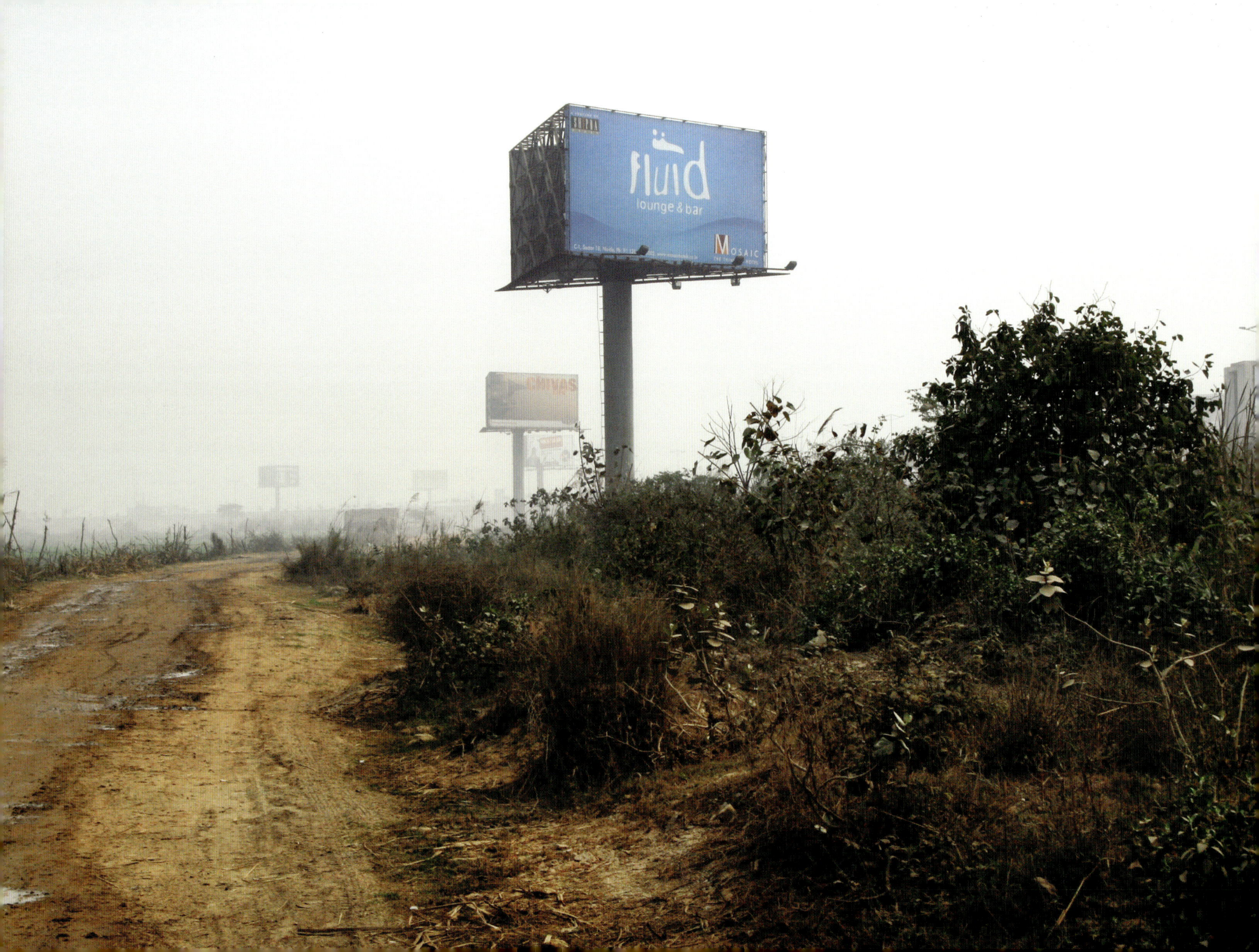
fluid
lounge & bar
MOSAIC
CHIVAS

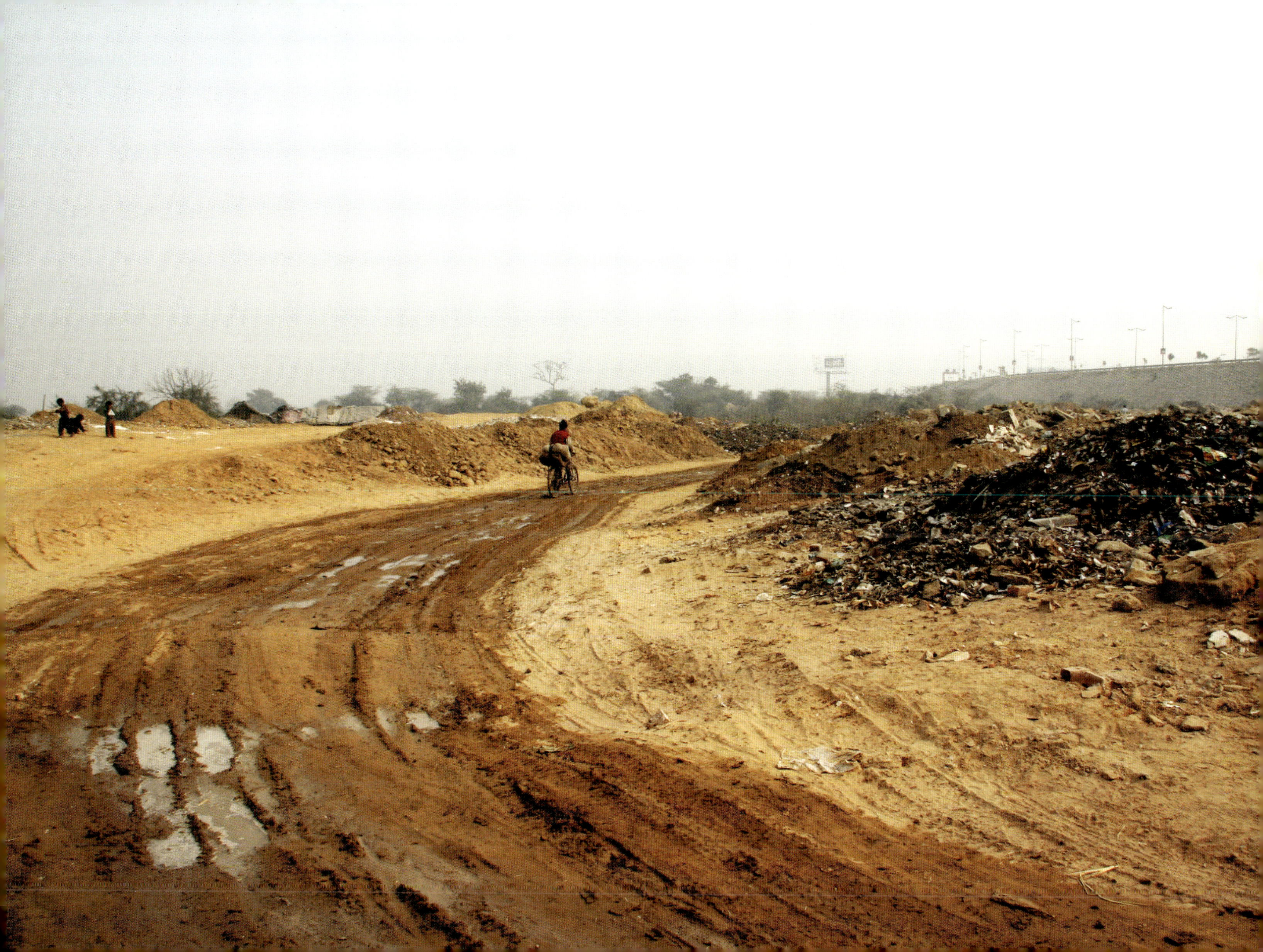

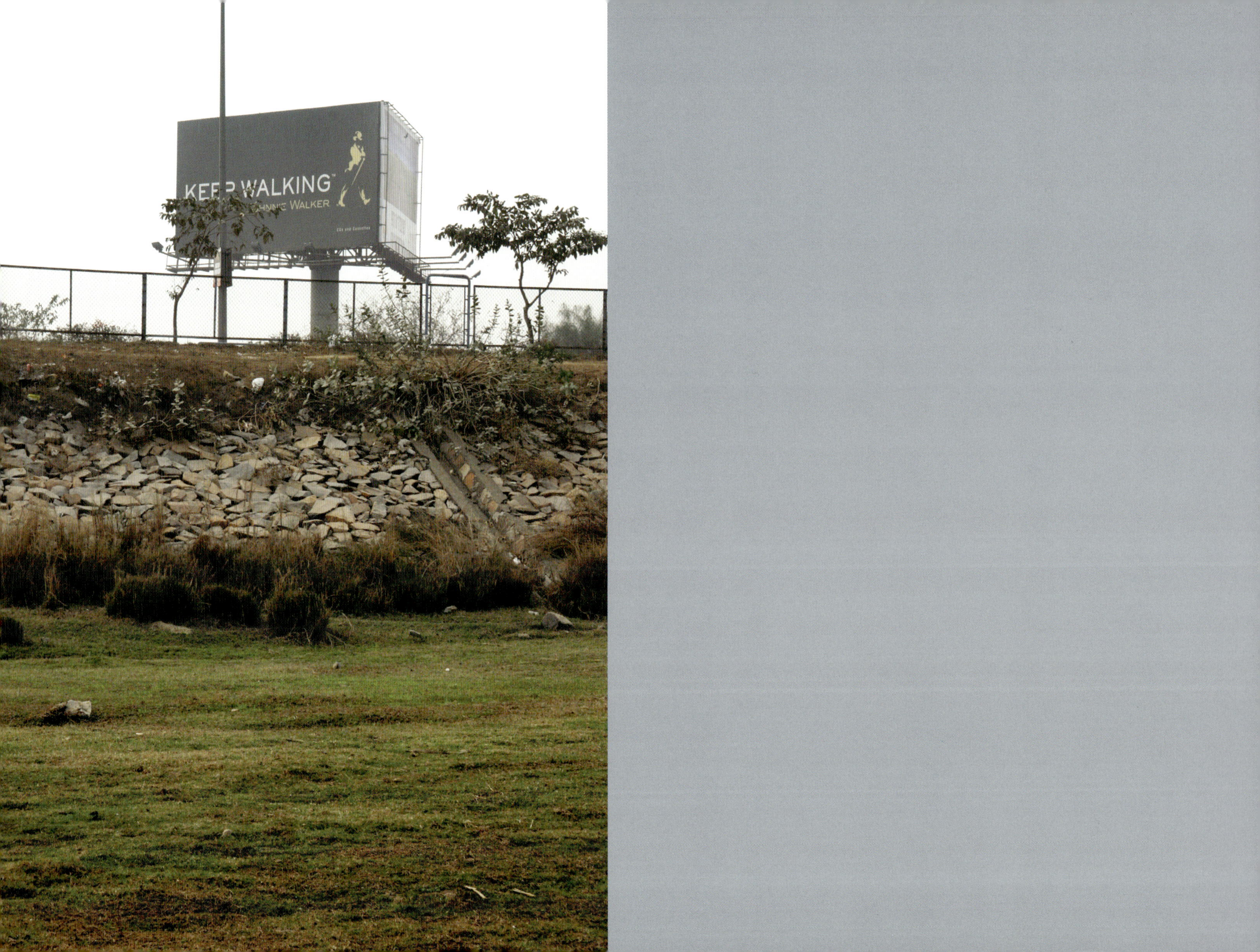
KEEP WALKING

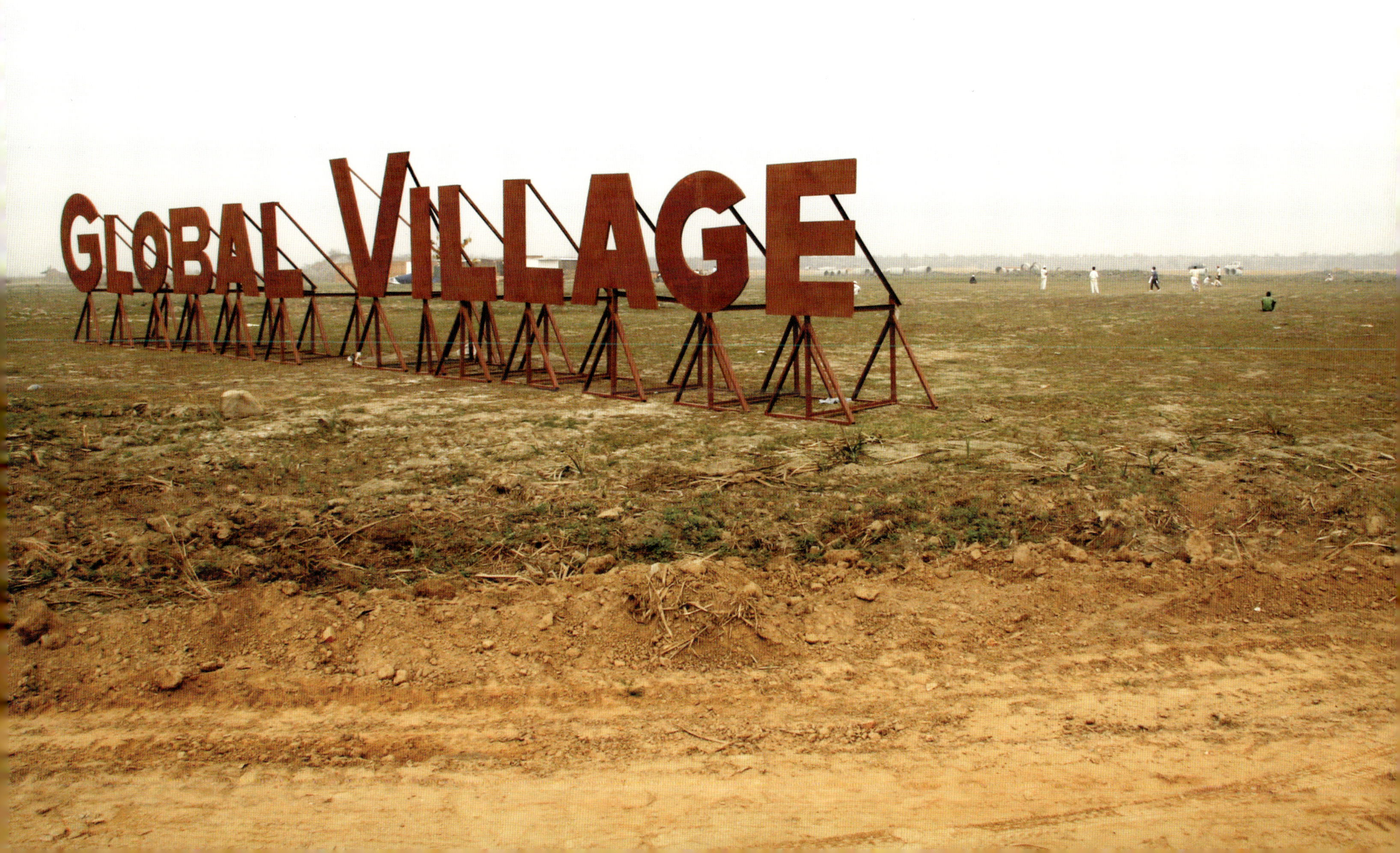
GLOBAL VILLAGE

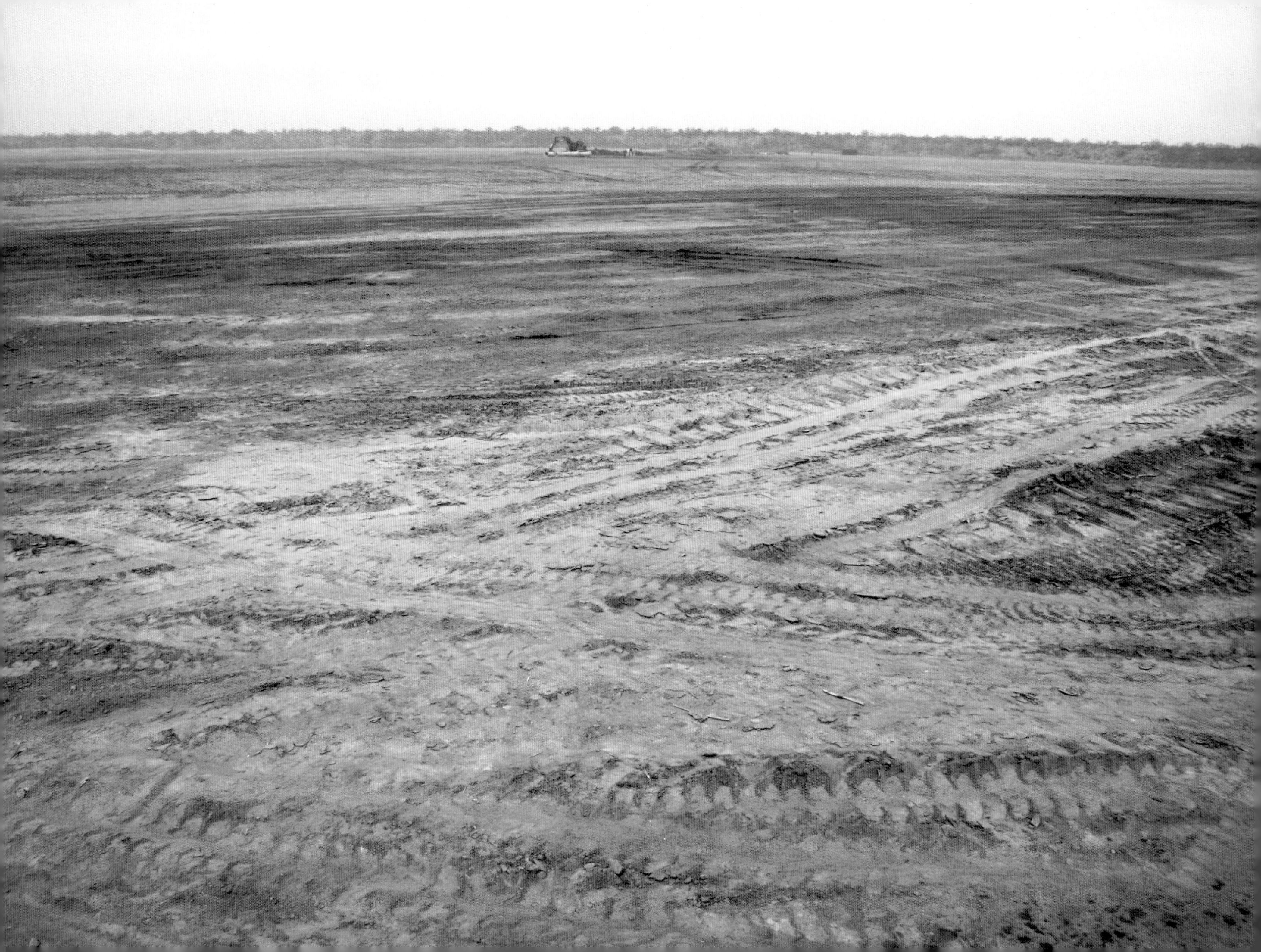

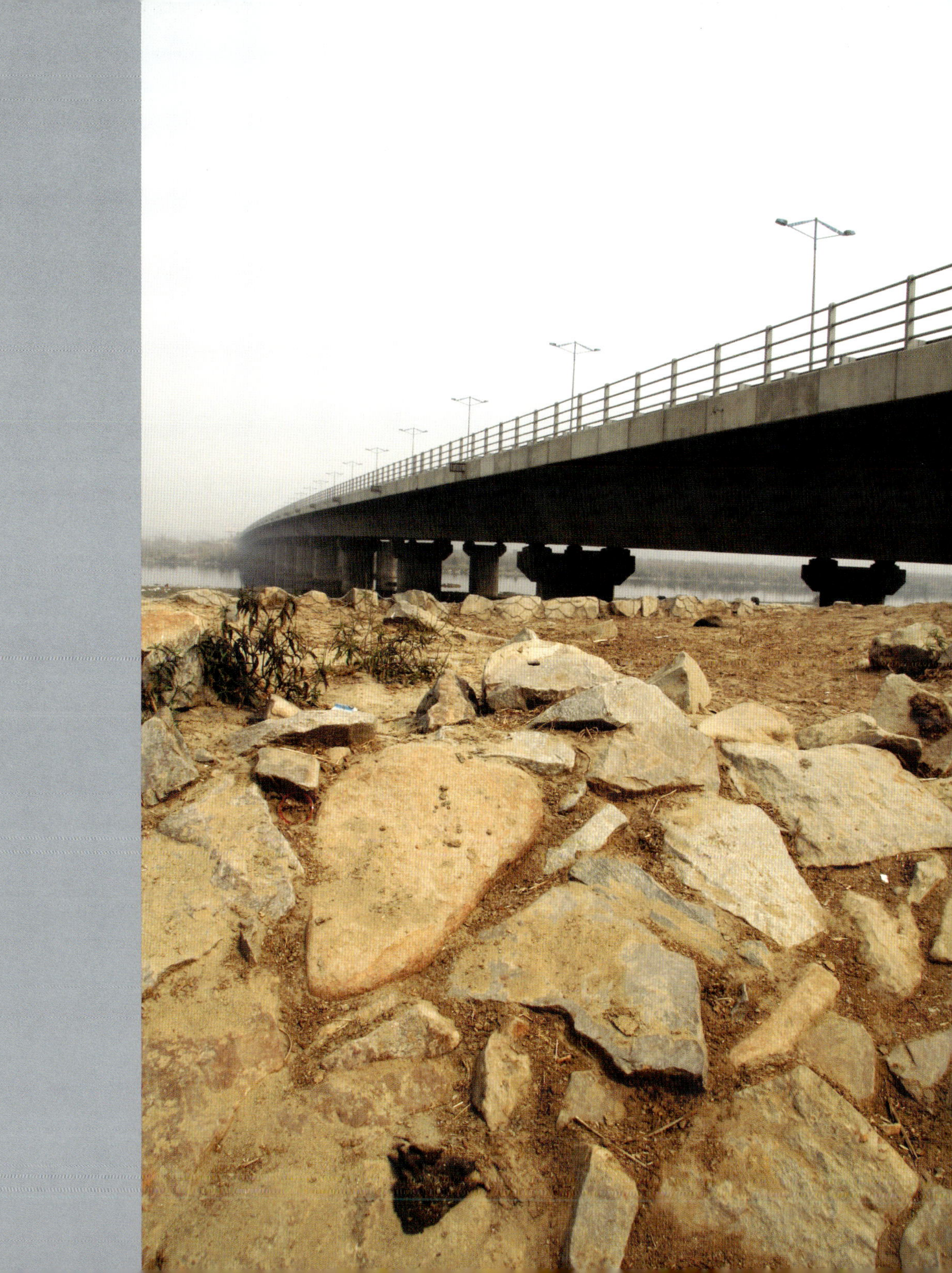

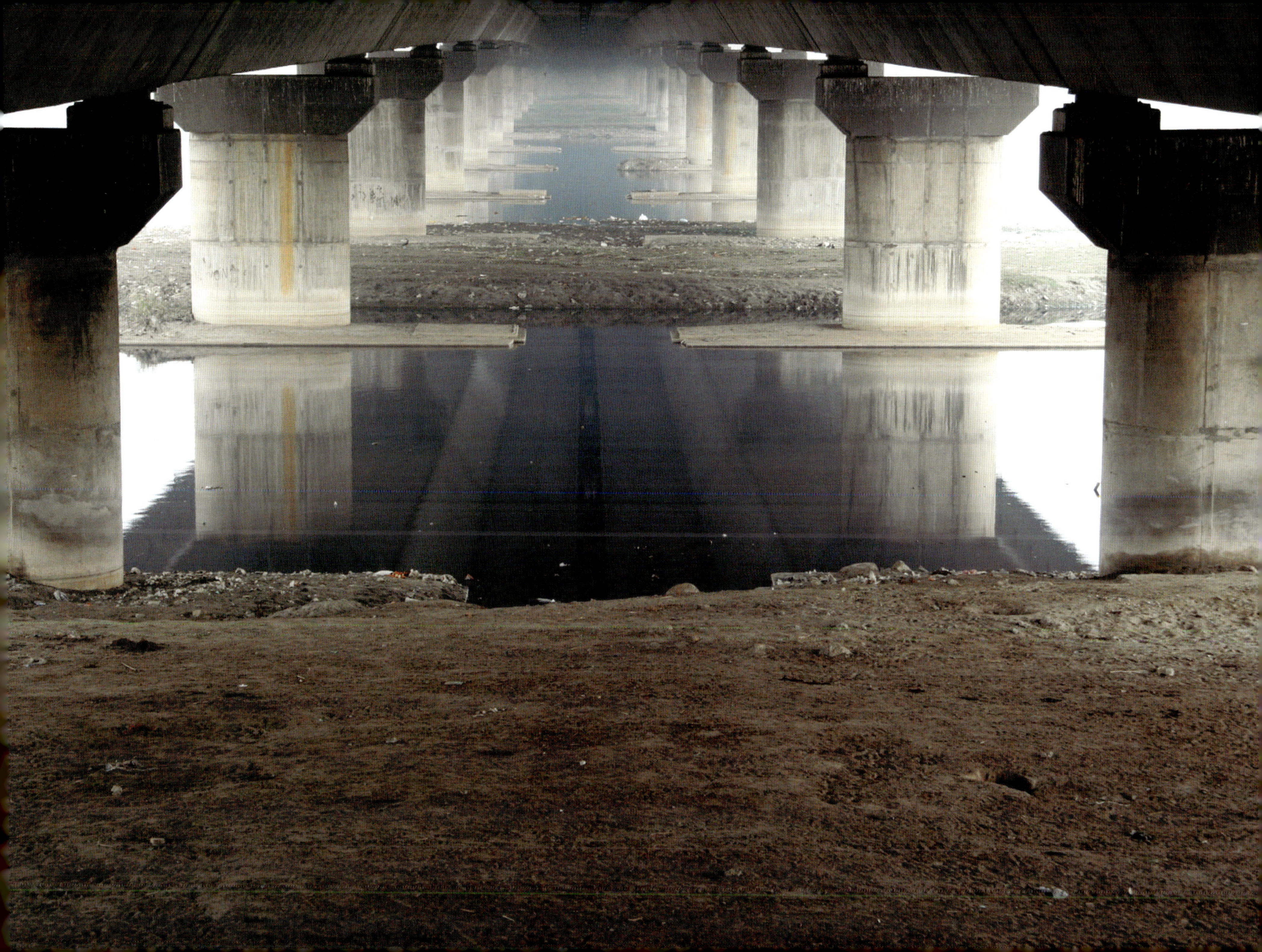

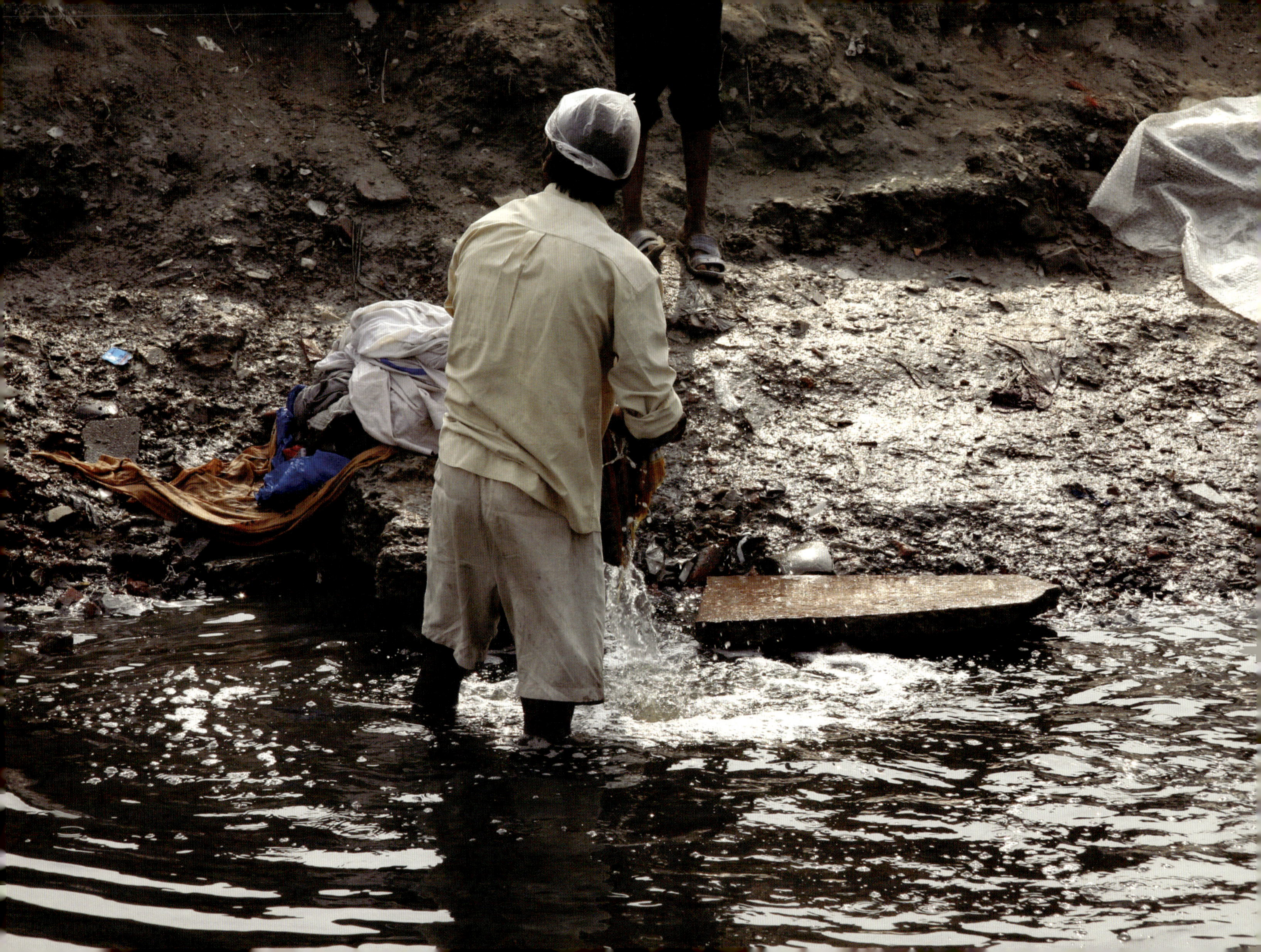

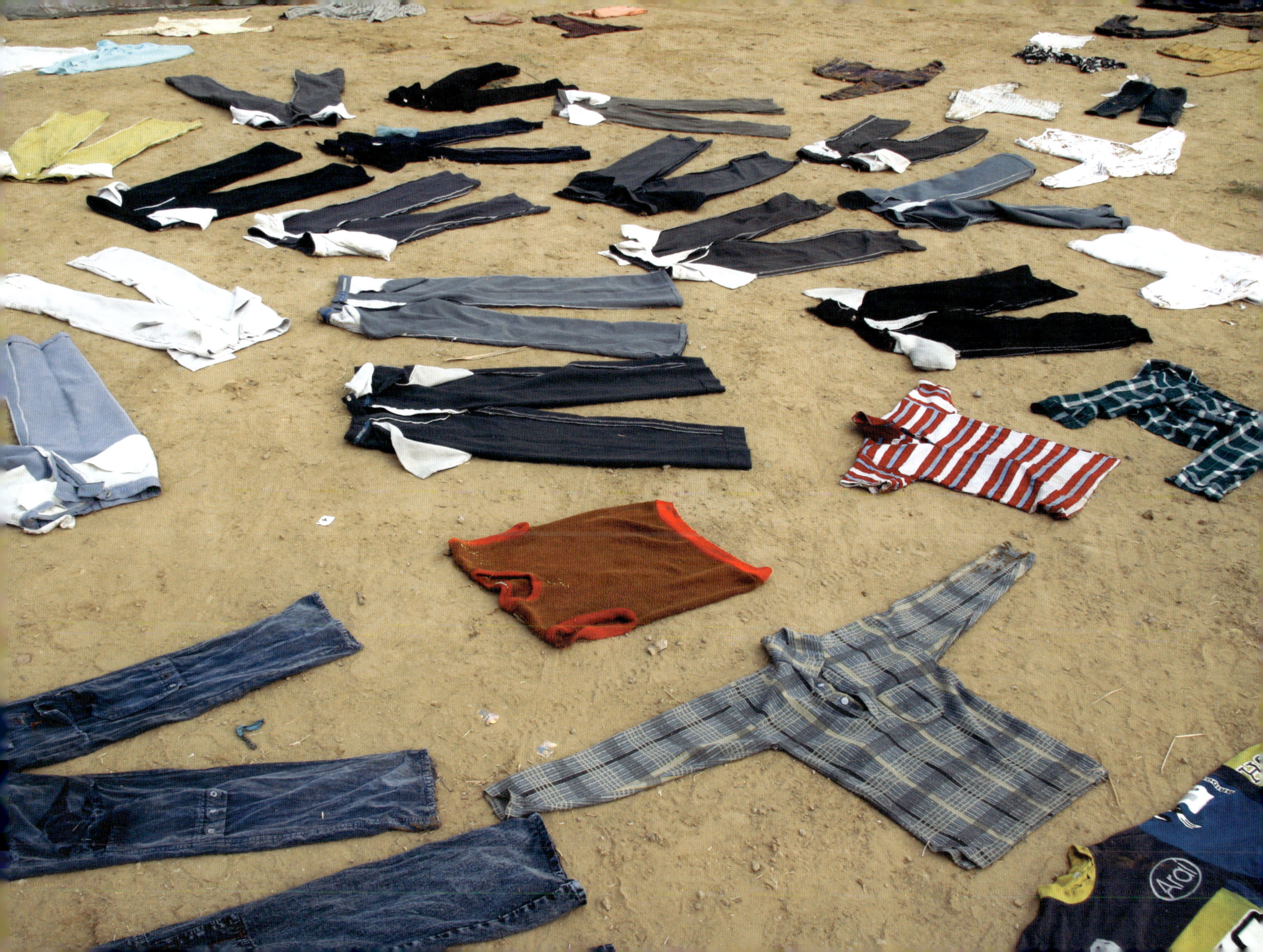

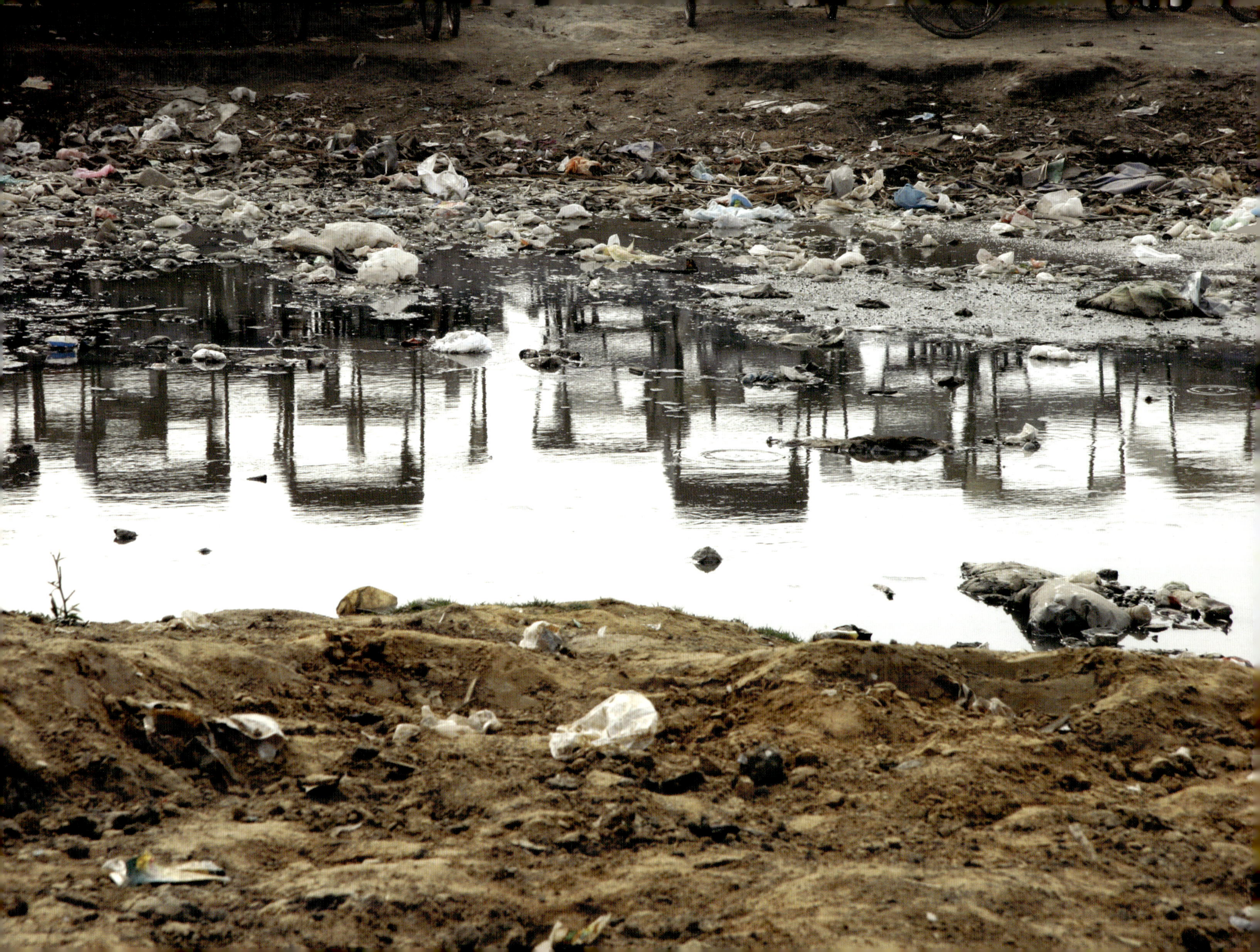

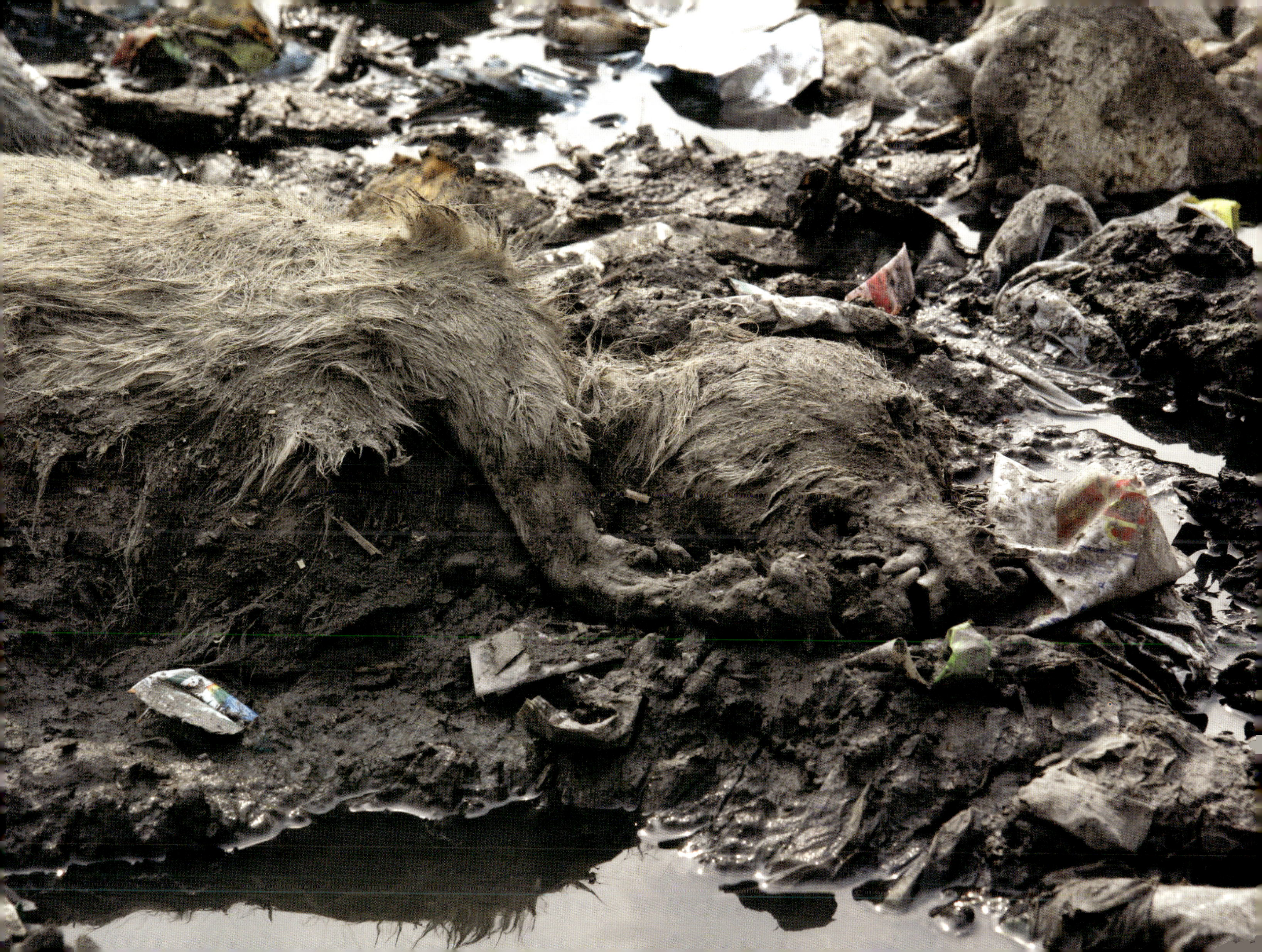

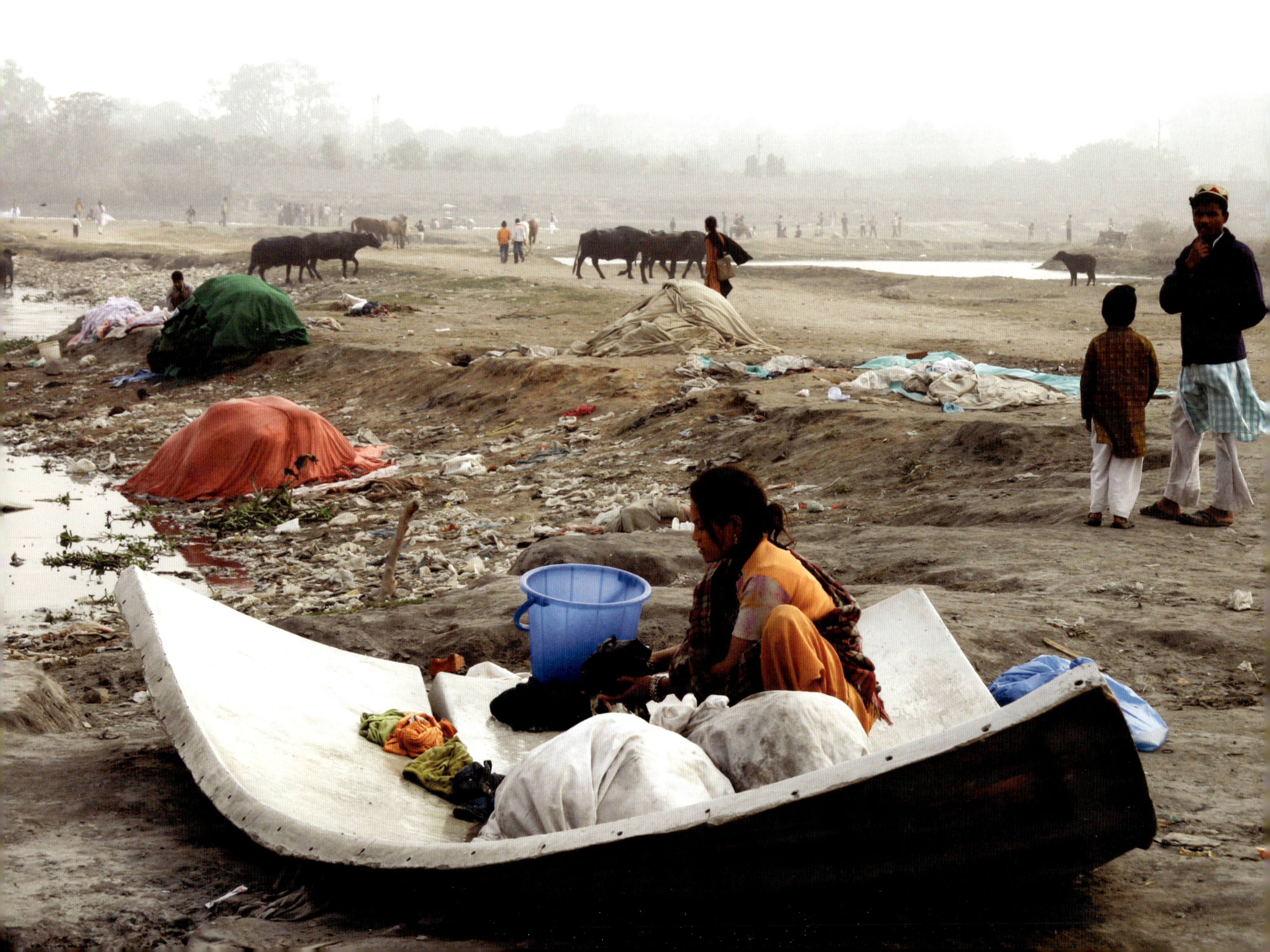

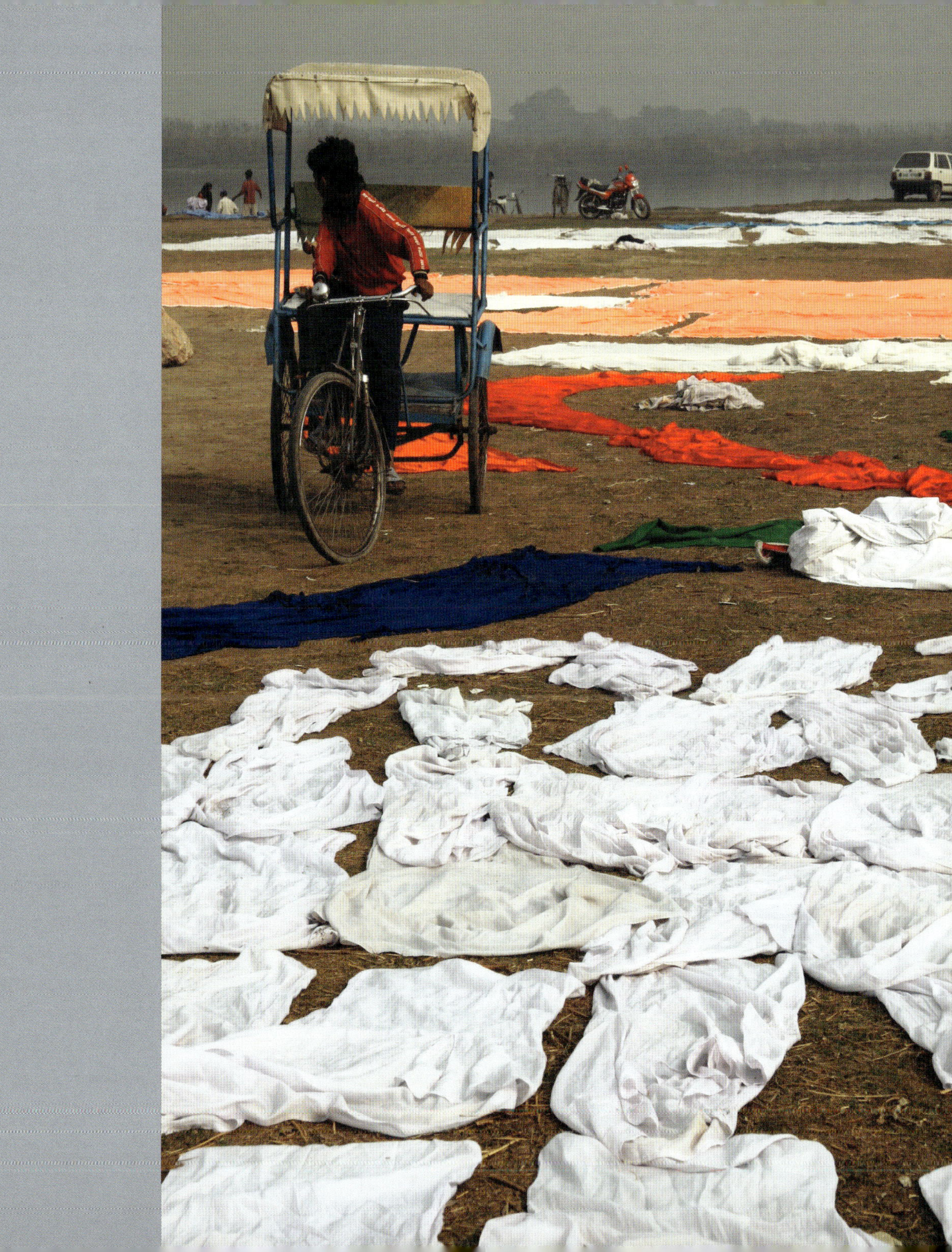

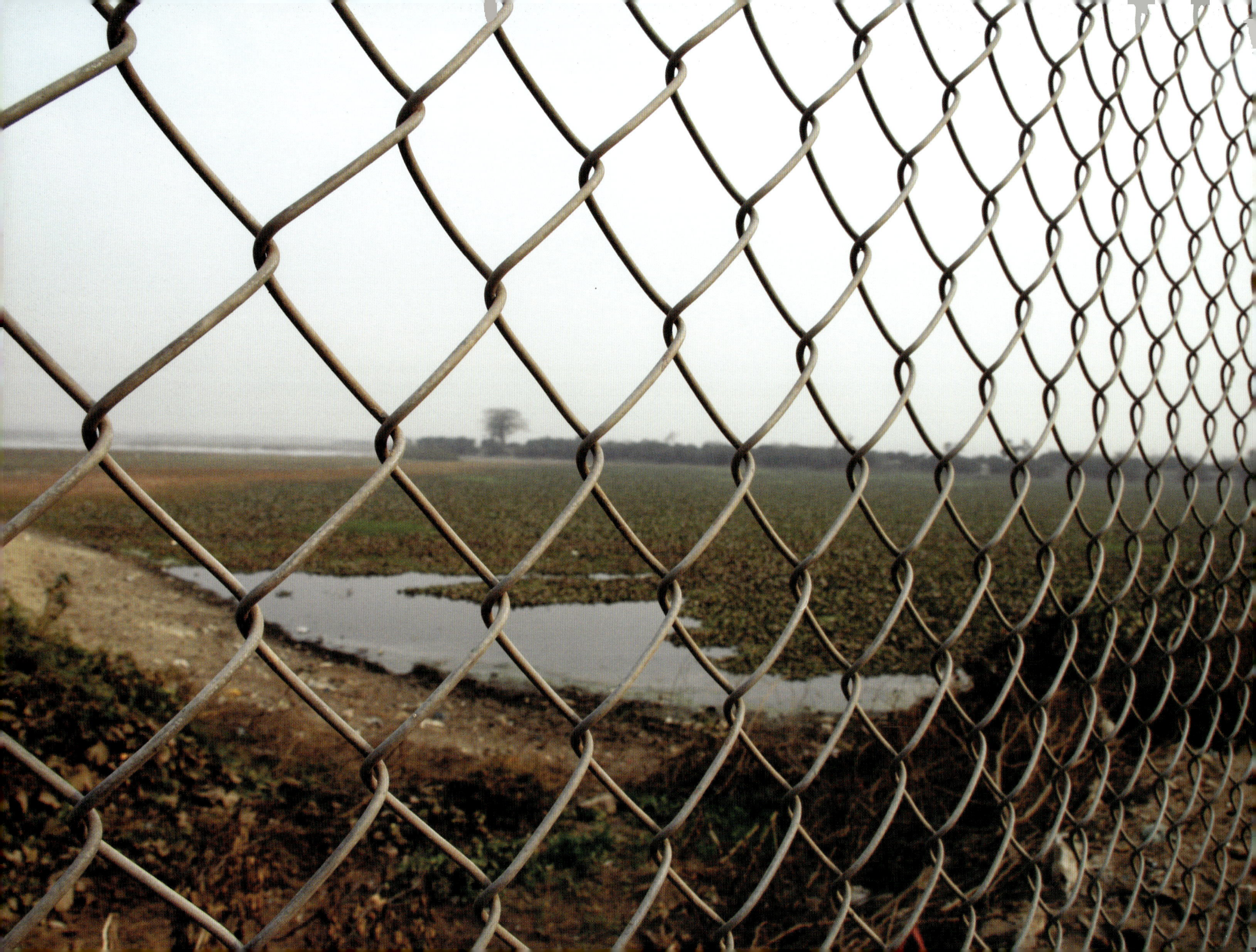

22KM: A JOURNEY INTO THE PRESENT

BY MALIHA NOORANI

"...it took me four days of walking around six hours a day. The attempt was to walk along the water, to engage with the river as it flows through Delhi. The pictures and the text document my attempts and where I was forced to take the road or a boat, and where the city totally forgets the river..."[1] — ATUL BHALLA

Born out of Bhalla's KHOJ[2] international residency in 2007, *Yamuna Walk* visually logs Bhalla's journey along the banks of the Yamuna River. Beginning where the river meets rural Delhi at Palla Village, Bhalla walked a total distance of 56 km. The urban leg of his journey, which flowed through Delhi, was 22 km and reached into the neighboring state of Uttar Pradesh (U.P.). The series highlights the visual hybrid composite of photo-performance and photo-documentation often visible in Bhalla's oeuvre. The images are un-doctored and unfold in a sequence that enables the viewer to simulate the experience of Bhalla's journey. The tone of the work is often quiet, subtle, open-ended, and brings forward the Yamuna's different faces. Through Bhalla's lens the Yamuna does not exist in binaries; the photographs depict the Yamuna as both divine and in decay, inhabited and forgotten. This dichotomy is one of the defining trajectories of this series and indeed of much of Bhalla's work and his process. The sensibility of the work is documentary and thus avoids polarized narratives. Bhalla's photographs are as complex as the issues and preoccupations that revolve around the Yamuna, his position subtly inferred and his approach nuanced.

Bhalla's method often infuses the poetry of performance and the pragmatism of visual documentary. The performative aspect of the walk was physically strenuous. As the photographs illustrate, walking along the Yamuna was a process as non-linear as the river itself. Mirroring the intrinsic nature of water, Bhalla was forced to adapt his course, bending to the dictates of topography and urban development.

"The Earth. the river. me?" So begins Atul Bhalla's journal on the first day of his walk down the river Yamuna's banks. The conjugation of these elements forms one strand of inquiry that underlines Bhalla's work: locating the self (singular and collective) within the realm of nature and vice versa. Water runs through Bhalla's work as it flows through and shapes India's landscape. He examines its ordinary, yet extraordinary, nature and its shifting role in contemporary India. The recent acceleration of urban development in India has refigured the ways in which urban communities engage with water. Bhalla's particular muse is the river Yamuna and the layered history it shares with the city it has sustained for centuries to the present day — Delhi. The river Yamuna features as the site of the works in this series, as both a source of sustenance for daily life and a metaphor for the divine.

To contextualize the spiritual value of the Yamuna, a trial by water as elaborated in the following exchange from the Mahabharata,[3] the ancient Indian epic of two warring royal families, is considered the ultimate test of purity in Hinduism and highlights the place of water in Indian thought. Toward the end of a twelve-year exile in the forests, the wise Pandava king Yudhishthra must answer questions of a yaksha, a water spirit, before he may drink from its lake.

yaksha: first, answer my questions then i will let you drink.
Yudhishthra: examine me.

yaksha: what is quicker than the wind?
Yudhishthra: thought.

yaksha: what can cover the earth?
Yudhishthra: darkness.

yaksha: what is the cause of the world?
Yudhishthra: love.

yaksha: what is your opposite?
Yudhishthra: myself.

According to Amita Sinha and D. Fairchild Ruggles, "Hindus apprehended divinity in everyday life, and deities inhabited the landscape and built [an] environment around them so that the landscape was more than an object of vision: it was an animate, living being. The faithful viewer sought transcendental union, both visually and physically, between himself and the deified landscape."[4]

Bhalla's preoccupation with the relationship between Delhi and the Yamuna is apparent in prior installations such as *I Was Not Waving But Drowning II* (2005). The series of self-portraits depicting his slow immersion into the river's polluted waters can be read as a loaded double narrative — uncovering and pushing the idea of the sacred and the decrepit as a single entity. *Not Waving* is site-specific yet the visual conveys a sense of geographic ambiguity — the Yamuna could be any river. The cerebral quality of the water within these works also points to politics of depiction. With the absence of visible pollution in the water, Bhalla avoids didactic constructions and allows viewers their own experience of the images.

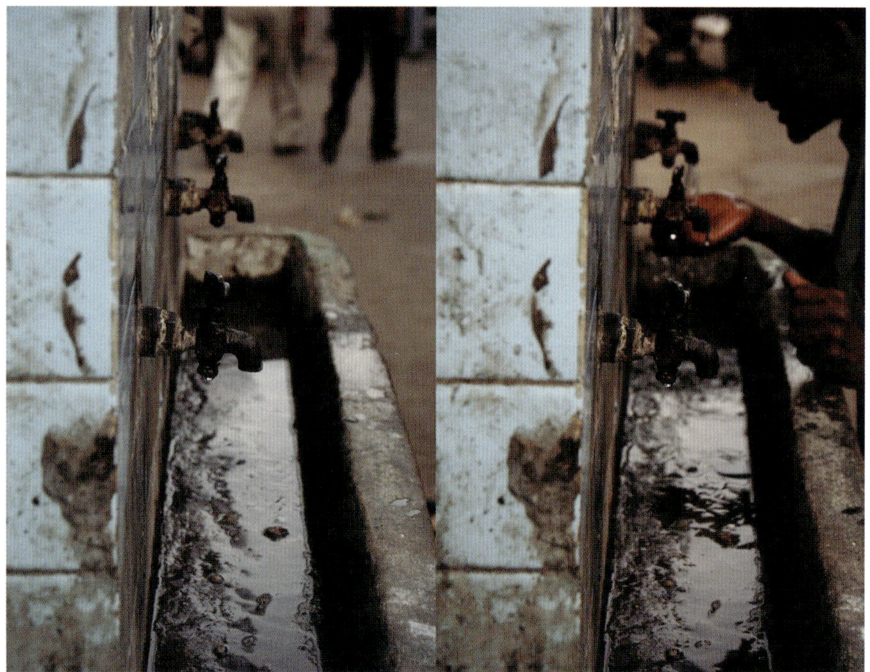

PIAU AT LALKUAN, 2007

Piau at Lalkuan (2007) examines the value of water as a metaphor for civic duty and generosity. 'Piau' in Hindi refers to the public faucets communally accessible in Old Delhi. Originating from the word paani meaning "water" and the word peena meaning "to drink," Piau literally means "where to drink." These faucets provide water sourced from the Yamuna and local wells. An initial reading of the diptych shows three taps placed over a cement basin that has been built into the wall. The taps face the street and are open to all passersby in need of a drink, or a wash as is shown in the second image. The diptych contextualizes the location and structure of these water-points and offers water as an emblem of social responsibility, under-cutting the idea of ownership, especially in an age in which water is a heavily commodified resource. This water belongs to the city and its peoples and is made accessible to all.

This idea is expanded in *Piaus-II* (2008), a sixteen-unit polyptych of photographs which serves as a visual inquiry and architectural survey of public faucets embedded in different forms around the city of Old Delhi. Again, this series highlights the politics of depiction as the images are quiet and intimate and involve the process of uncovering what is present but unseen, thus acknowledging the city's complicated and often overlooked relationship with water.

Issues around urban development are a visible preoccupation in *Yamuna Walk*. The photographs point to urban life along the river while indicating signs of new construction and development. The silhouettes of cranes and trucks laden with cement call into question the idea of responsible development, particularly since images of a visibly littered and decrepit Yamuna are interspersed throughout the photo-performance. This series highlights Bhalla as an artist preoccupied with process. Most of the works referenced involve elements of the performative and create layered narratives. They address the politics of water and the trajectories that extend from it: social, ecological and historical. Bhalla's work, particularly in *Yamuna Walk*, straddles the political with the personal and in doing so sidesteps the danger of engagement with a single story. The open-ended quality of these images is what compels us to revisit them.

Undulating over a distance of 1200 km, the Yamuna originates from the Yamunotri Glacier in the Himalayas and flows eastward past the cities of Delhi, Agra, and Allahabad, where it merges with its divine sister, the river Ganges. According to

Hindu scripture, this holy river flows through the forest of Vrindavan where the young god Krishna played with the gopis (devotional cowherds), and bathed in its waters. Yamuna's divinity is amplified through her place in Hindu mythology; as Krishna's chief consort, she features repeatedly in allegorical form within his stories. Devotees today worship the goddess Yamuna and the river itself at different points along its bank. Each day thousands seek these waters to cleanse themselves and experience spiritual rebirth.

The Yamuna is woven tightly into the fabric of Indian cultural and social history as well as its subconscious. Delhi has been a historically important city, for its advantageous location within the Indian subcontinent and because it sits on the banks of the river. A cursory glance through time provides us with examples of the Yamuna's place in Indian history; it was the site where Turkish invaders settled and ruled for approximately three centuries as the Delhi Sultanate. It frames the Mughal architectural magnum opus, the Taj Mahal in nearby Agra; it was a traversable river during the time of British colonial rule and was used to transport passengers from Delhi to Calcutta,[5] and is of course the source of water and irrigation for the country's capital city.

Ironically, however, the purifying waterway is now an environmental health hazard as a result of irresponsible urban development and heavy pollution from sewage and industrial waste, particularly around Delhi. Bhalla's work draws attention to the ecological degradation of the river and its effects on local communities. The consequence of urban consumption occupies space in both the physical and psychological landscape of the Yamuna that is brought forward through the honest and open images of this series. This photo-performance unveils the paradoxical position the Yamuna occupies in India today. Embedded within Indian consciousness yet also relegated to the periphery.

"Daal on dung cakes."[6] Confronted with this entry in Bhalla's log, one must consider the breadth of the unexpected that is suggested in the works. Cooking lentils on cow dung (cow-dung patties are used in rural India mostly as a source of natural fuel) is a consequential adventure we learn of through Bhalla's log that serves to complement the images and amplify our own simulation of his experience. These logs were kept daily for the duration of the walk and consist of single words or phrases that lend an immediacy and context to the images.

peer baba[7]

gurudwara[8]

mandir[9]

stink

madness

forgotten way

climb up

the road

down

the yamuna

access

denied.

again and again

— ATUL BHALLA, 24TH JANUARY, 2007

The text allows for the images to speak to us in different ways and helps animate the physical process of this performance. The site-specificity of the project helps orient us to a terrain alongside the river that is both natural and manmade. The photographs are open-ended and invite our eyes to roam the expanse of the riverbank through wide-angle shots, drawing us close to peer through iron fences and under bridges. Tight compositions of industrial and human waste in toxic heaps unnerve, while the young farmers who pose unabashedly for the camera charm. The river is thus humanized; the images nudge us to reconsider the Yamuna with fresh eyes.

The cover image is a particularly haunting photograph — a boat lies submerged in the river, floating shallowly alongside the partially sunken mossy embankment. There is nothing outwardly remarkable about the image, yet it evokes a sharp sense of melancholy. A diffused light washes over the image and lends it a mystical air. The boat appears almost as an apparition, placed compositionally in the middle of near evenly divided planes. Water, the boat, and the mossy bank, all feature as equal protagonists in this image. A possible interpretation is that the boat signifies — in its placement and function — as the bridge, a connecting element between land and river. Yet both boat and land are submerged within the river, tying the entire visual to the Hindu belief of death, when the ashes of the dead are washed away into the flowing waters. The submerged boat, then, as a signifier of human presence, is a metaphor for the temporal nature of human existence, whereas the water is an element both holy and eternal.

In another image (pg 39), peeping bundles of marigolds sit on the banks of the river, with a fertile sprawl of green field in one corner, the river to its left and a small path between, and clear bright skies framing the landscape. This picturesque scene is at odds with other images that detail the Yamuna stagnant with muck. This photograph shows that the Yamuna, even in its most profane state, is capable of beauty. But the photograph also elicits our curiosity; why has Bhalla elected to show the Yamuna as a source of magnificence? Here, the political becomes personal as Bhalla subverts the usual associations with pollution. Polluted water does not have to be physically shown as dirty in order to be dirty.

The Yamuna is a forgotten source that, despite human neglect, feeds the urban and rural spaces that surround it. The river is a manifestation of the divine; one could read the Yamuna to be a selfless source that will continue to sustain. However, the thoughtful quality of the series serves to remind us that the river is a silent but living entity and the flogging it endures through thoughtless practices comes at a very high price.

Having followed the *Yamuna Walk*, we are forced to consider the imbalanced relationship of river with the urban communities it sustains. Bhalla refrains from painting with broad strokes: the subtlety with which he presents this relationship enhances our subconscious reception of the idea. We have a multitude of visual references, direct and indirect, to underline this. Yet if the images indicate the danger of disrespectful methods of human consumption, they also highlight the rewards of respectful coexistence with the Yamuna. The plush, fecund fields that yield produce, the ecological systems that the river sustains in both the natural and human world.

Access to the river is often difficult, particularly around the urban and rural juncture of Jagatpur, forcing Bhalla to oscillate between riverbank and highway. This exercise also questions whether the river is being pushed into the periphery. As Bhalla noted during his excursion,[10] new housing developments are oriented with their backs facing the Yamuna in contrast to earlier times when Mughal structures built near the river were oriented to face and allow access to the river. It is a significant shift and a testimony to the level of ecological disaster the Yamuna has become.

Yamuna Walk is a layered series that anthropomorphizes the river. Bhalla's images succeed in capturing the many different facets of the river and its communities. Also evident through the quiet and honest photo-log is the artist's journey. Bhalla's images engage not only the river itself, but all that is associated with the Yamuna. The rural and urban landscapes that intersect the river bring forward different sets of consciousness towards the site. The ecological price that the Yamuna is paying to keep up with urban demands is referenced through the outline of machines in the far distance or the clutter of litter at the foot of a *ghat.*[11] Yet the series also pays homage to the resilience of nature. The images that *Yamuna Walk* presents us with—fishermen, school children at the banks, women collecting marigolds, temples—all suggest the possibility of a respectful coexistence. Bhalla's walk along and sometimes across the Yamuna can be considered a pilgrimage in its purpose to uncover and acknowledge, bringing this dialogue beyond local locations. *Yamuna Walk* is particular to India, yet holds a universality in its tone that transcends the subcontinent — and is appealing on its most basic level as one man's walk along the river.

NOTES

1. Atul Bhalla website, www.atulbhalla.com.
2. KHOJ is an artist-run alternative space for experimentation and global exchange based in New Delhi India, www.khojworkshop.org.
3. Carrière, *The Mahabharata.*
4. Sinha and Ruggles, *The Yamuna Riverfront,* 141.
5. Haberman, *River of Love,* 8.
6. Atul Bhalla, *Yamuna Walk* log.
7. Peer baba is an honorific term used for a holy man.
8. Gurudawara is a site of worship for Sikhs.
9. Mandir is a site of worship for Hindus.
10. HUAM (Harvard University Art Museum) 'In conversation with Atul Bhalla.'
11. Ghat is a wide set of stairs leading into a river, usually holy.

BIBLIOGRAPHY

"Atul Bhalla," sepia EYE, accessed August 5, 2011, http://sepiaeye.com/atul-bhalla.

"Atul Bhalla," Yamuna.Elbe, accessed July 30, 2011, http://www.yamuna-elbe.de/index.php?title=Atul_Bhalla.

Bhalla, Atul. 2005. *I Was Not Waving but Drowning II* [wall text], Harvard Art Museums/Arthur M. Sackler Museum.

Carrière, Jean Claude, and Peter Brook. 1987. *The Mahabharata: A Play Based on the Indian Classic Epic.* New York: Harper & Row.

Chamberlain, Gary. 2008. *Troubled Waters: Religion, Ethics, and the Global Water Crisis.* Lanham, MD: Rowman & Littlefield.

Haberman, David L. 2006. *River of Love in an Age of Pollution: The Yamuna River of Northern India.* Berkeley, CA: University of California Press.

"In Conversation with Atul Bhalla," South Asia Initiative at Harvard, March 3, 2011, accessed July 30, 2011, http://vimeo.com/20878460.

Narayanan, Vasudha. 2001. "Water, Wood, and Wisdom: Ecological Perspectives from the Hindu Traditions." *Daedalus* 130, (4):179-206.

Sinha, Amita, and D. Fairchild Ruggles. 2004. "The Yamuna Riverfront, India: a Comparative Study of Islamic and Hindu Traditions in Cultural Landscapes." *Landscape Journal.* 23(2):141-52.

Sinha, Gayatri, Paul Spencer Sternberger, and Brian Drolet. 2007. *India: Public Places, Private Spaces: Contemporary Photography and Video Art.* Newark, NJ: Newark Museum.

ACKNOWLEDGEMENTS

I am grateful to Esa Epstein, Pooja Sood and Pamela Auchincloss for their continuous belief in my work, without whose support this book would not be possible.

Ranbir Nerwal for all the technical support.

KHOJ-International Artist Association for providing the platforms for me to surprise myself.

Printed and bound in China

16 15 14 13 12 5 4 3 2 1

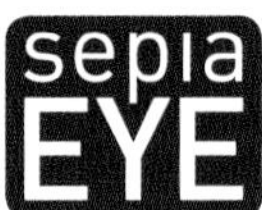

Editor: Esa Epstein
Book Design: Melanie Roberts Design
Sepia Eyes: Brian Corby, Sayuri Rupani-Hayes, Nandinee Phookan and Akemi Yoneyama

sepia EYE
41 West 57th Street, 6th Floor
New York, NY 10019
www.sepiaeye.com

UNIVERSITY OF WASHINGTON PRESS
PO Box 50096, Seattle, WA 98145, USA
www.washington.edu/uwpress

Library of Congress Cataloging-in-Publication Data
Bhalla, Atul.
Yamuna walk : 22 Km, a journey into the present / Atul Bhalla, Maliha Noorani.
p. cm.
Includes bibliographical references and index.
ISBN 978-0-295-99177-1 (cloth : alk. paper)
1. Yamuna River (India)–Pictorial works. 2. Delhi (India)–Pictorial works.
3. Landscape photography–India–Delhi. I. Noorani, Maliha. II. Title.
DS485.Y34B48 2012 954'.560532–dc23 2011042657

The paper used in this publication meets the minimum requirements of American National Standard for Information Sciences — Permanence of Paper for Printed Library Materials, ANSI Z39.48–1984.∞